We Fight to Win

The Rutgers Series in Childhood Studies

The Rutgers Series in Childhood Studies is dedicated to increasing our understanding of children and childhoods, past and present, throughout the world. Children's voices and experiences are central. Authors come from a variety of fields, including anthropology, criminal justice, history, literature, psychology, religion, and sociology. The books in this series are intended for students, scholars, practitioners, and those who formulate policies that affect children's everyday lives and futures.

Edited by Myra Bluebond-Langner, Distinguished Professor of Anthropology, Rutgers University, Camden, and founding director of the Rutgers University Center for Children and Childhood Studies

Advisory Board
Joan Jacobs Brumberg, Cornell University
Perri Klass, New York University
Jill Korbin, Case Western Reserve University
Bambi Schiefflin, New York University
Enid Schildkraut, American Museum of Natural History and
    Museum for African Art

We Fight to Win

Inequality and the Politics of Youth Activism

HAVA RACHEL GORDON

RUTGERS UNIVERSITY PRESS

NEW BRUNSWICK, NEW JERSEY, AND LONDON

LIBRARY OF CONGRESS CATALOGING-IN-PUBLICATION DATA

Gordon, Hava Rachel, 1974–

  We fight to win : inequality and the politics of youth activism / Hava Rachel Gordon.

    p. cm. — (The Rutgers series in childhood studies)

  Includes bibliographical references and index.

  ISBN 978–0–8135–4669–8 (hbk. : alk. paper) —

ISBN 978–0–8135–4670–4 (pbk. : alk. paper)

   1. Youth—Political activity.   2. Students—Political activity.   3. Youth movements. I. Title.

  HQ799.2.P6G65 2010

  322.40835—dc22

2009006028

A British Cataloging-in-Publication record for this book is available
from the British Library.

Visit our Web site: http://rutgerspress.rutgers.edu

Manufactured in the United States of America

CONTENTS

ACKNOWLEDGMENTS

First and foremost, I would like to thank Youth Power and Students Rise Up, two teen activist networks who granted me access to youth movements and to the lives of adolescent political organizers. The youth activists and adult allies who I came to know during this experience have changed me forever. They are among the most gifted educators I have ever met. Although I would like to thank them here by name, I cannot do so without breaching their confidentiality. To protect the identities of these activists, I have decided not to include certain citations throughout the manuscript that might compromise their anonymity. I thank sociology for bringing me to their worlds and to the brilliant work that they do. The future (and present) is in good hands!

Many thanks go to my mentors at the University of Oregon. Gregory McLauchlan was the first to give me the intellectual space and encouragement to pursue the links between age inequality and youth political organizing, and never once lost faith in my ability to write a compelling ethnography on youth activism. Special thanks go to Jocelyn Hollander, who has consistently been a friend and mentor to me. Sandra Morgen, Lynn Fujiwara, and Elizabeth Reis have all mentored me as a researcher, teacher, feminist, and scholar more than they will ever know. To me, all of you are shining examples of activist-scholars.

I could not have written this book without the intellectual and emotional support of my fellow academics at the University of Oregon, the University of Denver, and elsewhere: Barbara Sutton, Jey Strangfeld, Mara Fridell, Mark Hudson, Roxanne Gerbrandt, Khaya Clark, Lisa Gonzales, Sandra Ezquerra, Leontina Hormel, Maria de la Torre, Lisa Pasko, Lisa Martinez, Nancy Wadsworth, Kate Willink, Scott Phillips, Jennifer Reich, and Amy Wilkins. LeThi Cussen, Brad Gillies, Kim Gilbert, Amanda Levinson,

Kris Boesch, Erin Neff, Petra Caruso, Kristen Cardinal, Anne Britton, Jen Stocksmith, and many other good friends took the time to laugh with me, be silly with me, go dancing with me, travel with me, feed me, and remind me that there is a rich world outside of academia.

A big thanks goes out to Adi Hovav, my editor at Rutgers University Press, who patiently coached me through the writing of this book and has undoubtedly made it better with her feedback. I would also like to thank Myra Bluebond-Lagner, Amy Best, and the anonymous reviewers at Rutgers University Press who gave me critical feedback on earlier versions of this manuscript. Chapter 3 ("Allies Within and Without: Navigating the Terrain of Adult-Dominated Community Politics") is an expanded version of an earlier article published in the *Journal of Contemporary Ethnography* in 2007, and chapter 6 ("Gendering Political Power: Gender Politics in Youth Activist Networks") is an expanded version of an earlier article published in *Gender & Society* in 2008. I would like to thank the editors and anonymous reviewers at the *Journal of Contemporary Ethnography* and *Gender & Society* for helping me to develop the ideas that are now in these chapters.

I would also like to thank my family for their love, humor, and support. My mother, Marcia, and father, Gerald, offered me their wisdom just when I needed it the most. Their perspectives helped to shake me out of my difficult moments. I give a big thanks to my brother Joshua; his wife, Eve; and my sister Rebecca. This research would have been impossible without them. Without hesitation, they provided me with their house keys so that I could come and go during all hours of the day, sleep on their living room couches, eat their food, and otherwise interrupt their lives in the Bay Area to conduct this research. Along with my other siblings David, Steven, and Marcia, as well as their partners, they have listened to me talk through this project and have given me wonderful insights. I thank my siblings for being among my greatest gifts in life. My biggest thanks goes to Jason McKain, who has been a constant source of inspiration and laughter in my life. His unwavering commitment to social justice continually fuels my own. Jason read drafts of chapters, visited me while I was conducting research, and has spent hours upon hours talking with me about social, economic, and political issues. His love, friendship, bravery, integrity, and brilliance have carried me through this project, and I am deeply grateful to him. To our twins on the way: we can't wait to meet you!

I DEDICATE THIS BOOK to the memory of my father, Gerald S. Gordon. You were larger than life, a light and inspiration to all who were lucky enough to know you. You changed the world for the better and we will miss you forever.

We Fight to Win

Introduction

In February of 2003, mainstream media outlets covered the massive and simultaneous antiwar protests that shook hundreds of cities across the world. Activists from almost every corner of the earth marched in the streets, numbering in the millions, to protest the impending invasion of Iraq. Although the sixties are often identified as an apex of political activism, the 2003 marches made history in terms of the sheer numbers of people participating in the antiwar demonstrations. If the news cameras were to zoom in on the crowds and were to look beyond the spectacle of people's collective outrage spilling into the streets, they would have caught a variety of groups coalescing together: environmentalists, workers, antiglobalization activists, war veterans, elderly people, churchgoers, families, teachers, college students, and even children. These groups did not appear in the streets haphazardly or randomly; many were mobilized long before into carefully organized campaigns for social justice. Behind these massive demonstrations were leagues of civic organizations and tireless organizers who worked daily to organize their communities for social change. If the cameras would have zoomed in even closer, they might have noticed that some of these core community organizers were teenagers. Although already politically active, most of these teens worldwide did not yet have the right to vote in formal elections. Many of them were not even old enough to drive a car.

In one corner of the world, I first met some of these teenage organizers at a peace rally in Portland, Oregon, during the autumn of 2002. Under a banner that read in thick, black-painted letters "Students Rise Up," about twenty teens crowded together for warmth against the cold Oregon rain among hundreds of other antiwar Portlanders. This is the first time I met Curt, Shae, Troy, Joni, and other core organizers of the SRU student network, a group of politicized high school students across several Portland area high schools that began organizing against two troublesome and simultaneous developments: unprecedented school budget cuts and the impending war in Iraq. Over the next two years, I would come to know these and other student organizers in SRU. I would watch as sixteen-year-old Sara, outfitted in leggings and heavy black boots, waved her sign that read "Stop the war! Fund our schools!" high above her head and skipped to the front of the weekly antiwar marches in Portland. She and her friends would bounce to the beat of the raggedy antiwar drum corps that kept the marchers moving through the streets. I would witness seventeen-year-old Travis sneak away from a wide circle of students protesting school budget cuts inside the Oregon State Capitol. I would watch him as he climbed a huge marble staircase to unfurl a gigantic banner spray-painted in capital letters "SMART KIDS, NOT SMART BOMBS," only to see him be swiftly shooed away by a security guard. I would walk behind sixteen-year-old Troy, dressed in all black, who coolly and confidently led several hundred youth through Portland's streets in a solemn march protesting what SRU called the "death of education." Behind us, in a sea of youth, SRU students held high a huge papier-mâché coffin in which other students ritually laid to rest their school textbooks.

The core SRU organizers were all white and middle class, and openly recognized the white, middle-class dominance of the SRU network. In meetings, SRU organizers expressed vexation over their inability to draw more students of color from Portland schools that were located in the city's largely segregated Latino and black communities. The SRU pioneers, boys who were marginally active in the anarchist movement in Portland, recognized that there were no clubs at their schools that provided good vehicles for antiwar activism or activism around school budget cuts. They identified a need for a student movement that could connect these two concerns and that could span several high schools. They lamented that there were no school clubs that allowed for direct action tactics and vowed to cultivate some.

Just over six hundred miles south of Portland, I first encountered Youth Power (YP) teen organizers the following spring at a proeducation, anti-incarceration coalition meeting in downtown Oakland, California. Coming to this meeting from high schools all over the East Bay, black and Latino teens as young as fourteen years old introduced themselves and the youth organization they represented. On this particular day, Malcolm X's birthday, each teen also shared something they found interesting and important about Malcolm X. As they spoke easily about his beginnings, the evolution of his political ideology, and the alliances he had forged with other movements, it quickly became apparent that their knowledge of the famous black leader and the racial justice legacy he represented far outshone my own, or that of most progressive adults I knew. It was here that I first met some of the magnetic YP organizers I would come to know over the next two years: Salvador, Gayle, Jazmin, Pilar, James, Tevin, and many others. Later that year, they would allow me to march with them during their protest against the California High School Exit Exam. Surrounding the state school board in Sacramento, we shouted "We are the students! The mighty, mighty students! Fighting for our rights! And equal education!" while school board members looked on from behind their second-floor windows. I would grow to deeply admire the pedagogical styles of Salvador, Jazmin, James, and Naomi as I watched these teens lead groups of freshmen in educational workshops on oppression. They explained ageism, sexism, and classism as systemic, interpersonal, and internalized forms of oppression to a large group of students in a powerful yet accessible way, so that even high school freshmen new to social movement politics could understand these concepts. I would witness sixteen-year-old Jazmin run up onto the stage in her school's auditorium during a YP organized rally against interracial violence, grab the microphone, and invite students to get up on stage with her and speak their minds. When Latino and black students began using their opportunity on the mic to battle each other onstage and to even invoke longstanding turf and gang wars, I watched Jazmin quickly interrupt them to diffuse the tension and make peace.

Youth Power in Oakland began in the mid-1990s as a response to increasing interracial violence in several East Bay schools. Young adults from area social justice organizations and larger state coalitions met with students to create YP, taking students' lead as to what needed to be done about the violence. Students asserted that interracial violence on school grounds mirrors the larger tensions between racially segregated communities and could be partially remedied by the institution of ethnic studies programs in schools. They also argued that school violence is directly linked to students' (particularly students of color) powerlessness in both school and community decision making and that the problem of student violence can be solved only by organizing high school students into a collective movement for multiracial justice, in which youth—not adults—would be the key leaders.

The youth activists in Students Rise Up and Youth Power did not want to blend themselves seamlessly into adult social justice groups. They did not wait for their teenage years to be over before they became actively involved in politics. They did not necessarily long to be adults. Although marked by many differences shaped by race, class, and even gender, these youth all recognized that there was something special about being a teenage activist. While able to clearly explain the many ways in which they experienced subordination in an adult-dominated society, they also strongly believed in their own unique potential as youth to effect social change. SRU activist Troy explained the promise of teenage activism in this way:

> Well, in high school, you are really energetic. You really want to do something. And like, a lot of the adults don't have our energy. They are burning out. They are constantly telling themselves, "I'm not going to do anything anymore. What I'm doing isn't working anymore. I'm tired." I mean, break out of it! You've got to liberate yourself! You need to feel like you can do something. And that's the thing. *Kids fight to win.* Kids don't say, "Well, we'll try this, but it might not work—so we need to be ready to lose." Kids say, "We are going to do whatever it takes. We are taking city hall, we are going to the Capitol, and we are going to yell at them until they come down to talk to us."
>
> So I think that's one of the coolest things about the youth movement. We can take radical direct action and be totally accountable for it. Because if they are not giving us a voice, then fuck them. If we are not going to be able to participate in the system, then we are outside of the system, and there it is.

The SRU movement in Portland and the YP movement in Oakland awoke me to the world of teenage political activism. Between 2002 and 2004 I charted the struggles, successes, and defeats of SRU and YP organizers. I joined them in their rallies and protests, attended their weekly meetings and weekend organizing retreats, interviewed them, and listened to their stories. As I followed them on their activist journeys, I began to see the ways in which larger systems of inequality such as race, class, and gender differently shaped their collective strategies, ideologies, victories, and failures.

Their sharp critiques of adult power also underscored the significant ways that ageism impacted their lives and their approaches to activism. By explicitly identifying and politicizing ageism, these youth put into words something I had known myself since I was a teenager but was largely unable to find as a consistent and systematic theme in sociological works: the ways in which age constitutes a significant axis of social power and specifically how adolescence constitutes a subordinated social category. Even more invisible in sociological examinations of youth and inequality are the ways in which young people consciously and collectively contest adult power, other social inequalities like racism, classism, and sexism, and their own subordinated status as youth. The SRU and YP activists opened my eyes to a world of teenage political activism, one which stands at the nexus of intersecting social inequalities, history, geography, and, most importantly, social and political agency.

Adolescence as a Social Construction

To fully understand young people's social movements—how they arise, how they succeed, and why they fail—we must first confront age as a socially constructed category of difference and inequality rather than as a simple reflection of biology. This is what Nancy Lesko (1996) has referred to as "de-naturalizing adolescence." Social constructionist analyses of large-scale social inequalities such as race (Omi and Winant 1986) and gender (Lorber 1991) have emphasized the role of history, power, and social agency in the making of inequalities. Despite popular discourses that continuously refer to "the teenage years" or "adolescence" as a universal and inevitable part of a linear human development process, a closer look

reveals that both the teenager and the adolescent are socially constructed
categories with traceable histories.[1] While social constructionism has been
crucial in challenging essentialized notions of gender and race, this theoretical perspective has been used less frequently to dismantle the ways in
which adolescence is represented in both popular discourses and even in
social science research. Biological and cognitive explanations for youth
sexuality, deviance, delinquency, and instability imply that young people
are somehow isolated from the processes of history, social structure, and
culture, as youth are often discussed only in terms of their cognitive
processes and their physiology. Despite the lingering dominance of these
essentialist theories in the literature on adolescent development, social
constructionist arguments have been fundamental to tracing the ways
in which the concepts of childhood, youth, and adolescence vary cross-
culturally and over time.[2] Much of this social constructionist work on
youth can be attributed to the paradigm shifts associated with the New
Childhood Studies, a set of fresh perspectives on youth that emerged in the
last few decades and broke with previous models of child development.
Instead of viewing children and youth as passive social actors constantly
becoming and developing but never quite being, New Childhood Studies
scholars began to view youth as autonomous, engaged, independent social
actors and producers of culture in their own right. These studies also repudiated the universalist tendencies of the reigning child development models, helping to lay the groundwork for how we might conceptualize youth
through the lens of social inequality and not just development.[3]

Adolescence as a Social Inequality

While social constructionist, historical, and cross-cultural studies have
thrown doubt on the notion that adolescence is a clear biological and universal phenomenon, not all of these studies emphasize generational issues
of power and inequality in the making of childhood and adolescence.
To fully grasp the reasons why and how young people organize their social
movements, we must also recognize that age is an axis of inequality and
not just a socially constructed difference. As Lesko (2001) notes, adolescence has long been drawn as relational and oppositional to adulthood,
and in this sense it has been and continues to be an important tool in

defining adulthood as much as it defines youth. Furthermore, we know from social constructionist works on gender and race that systems of difference in modern Western societies are also systems of inequality. Mike Males (1999, 1996), for example, argues that generational inequality constitutes a veritable "war on youth," one that is waged by a segment of adult society that advocates warehousing youth in expanding prison systems while cutting their education, impoverishes them while commodifying them, and scapegoats them for larger social problems like teen pregnancy, poverty, drug use, and violence. These studies of youth as reflections of generational inequality focus on the ways in which adolescence, as a social and historical construction, functions to maintain adult identity, value systems, and power, and results in young people's actual lived realities of political, economic, and social oppression.

Even with these studies, we have little understanding of how the social construction of youth manifests as an ongoing process within the everyday life-worlds of teenagers in schools, families, and other institutions and public spheres. How exactly do adults and youth maintain, modify, or resist age inequality in their interactions with each other? In a general sense, social researchers understand that social inequalities are maintained on institutional/systemic levels, interactional levels, and internalized/individual levels. In terms of age inequality and adolescence, it is these latter two domains of social constructionism that have been the least explored in research on adolescence as a social inequality. This study of youth activism reveals the actual processes of youth subordination in the everyday interaction between youth and adults and youth and each other as they build their own movements for social change.

Furthermore, existing studies of age as a social inequality, in their nearly exclusive focus on macroinstitutions and macrodiscourses, tend to leave out young people's voices and agency. Although New Childhood Studies perspectives strive to understand the ways in which children are active agents, in the sense that they are "active in the complex negotiations of social life and contributing in significant ways to the everyday construction of the social world, not as subjects-in-the-making but as subjects in their own right" (Best 2007, 11), many studies of age as a social inequality omit this focus on young people's agency, inadvertently reifying young people's political passivity and silence and portraying them as social objects unaware of social problems. Although these studies illuminate the ways in which youth is a socially constructed category, we are left wondering whether or not young people know that they are a subordinated group. Are they aware of their own subordination? Do they care that they are subordinated? How do they understand and contend with their own social status as developing but "deficient" adults? How do they respond to this subordination? In short, I wanted to explore how young people themselves also participate in the social construction, and sometimes the reconstruction, of youth. As Allison James argues, "It is clear that the particular character of that structural space of 'childhood' is not only determined by macrosocial, economic, and demographic processes. Children themselves, those who at any point in time inhabit that space, may also make their presence felt and contribute to shaping what childhood is" (1998, 60).

Youth as "Citizens-in-the-Making"

Central to the construction of adolescents as a subordinated group and of age as a system of inequality is the maintenance of what I call "citizenship-in-the-making": a model of ambiguous social belonging where young people's political participation can be imagined, but only in terms of their adult eventuality. As John Holt observes, modern Westernized notions of childhood construct children as a mixture of "expensive nuisance, fragile treasure, slave and super-pet" while deeming childhood to be "a kind of walled garden in which children, being small and weak, are protected from the harshness of the world outside until they become strong and clever enough to cope with it" (1975, 22). The often uttered phrase "the children are our future" expresses this very idea: young people will be those who make political decisions as adults; they will be the gatekeepers of democracy and the caretakers of future generations. They will accomplish all of this in the context of adult political subjectivity. They are our "precious resources," our future incarnate (Gaines 1991).

Chris Jenks (1996) argues that children, as they are constructed in modern Western society to be fundamentally different from adults, become objects to be nurtured and cherished in their potential as the next generation of adults. They are citizens in the very abstract sense that they are rendered as voiceless caretakers of an uncertain future. Audrey Osler and Hugh Starkey (2003) note that this represents a "deficit model" of social citizenship: a presumption that young people are politically ignorant and uncaring, largely unaware of their rights and social responsibilities. According to this model, youth are socially constructed as citizen participants only in future tense: ill-equipped to participate in social and political decision making as youth, only capable of this participation as adults. Furthermore, this deficit model also necessitates that adults intervene to "create" citizens out of youth through educational processes. Actualized citizenship, in this scenario, is the province of adulthood. The generalized assumption that youth are always developing and lack the cognitive capacities to engage responsibly in social decision making provides the rationale for why the voting age is set at eighteen years of age. By socially constructing adolescents as cognitively and socially deficient compared to adults, as always "becoming" but never quite "there" (Lesko 2001), we foreclose the possibility of adolescent political participation in society. Hidden in the benign, hopeful phrase "the children are our future" is a segregation between adult and youth worlds, one that has real implications for leaving young people with very little political power.

The deficit model and the model of citizenship-in-the-making are further complicated by young people's social locations in race, class, and gender hierarchies. As Noel Smith and others note, "The status of young people as citizens in the context of social policy could be described, at best, as ambiguous" (2005, 427). Young people must be eighteen before they can vote, own land, sign most contracts, and marry without parental permission. Yet increasingly, youth below the age of eighteen can be tried in adult courts and can be sent to adult prisons. These contradictory variations in the classification of young people's citizenship are often rooted in larger social inequities. As Ann Arnett Ferguson (2001) argues, youth of color in particular are "adultified" in ways that deny them the protections of childhood innocence often accorded to white, middle-class children. For youth of color, Holt's notion of childhood as a "walled garden" does not adequately explain their alienation from the rights and responsibilities associated with social citizenship.

Furthermore, the adultification of youth of color does not provide these youth with the kind of adult privileges that facilitate their political participation and social inclusion more generally. Importantly, adult groups are also highly differentiated as citizens according to their sexual orientation, immigrant status, and positions in racial and class hierarchies. Although actualized citizenship is the province of adulthood in an age-stratified society, clearly not all adults share equally in the benefits of this citizenship. In short, citizenship—as political subjectivity and social belonging—represents a confluence of social and historical processes that create patterns of political inclusion and exclusion. This is as true for youth as it is for adults.

Rather than conceptualizing youth as just naturally ill-equipped for political participation due to their perceived developmental and social deficiencies, I advocate an examination of the processes by which adolescents are actually *diverted* from political action and are socially constructed as nonpolitical beings. My findings suggest that, at times, when young people insist on claiming a political, collective voice in local decision-making processes and social movements, they are subtly and overtly thwarted by adults, and sometimes even other youth, who read this political action as precocious, transgressive, and out-of-bounds of proper adolescent behavior. Examining the processes of adolescent political organizing provides a unique window into the construction of youth as citizens-in-the-making rather than as actualized political actors, as teens' struggles to form political movements bump up against the many prescriptions for their political silence. Young people's exclusion from political participation is not a biological inevitability: it is the result of institutional and interactional social processes, which young people themselves resist using various strategies.

Youth Resistance: From Subculture to Social Movement

There is a notable silence in the social science literatures on adolescence and political action. The sociological focus on politics and youth has waned in the decades since the college student movements of the 1960s and 1970s. In most social movement theorizing, the implicit assumption is that the social movement actor is an adult. In social constructionist works on adolescence, there is hardly any mention of youth political action at all. It appears that many sociologists take for granted that adolescents are nonpolitical beings, and the naturalized assumption that adolescents are always developing and are citizens-in-the-making but are not yet capable of actual political participation largely goes unquestioned or unchallenged. The assumption that teens are, at best, "practicing for the real thing" but are not yet real political actors might account for some of the sociological silence regarding youth political organizing.

Another important reason why adolescent political activism has not become a major focus of sociological research (neither in social movement literature nor the literature on adolescence) is because adolescent activism often takes place on school grounds and away from adult society and larger adult publics. Their marginality and relative invisibility as political actors speaks to their social and spatial segregation from the world of adults, and thus from the spheres that adults usually recognize as political and public. While the activists in this study aimed to coalesce with larger social movements in their communities and tried to make their movements visible to other adult activists and adult publics in general, preceding these public appearances were efforts toward collective political action that were confined to youth spaces such as schools. Given that secondary schools play a key role in constructing youth as citizens-in-the-making, it is not surprising that many teenagers' conscious efforts toward political organizing never come to fruition on school grounds. As a result, these efforts escape the attention of both adults and other youth alike.

The major studies that do edge toward examining forms, or at least glimmers, of youth political agency are subcultural studies of youth resistance. Profoundly ethnographic in nature, works by subcultural theorists such as Donna Gaines (1991), John Clarke and others (1975), Dick Hebdige (1979), Angela McRobbie and Jenny Garber (1975), and Paul Willis (1977) have highlighted collective forms of youth agency in studies of youth cultures' music, style, and leisure. It is within subcultural studies on youth, and their relationships to parent cultures and class conflict, that researchers have raised the question as to whether or not this resistance can be considered legitimately political.[4] These debates about whether or not youth subcultural resistance represents true political resistance are undoubtedly important, as it is likely that many more youth "resist" through youth cultures rather than through social movements. However, it is telling that while some researchers have become experts at teasing out the potentially political threads of youth subcultural style, music, dress, and leisure, most have maintained a curious silence regarding young people's overt political resistance through social movement activism. Furthermore, studies of youth subcultures overwhelmingly focus on the cultural dimensions of youth resistance rather than on their potentially political dimensions (Garrison 2000; Kearney 1998), further obscuring our understanding of young people's political resistance.

Although this study of youth activism, like studies of youth subcultures, relies on ethnographic methods to make visible forms of youth agency, I do not speak of Portland teens in Students Rise Up or Oakland teens in Youth Power in subcultural terms. In fact, the great accomplishment of youth movements like SRU and YP is that they are able to draw together many different types of youth and even cross traditional clique boundaries through a shared political culture. For example, in YP, Shandra and Alisha, two black girls, wore oversized, black T-shirts, baggy pants that hung from their hips and fell no farther than their calves, and cornrows in their short hair. Shandra almost always wore a black winter hat on her head, even in summer. They both wore rainbow necklaces that identified them as queer youth. Alisha was best friends with Salvador, who identified himself as Raza instead of Latino or Hispanic. Salvador wore his long, black hair slicked back and always wore an oversized black-and-white flannel coat. Salvador listened to Tupac Shakur and Mexican pop music and carried all his CDs with him in a little black case wherever he went. Alisha said she preferred heavy metal but listened to Salvador's music with him, one of his headphones in her ears. Often I found them like this, their heads together, listening to music before the beginning of an organizing meeting. Pilar and Shandra had also become best friends through YP organizing. Pilar looked the complete opposite of Shandra. Pilar had long, dyed-reddish hair, which she ironed flat. She wore heavy eye makeup and dark lipstick and dressed in miniskirts. Pilar (who identified herself as Raza and a queer ally) and Shandra often led workshops on racial stereotypes together for incoming YP freshmen. Guillermo was also a major organizer in YP. He played football for Patterson High and struggled to balance his political organizing work with the demands of his football practice. With short, cropped hair, white T-shirts, and clean shorts, he looked to be the classic jock and in this sense stood in sharp contrast to organizers like

Shandra and Alisha who did not participate in school activities like sports. These organizers represented an impressive array of youth cliques that are usually segmented by class status, racial/ethnic identity, sexuality, and orientation to schooling as an institution.[5] They were the jocks, the brains, and the freaks.

I found the same heterogeneity among SRU organizers, and, indeed, both YP and SRU organizers took a great deal of pride in having created a network of students that cross common student divides. SRU organizer Troy, a self-described anarchist, looked the picture of Portland anarchism: dark, ripped clothing, mussed up hair, shoes held together with duct tape. Stephen wore short, thick dreadlocks and brightly colored bell-bottom pants, while Shae, who looked like the classic cheerleader, had long, perfectly combed blonde hair and wore pink eye shadow and pastel-colored clothing. The first photo story of SRU in a local Portland paper disappointed SRU activists, who claimed that the paper featured "the most extreme looking" teens like Stephen and Troy, while overlooking the more "normal looking" teens like Shae. Troy, Stephen, and Shae, as well as other SRU activists, felt this coverage obscured how vast the SRU student movement had become and had relegated their movement to more of a depoliticized inside look at a strange and new youth culture rather than a real political movement.

As Alain Touraine writes, "In situations which are generally interpreted in terms of participation or exclusion, of conformity and deviance, the idea of social movement introduces a different approach because it tries to evaluate the capacity of various categories to transform themselves into actors of their own situation and of its transformation" (1985, 783). By describing youth organizing in social movement rather than youth subcultural terms, I highlight adolescent political agency. This perspective positions adolescents as active agents in their own social construction, beings capable of explicit critique and organized political action.

Feminist Notions of Intersectionality

In examining the politics of youth activism, I draw on multiracial feminist notions of intersectionality. These feminist perspectives have drawn attention to the overlapping and intersecting systems of racial, class, and

sexual oppressions in the making of gender inequality. The development
of an intersectional perspective on gender and race is rooted in the work
of activists and scholars studying the lives of women of color, who occupy
social locations that are not easily explained by gender or race analyses
that fail to grasp the simultaneity and intersection of these systems.[6]

Similarly, I approach youth subordination and agency through a multiracial feminist lens, focusing on the complex ways that youth subordination speaks through and intersects with racist systems of power, gendered
systems of subordination, and poverty. Just as all adults do not share a
similar lived experience of adult privilege, the processes of youth subordination and empowerment, and the construction of youth as citizens-in-
the-making, are not the same for all youth even though they all share a
subordinated social status in an adult-dominated society. A feminist intersectional framework allows us to understand that although age is always
salient, it does not constitute a unidimensional axis of inequality. As Lesko
explains,

> Each group and each individual has to come to terms with the
> modern scientific definition of adolescence and its reverberations
> in public schooling, therapeutic talk, and expectations for maturity,
> self-discipline, and well-planned futures. Since adolescents have
> been defined as not adult, this opposition to adults, or at least the
> assumption that adolescents are distinctive from adults, will influ-
> ence all cultural and class groups, although these ideas may have
> different implications and interpretations in particular moments
> and localities. (2001, 12)

Multiracial feminist theory maintains that systems such as gender and
race, which are socially constructed, not only structure individual identities but also provide organizing principles for our social world (Collins
1999), and these categories are mutually constituted to reproduce and
maintain social hierarchies. The notion of intersectionality also draws
attention to the relationship between disadvantage and privilege. Young
people's individual and collective social locations in gendered, racial, and
class hierarchies produce different social movement tactics, frameworks,
identities, and relationships to adult society. These are all shaped by young
people's privileges and disadvantages stemming from other systems of

inequality, as they are lived through the structures, processes, and experiences of youth subordination. Beyond simply applying intersectional theory to the study of youth movements, I am weaving another thread into the theory itself. I move beyond the usual feminist categories of gender, race, class, and sexuality and expand the intersectional lens to demonstrate how *age*, as another axis of social power, shapes young people's racialized, classed, and gendered struggles for political power. In short, young people's struggles are not just qualitatively different from each other's because of the many racial, ethnic, class, and gender differences that divide them. Their struggles are also distinct from adults' political struggles, as they grapple with age inequality while trying to claim political power.

The Focus of This Book

While the behaviors, consciousness, and political orientations of the youth activists featured in this study are not meant to stand in for all adolescents (most of whom are not political activists), they do reveal the larger mechanisms of how young people are produced as a subordinated group, the resources that are available to youth to counter this subordination, and the possibilities for youth political agency. Furthermore, the specific strategies, successes, and failures of the youth movements described in the following pages teach us how these larger mechanisms of youth subordination and resistance are powerfully shaped by systems of race, class, and gender.

Chapter I provides the larger historical and geographical context for the rise of Youth Power (Oakland) and Students Rise Up (Portland)—the two youth movement networks featured in this book. I begin with an examination of the political geographies of both Portland and Oakland, two cities with vibrant political and countercultural infrastructures that have been crucial to facilitating adolescent activism in these urban areas. I describe the rise of a politicized hip-hop culture in Oakland that has helped to provide the language, consciousness, and shape of youth organizing, and I contrast this picture of Oakland with that of Portland, a city that is known for its thriving DIY ("do it yourself") culture. In this chapter I also outline some of the social crises that have spurred youth activism and motivated students to take political action, and I end this chapter with a consideration of the paradox of how youth social movement has developed in a historical moment when adult commentators have discussed concerns over increasing youth civic apathy. I provide accounts of how youth activists themselves perceive the political inaction of their peers and their generation more broadly, as well as how they envision routes to their political power.

After the historical and geographical context for the formation of youth movements have been established, chapter 2 traces the development of teenage political activism on school territory. While the teens in this study eventually merged with larger social movements in their cities, they first began their activist journeys on the grounds of their individual schools. In this chapter I detail the battles that youth waged in Oakland and Portland to integrate youth movements into the social and academic life of their schools.

Chapter 3 focuses on these student movements as they develop beyond the schools and into adolescents' larger communities. In this chapter, I delve into the complex and sometimes problematic relationships that youth have with adult allies in local social movements. I analyze how these relationships with adult allies prompt teens to conceptualize and politicize age inequality in specific ways and to structure their movements in each city according to these understandings.

Chapters 4 and 5 document key strategies that adolescent activists use both in their schools and in their larger communities to establish legitimacy and leverage as political actors in the eyes of adults. I argue that adolescent activists encounter larger social expectations for their political silence, passivity, and social marginality and thus develop strategies to navigate what I call the "adult gaze" to achieve student movement goals within their schools and larger communities. Chapter 4 foregrounds Oakland youth and their strategies for political legitimacy as they fight to change their school conditions, while chapter 5 focuses on Portland youth activists' strategies to gain political leverage by harnessing local media coverage.

The final chapter of this book explores the way in which gender differences impact young activists' abilities to counter the model of citizenship-in-the-making in their communities. In this chapter, I demonstrate that young people's potential to counter the deficit model of social citizenship is powerfully shaped by their gendered positions within their families. I analyze the gender politics of both YP and SRU to ultimately show that adolescent subordination and political empowerment, in relation to the adult world, operate along gendered lines of privilege and disadvantage. I complicate this story of gender politics in youth movements by revealing how these politics are also structured by divergent racial, ethnic, and class contexts.

As Richard Farson wrote in 1974, "In the developing consciousness of a civilization which has for four hundred years gradually excluded children from the world of adults, there is the dawning recognition that children must have the right to full participation in society, that they must be valued for themselves, not just as potential adults" (3). The following chapters explore the struggles of young people to become vocal, embodied, political subjects rather than the objects of adult inevitability: the invisible and silent citizens-in-the-making.

1

The Development of Urban Teenage Activism

Opportunities and Challenges at the Turn of the Millennium

One day, sixteen-year-old YP student organizer Salvador and I roamed around East Oakland on city bus after city bus, trying to find local restaurants that might be willing to donate food to Youth Power. That day, Salvador told me this story of his lone attempt to access the highest executive power in the United States:

> I wrote a letter to the president, and he sent me an autographed picture. Like, I talked to him about all the issues around my neighborhood and stuff, like drug dealing and violence. And he sent me a response saying, "Well, here's the information you requested." And it's like, I didn't request any information! It's like, "Thank you for writing," and this and that, and "Here's an autographed photo," and this and that. And, you know, that shows how ignorant he is. When my brother went off to war [in Iraq], my father just ripped that photo up. He *burned* that picture.

As he spoke, we passed blocks and blocks of dilapidated houses that crept up the low Oakland hillsides like Brazilian favelas—the closest thing to shantytowns one might find in the United States. Salvador shook his head in disgust as recounted to me this first and last attempt to access political power as an individual teen without a movement behind him. In light of the controversies around election fraud, the electoral college system, and low voter turnouts, individual access to executive decision making is certainly problematic even for voting adults. For teenagers who are, by definition, without voting rights at all, it is nearly impossible. As Salvador illustrates, the paths to political agency open to youth are few and far between. Adolescents do not have established channels for political participation through which they can speak to and be heard by powerful adult decision makers. This poses a problem for many young people who are both aware of and concerned about the political, social, and economic crises affecting their communities. These crises are many and are propelling young people to seek agency and influence through one of the few political routes open to them should they claim it: social movement activism.

But why do youth form youth movement networks, networks that articulate with, but are distinct from, adult movement organizations? Why don't they simply join any number of social justice organizations that already exist in their communities? The fact that students seeking political participation in social movements seldom walk out of their usual settings like the family, school, or mall and into any number of social justice groups in their communities speaks to the extent to which social movements, like electoral politics, are often adult dominated and age segregated. Many of the youth featured in this book told me stories of how they had been dismissed, overlooked, or shut out by adults in adult-dominated organizations such as local peace organizations. Some had never even joined adult groups, as they anticipated that they would be marginalized. Thus, it never even occurred to them that adult organizations could be a route to their own political participation. Indeed, youth movements stand as testaments to the way politics is not meant for adolescents, whether electoral or social movement–oriented. At the same time, youth movements also signify an instance of collective youth agency, which, unlike many forms of subcultural agency, is explicitly and self-consciously political. Adolescents' battles to weigh in on important social and political issues require that they transgress the line between symbolic, developing, and eventual political beings and actual political actors with voices and presence.

This chapter outlines the larger geographical and historical contexts for rise of youth movement networks such as Youth Power (Oakland) and Students Rise Up (Portland). Youth social powerlessness is constructed within particular historical epochs and geographical locations. Indeed, the strength of taking a social constructionist view of youth is that it focuses our attention on the ways in which age, as an axis of inequality, changes over time and across place. Young people's strategies for contesting their subordination are also geographically and historically bound. Thus, to understand the ways in which youth constitute a subordinated group in society, and also to understand sources of youth political agency through collective movements, we must turn to the larger historical processes and political developments that shape young people's lives. In setting the stage for the emergence of youth activism at the turn of the millennium, this chapter focuses on the ways in which young people themselves identify and interpret the social crises of their time. Although I establish these crises and contexts piecemeal, they work together to create the conditions that structure adolescence and generational relationships, and spark the formation of youth movements.

Youth Movement and the City: Oakland and Portland

This research was conducted in two West Coast urban areas: Portland, Oregon, and the larger East Bay of the Bay Area in California. I began the research process in the Fall of 2002 and continued through the summer of 2004: a historical moment in which youth and adults alike witnessed a rush of rapid and profound changes to the structure of U.S. government and its foreign policy. In the wake of the 9–11 terrorist attacks just a year before, the Bush administration ushered in a two-fronted war in the Middle East: first in Afghanistan and then in Iraq. The administration established a new security wing of government: the Office of Homeland Security, which later morphed into the Department of Homeland Security. In the shadow of the new "war on terror," the Bush administration also established the No Child Left Behind Act (NCLB): a sweeping standards-based education reform act, which established that federal funding for education should be contingent on standardized test performance as the main measurement of school, teacher, and student "accountability." NCLB skillfully wedded national education reform to U.S. militarism, specifying that schools furnish to military recruiters the name and contact information of every public school student in the nation, unless students or their parents specifically opt out. These rapid national changes filtered down from the upper reaches of the Bush administration into students' own lives and became the targets of youth political opposition.

These changes hit the ground in Oakland and Portland, cities with their own rich histories of social movement activism. The two cities' cultural legacies were fundamental to shaping youth movements during this historical moment. In particular, these urban spaces provide politicized centers for meeting, reading, learning, and organizing that are somewhat open to youth mobilizing and provide students with the spaces they need to develop movement organizations. Sara Evans and Harry Boyte term these spaces "free spaces," defined by their "roots in community, the dense, rich networks of daily life; by their autonomy; and by their public or quasi-public character as participatory environments which nurture values associated with citizenship and a vision of the common good" (1986, 20).

In the Bay Area of California, an older history of civil rights, black insurgency, Third World Liberation (Ferreira 2004), and people of color movements have found their new incarnations in a more recent wave of multiracial justice movements and immigrant rights movements beginning in the early 1990s (Martínez 1998). During this period, youth of color have increasingly become the targets of increased police repression, violence, and incarceration (Males 1996; M. Davis 1991), while the schools they attend have been slated for budget cuts. Because of this history, many movements to organize and empower communities of color have focused on youth, bringing youth into the fold of larger social justice movements. Because youth gang, turf, and interracial violence have increased since the institution of new anti-immigrant and racist legislation in the early 1990s, many youth and adults alike have identified that encouraging "youth empowerment" (although the definition of this term varies widely from organization to organization) or, at the very least, providing youth with more activities, is one way to stem gang violence both in schools and on the streets. Thus, youth empowerment has been instituted in a wide range of nonprofit organizations.

Beginning in the early 1990s, high school students from across the Bay Area (as well as in Los Angeles) began organizing student strikes and mass school walkouts to demand an end to racist educational practices and right-wing legislation. These walkouts were inspired by the college student movements at San Francisco State and University of California at Berkeley that were also demanding ethnic studies around the same time. Nearby college MEChA chapters were especially instrumental in helping to shape teenage student organizing, since these chapters began to extend their organizing work to local high schools.[1] The black student unions and Asian student unions that coalesced with MEChA during the fights for ethnic studies in the early 1990s also began to reach out to high school students. For many college students of color, organizing exclusively on college campuses took on, as twenty-five-year-old YP ally Javier noted, a "bourgeois kind of quality." Twenty-five-year-old YP ally Yesenia remembered, "Yeah, [college organizing] was too academic, and I felt that it was too campus-oriented. You know, all the time I would be in my mind, 'I can't believe we are here and we are just five miles away from Oakland,' you know. 'There are murders going on and stuff, and we are here arguing over a flyer,' you know?"

While politicized college students were finding new inspiration from extending their organizing to local communities and working with high school students of color, high school students hungry for young adult mentorship were also reaching out to college students. Fledgling high school student organizers were inviting college students to come speak at their high schools. Twenty-seven-year-old YP adult ally Emily recalled this synergy between high school and college students:

> Those folks were feeling really gratified by just their relationship with these high school students who were also looking for those political people that we were looking for in college, right. So we were out maybe gravitating toward professors that meant something to us. You know what I mean? . . . Like, they were finding it with us. And I think that was sort of, like, an instant thing.
>
> Here you have this high school student who is, like, calling up at night going, "I just called to say hi," you know, and you knew something was happening, and you saw them struggling with the same questions we struggled with when we were in high school, but nobody was there to help us answer them.

During the early 1990s, foundations started to fund youth organizations all over the East Bay (although the funding is always problematic and never enough). One result of this support has been the emergence of youth media councils, youth radio, youth hip-hop organizations, art programs, and several new multigenerational coalitions working to raise awareness of the simultaneous defunding of schools and the ever-expanding prisons in California: a funding trend that has the effect of channeling young people of color out of the schools and into the prisons.

The youth movement in the Bay Area is both expansive and disconnected in points. Many of these disconnections are due to different visions of youth empowerment, different roles for youth, different visions for solving social problems, and of course different funding sources that impose constraints on organizational strategies and missions. Some youth organizations are not overtly political. Many groups such as Teens on the Move or Youth Against Violence focus on violence prevention, while some like Youth Arts focus on channeling young people into positive activities like making music and art (which can be political), without necessarily introducing a political framework to organizational activities. Despite these different orientations of youth organizations in the East Bay, there are notably more opportunities in the urban environment than there are within school walls for young people to gain organizing skills, to form coalitions with other youth and multigenerational groups, and to access political frameworks for understanding social injustices: in short, to become political actors.

In Oakland, youth and student activism cannot be understood outside of hip-hop cultural, political, and spatial forms.[2] Murray Forman notes that over the last three decades, hip-hop has "associated the urban core with authenticity and the city's streets as a legitimating space of cultural value among youths" (2002, 46). While policy makers, social scientists, mass media, and a whole array of adult professionals have pathologized urban youth of color and the city ghettos and barrios in which they live, young people themselves have spun an ever-evolving, complex hip-hop culture that analyzes the urban terrain and humanizes their own existence.[3] As Forman explains, hip-hop as cultural and political expression extends well beyond music. It fundamentally appropriates and creates urban spaces:

> The culture of hip-hop embodies a range of activities that not only display but consciously foreground spatial characteristics, whether through the sonic appropriation of aural space, the appropriation of street corners (where, at an earlier stage in hip-hop's development, rap improvisation and break dancing were common), or the

> appropriation of the city's architecture through the ubiquitous dis-
> play of spray-painted graffiti tags, burners, and pieces. Hip-hop
> comprises a deliberate, concentrated, and often spontaneous array
> of spatial practices and spatial discourses that are both constituted
> by and constitutive of the spaces and places in which its primary
> cultural producers work. Its expressive forms have therefore been
> exceedingly influential in both the representation and the transfor-
> mation of the urban environment throughout the 1980s and the
> 1990s. (42)

In this sense, hip-hop political culture has held the potential to reinvigorate civil society among youth of color. In his historical analysis of hip-hop,
Neal notes that urban hip-hop radio DJs have long addressed specific
urban neighborhoods, housing projects, schools, workplaces, and streets
as part of their on-air radio shows, thus contributing to a black public
sphere. He observes, "Hip-hop recordings began to resemble digitized
town meetings" (1999, 161). Traveling on the BART from West Oakland, to
downtown Oakland, and into the heart of deep East Oakland, one can see
the ways in which hip-hop culture has reclaimed the urban environment.
Sides of buildings, carcasses of industrial centers long abandoned to deindustrialization, and trains are covered in bright explosions of murals and
graffiti. A youth center in West Oakland that hosts five youth nonprofit
organizations is a tall metal building with no windows. Nested in the shad-
ows of a factory that spits toxic plumes of smoke, the otherwise drab youth
center is immediately recognizable as a youth space with its murals and
taggings on the outside walls.

   This center, aptly called the Youth Empowerment Center, is a nexus of
youth cultural expression and community political campaigns. It is also a
veritable monument to hip-hop. One youth organization inside the center
is devoted entirely to the arts. Here, youth of color from all over Oakland
learn to deejay, freestyle, break-dance, write poetry, and silk-screen.
During the summer, YP teams at each school site across the East Bay built
solidarity by creating T-shirts, CDs, or murals together after attending
workshops on oppression, movement histories, and political organizing
strategies. A young person can walk out of this organization and into
another one that gives workshops on California's prison industry and

educational justice, or can walk upstairs to a library and read histories about political movements, music, and the arts.

Hip-hop weaves political analyses and dissent with artistic forms of expression. Almost all Youth Power events, if they are meant to mobilize and recruit new youth, involve hip-hop political expression. Marissa Bloom and Marianne Cariaso (2004) observe that across the Bay Area, multiracial youth political gatherings are almost always embedded in hip-hop performances (including music and dance) and entail an element of youth freestyling—giving youth a chance to "step up" and "get on the mic" to voice their perspectives on their schools, neighborhoods, country, and the world. Thus, hip-hop culture weaves together disparate communities of youth of color and often helps to align otherwise disconnected youth organizations into regional youth and student campaigns (Bloom and Cariaso 2004; Martínez 1998). Indeed, Andreana Clay (2006) argues that hip-hop is a vital tool for political organizing and consciousness raising among youth of color in a post–civil rights movement era. As twenty-nine-year-old YP adult ally Estella noted, "Performances are usually what brings in the crowd, you know. Once the music starts and once people get up there on stage, students focus. Students come in. The music really brings people in." YP chants meant to turn on new students to political action are politicized versions of popular hip-hop songs. YP student organizers even used political hip-hop songs such as "They Schools" by Dead Prez to teach incoming freshmen students about Eurocentric education and racism in school curriculums.[4] While hip-hop has provided the language, consciousness, and shape of youth organizing in the East Bay, the explicit goals of YP went far beyond what hip-hop alone could accomplish: more youth decision-making power within the schools, the institution of ethnic studies programs in high schools, and increased school funding. YP students opposed the war in Iraq, military recruiting on campuses, and the expansion of prisons and zero-tolerance policies (Giroux 2003a) that disproportionately affect youth of color in impoverished urban neighborhoods.

Portland, in contrast, lacks this vibrant homegrown politicized hip-hop youth scene. Without a large, politically active, local, and visible hip-hop youth culture that has the potential to catalyze politics and creative expression among young people, and without the highly visible wave of youth violence that has helped to trigger both community attention to the particular life conditions of youth of color and a trickle of funding to sustain youth-centered organizations (as in the East Bay), we find that in Portland there is instead a mostly adult-dominated progressive network of social justice organizations.

Despite Portland's lack of organizations that have created spaces specifically for adolescent activists, there are spaces within the radical wing of the mostly white, progressive activist scene—namely the anarchist movement infrastructure of bookstores, cafes, and other movement spaces that have spurred more radical direct action movements (and have made Portland famous for being a politically liberal city since being dubbed "Little Beirut")—that have provided Portland's white, progressive youth with accessible public and politicized spaces to develop student movements.[5] Sara described the opportunities that "liberal" Portland has given her for political agency:

> I was living in this really conservative, small town in Ohio, and everyone was really Republican. And then I moved here to Portland and it was a lot more liberal. And I embraced that so much that it completely changed me. It changed who I am. And, that's part of the direction I was going in, just seeing a lot of the problem where I came from and wanting to fix that. And I was lucky enough to get involved with the Vista High kids and the kids that got together from all the other schools. And we started planning things.

Some of Students Rise Up (SRU) students attended liberal-leaning middle or elementary schools in Portland, centers for liberal education that do not exist in many places such as the small town in Ohio that Sara describes. Indeed, middle-class institutions like these community-based, alternative schools fuel the image of Portland as an independent and "livable" city. SRU organizers who attended these schools credit them for the development of their social morals and sense of political responsibility. SRU activist Jacob reflected on his middle school experience:

> Personally I feel like I started self-consciously. I went to the Eco-Alternative Middle School and that was strange, and I was really surrounded by that community-based way of communicating and organizing and acting. I think most of my ethics and morals come

from that school. That's one of the greatest places; it's just a beautiful school. . . . They have gardens all over the place; they go on field trips every Tuesday and Thursday. There are murals all over the school.

Jacob noted that while his middle school experience was formative for the development of his environmental and community ethics, his school didn't provide him with an outlet for sustained political action: "I would say my opinions were radical in junior high, but I don't think I knew what to do. Like, there were several times in junior high I called, like, a local city task force and I was like, 'I don't know how to get involved.' But here I am, just a seventh grader; what am I going to do?" Nevertheless, urban alternative school spaces such as Eco-Alternative Middle School in Portland have been instrumental in awakening the social consciousness of many high school students.

Stephen credited the Portland activist street scene, which includes direct action groups who "reclaim the streets," and an explicitly anticorporate (Starr 2000) bike-oriented counterculture for his early entrée into community politics:

> I got into the real, like, *recreation* activism, like critical mass and things like that. Where it wasn't really, it wasn't really activism—like rallies and marches and that sort of thing. But it kind of had that overtone to it. And it kind of grew from there. Like, I met people. I got more and more involved.

Portland is also home to a thriving DIY ("do it yourself") culture, which stems from a youth-oriented punk movement and includes homegrown networks of independent record labels, cafes, zines, publishers, art venues, and clubs. Amory Starr notes that the anticorporate leanings of DIY culture "are teaching young people about alternatives to corporate-dominated economies and building theory and community around youth alienation" (2000, 132). When Portland students ventured into DIY territory, they accessed important critiques of corporate culture and began to critically analyze how corporate power has reached into their homes, schools, and communities.

Many of Portland's DIY spaces are also anarchist spaces or anarchist-friendly spaces. The culture of these establishments are somewhere between adolescent and full adult, allowing an access point for youth participation. These anarchist spaces are also explicitly antiauthoritarian in their political leanings and structures: they are collectives and cooperatives instead of hierarchically structured businesses. Thus, they create possibilities for subverting the age hierarchies and adult authority that reign in the larger society. The anarchist scene in Portland is a fairly young one, and very white, matching the demographics of SRU activists. In popular parlance, anarchism *is* a youth movement (Starr 2000; Nehring 1993).[6] So when students in Portland decided to thread their student unions and activism together, they ventured into anarchist territory to do this, because it seemed to be a territory less likely to be governed by adult power. As Starr writes,

> While anarchism is not a vibrant, rapidly growing movement, and while it languishes under discrediting stereotypes, its survival is significant for several reasons. . . . It provides a political space for a youth constituency and nurtures radicalism. Youth movements' sustained enthusiasm for anarchist thought, statistically insignificant though it may be, is important in delegitimizing liberalism and homogenizing consumerism; it is one of the few alternatives for youth. (2000, 114)

Portland is also unique in being so politically active for its relatively smaller stature (compared to other West Coast cities such as Seattle and San Francisco). Because of its relatively manageable size and its whiteness, it has the reputation for being a safe and progressive city. The city's central spaces that are mostly white and gentrified (read: "safe") and its reputation for being livable have made it somewhat easier for white student activists to get parental permission to explore Portland's progressive activist scene (although obtaining parental permission is often a gendered phenomenon for student activists in both Portland and Oakland: see chapter 6). Positioning Portland in opposition to a "weirder" city like New York City, Kristin explained,

> Portland is a really great community as it is; there are a lot of groups who are really active. And being like a smaller, safer scene . . . we can get out more. My parents are more trusting with letting me do things than they would be if we lived in New York, or whatever,

where there are a lot of weird things going on. People feel safer around here.

This motif of a safe and progressive city, which enables student organizing in manageable urban environments like Portland, is notably absent from Oakland student narratives. In fact, the prospect of youth of color venturing into embattled and impoverished urban spaces to attend political meetings, rallies, or protests generated significant parental worry. The presence of adult protectors like YP adult allies helped to facilitate the safe transport of students into urban public spaces and also helped to diminish parental worry and increase parental support for student organizing (see chapters 3 and 6). White students in Portland venturing into "safe," mostly white, urban spaces did not require this same adult protection.

As in Oakland, local independent media venues in Portland have helped to facilitate student mobilizing. The Portland Independent Media Center (Portland IMC or Portland Indymedia) is one example of local media where all kinds of organizations can post their activities online. Portland has an especially visible and active Indymedia, infused with an anarchist bent that has made it scandalous, drawing fire from political conservatives such as Rush Limbaugh. During the anti–Iraq war rallies, protests, and vigils of 2003–2004, Portland Indymedia was the central clearinghouse for information for activists. Importantly, the emergence of Indymedia in both Oakland and Portland also allows anyone with access to the Internet, regardless of age, to participate in online political discussions. Not only this, but groups like SRU can post their own meeting information, calls for action, or needs for resources directly to the activist public (Beckerman 2003). Middle-class youth with easy access to the Internet can do this without having to pay for access to the site and do not have to have their words filtered through adult gatekeepers and editors.

Indymedia is a relatively recent development that has helped to facilitate young people's entry into social movement activism. It has also helped to increase public recognition of young people as political actors. Youth Media Council in the East Bay has served a similar function for organizations such as Youth Power, although because YP had more points of contact with a larger network of social justice organizations than did SRU, it was less dependent on media for public visibility.

Despite the vibrant Indymedia and reputation for safety that Portland has, when SRU activists moved through urban spaces outside of their schools, they had to constantly watch out for a growing police presence. When SRU activists described urban spaces and the physical landscapes in which they strategize, rally, protest, and hold actions, they inevitably discussed encounters with police and worries about police surveillance.

Portland has indeed seen a visible increase in the police patrolling of urban spaces over the last decade.[7] Walking around downtown Portland on a weekday afternoon, one may glimpse a fleet of police on bicycles, a pair of sergeants on horses roaming the areas near the waterfront (said to be the center of Portland's heroin trade), and police cars zooming up and down Burnside Street, the thoroughfare that bisects the northern and southern quadrants of the city. In the late 1990s, Portland created the Joint Terrorism Task Force to patrol leftist groups such as environmentalists, animal liberationists, anarchists, communists, and other groups, even before terrorism rose to the top of the national political agenda in the wake of 9–11.

There is good reason for young people and social justice activists in general to worry about police infiltration. Stories of police surveillance of activist groups in Portland over the last two decades began to surface at the beginning of the new millennium, prodding the expansion of a "security culture" throughout Portland's radical social movement spaces.[8] It is not surprising that politicized youth activist identities formed in these spaces entailed a definite element of distrust and dislike of police. Student activists who began to see the first glimmers of their political agency in these radical spaces also began to view this newfound agency as being potentially undermined by police. Sixteen year-old SRU activist Troy connected his politicization as an anarchist to his realization that he was a "second-class citizen":

> I mean, it's a great thing, going down there to the People's Collective [a local anarchist collective]. I mean the first couple of times I was there, I realized I was a second-class citizen. My friend and I were walking out of the federal building, after one of our, I can't remember what it was, but we were walking outside the federal building and we got followed for four or five blocks by a couple of guys who were undercover. And my friend was like, "They are following us,"

and I was like, "You're right," so we kept on walking, and we walked back into People's Collective, and they left.

Many of the SRU youths experienced Little Beirut firsthand, before they formed SRU. They rode their bikes downtown and went to their first protests as middle schoolers and younger high schoolers. They attended the May Day March of 2000 and the Bush Protest of 2002. These were events in which police presence was heavy and police violence broke out. Young people quickly learned that police would target them specifically, particularly if they were dressed in anarchist DIY style: the black clothes, the bandana over the face, the patches sewn haphazardly on their pants or knapsacks. Young people were charged by police horses, knocked on the heads by police batons, pepper-sprayed in the face. At these protests they were no longer innocent (read: white, middle-class) youth. They became enemies of the state.

These collisions with police violence both infuriated and motivated students. They experienced firsthand the limits to their right to organize in the streets. They witnessed activist groups and protesters coming together to voice dissent and the violence inflicted on those communities once they did this. These street experiences helped to politicize youth, introducing them to a mode of political expression that was both empowering and yet also subjected them to police repression. The experience of occupying public spaces to voice political dissent, for these students, was always connected to the potential for police harassment and violence.

Not insignificant to the rise of SRU in Portland is Little Beirut's geographical proximity to Seattle and the landmark WTO protests of 1999 in that city. High schoolers who organized SRU in early 2002 were junior high students or younger high schoolers in 1999 during the widely publicized protests against corporate-led globalization. Their older siblings and friends returned from the WTO protests with pockets full of rubber bullets they had picked up in the streets as evidence of police violence and stories of how direct action at the "Battle of Seattle" helped to delegitimize a global behemoth like the WTO. The WTO protests were profoundly influential for SRU organizers. As eighteen-year-old Curt explained to me when I first met SRU at a peace rally in the fall of 2002, "We're kind of like the WTO [activists] of high school clubs."

Although Portland's anarchist scene provided a kind of politicized youth-oriented culture within which to organize a youth activist network, not all SRU activists identified explicitly as anarchists. SRU activists viewed themselves as a proeducation, anticorporate, and antiwar high school student network. While all SRU activists were guided by these overarching ideals, they were ideologically split between being simply peace-oriented and identifying as anarchist. At times, such as during students' school sit-ins for education funding, these two political identities dovetailed and became less important and less distinct. At other times, such as during street protests, these identities clashed and the ideological split between SRU members became more salient.

The social movement legacies and activist cultures of Oakland and Portland provided the soil that nurtured the growth of youth movements. But it was also the crises at the turn of the millennium that propelled these movements forward. Landmark school budget cuts, skyrocketing prison expansion, an unpopular war in the Middle East, marked interracial and interethnic violence, and rampant consumerism were not just headlines that made local and national newspapers. Youth identified these crises to be the most pressing social problems in their own lives. Once the roots of their social subordination, these crises now became the targets of their organizing.

Global Transformations, Local Youth Crises

Neoliberalism, Deindustrialization, and Social Divestment

Perhaps the overarching phenomenon that not only structures youth but also fostered systems of dominance and subordination at the turn of the millennium is the ascendancy of neoliberal ideology. This ideology promotes economic growth and free trade above all else and insists that both social and economic progress means individual entrepreneurial freedom (Bourdieu 1999). According to the ideology, individual freedom is maximized by smooth-functioning free markets unencumbered by government interference. The ideology, which has guided international lending by the International Monetary Fund (IMF) and the World Bank, advocates the shrinking of government and the downsizing or privatization of public goods such as transportation, health care, and even schooling. During

recent decades (largely since the Reagan/Thatcher era) we have seen neoliberalism move from the margins of economic philosophy to the center of
global economic restructuring policies (George 1999). According to Susan
George, neoliberal ideology's central value of unfettered market competi-
tion means that "the public sector must be brutally downsized because it
does not and cannot obey the basic law of competing for profits or for market share" (3). Neoliberal economic policies, both globally and domesti-
cally, have shifted social policy from public investment and social spending
to private investment and corporate welfare, precipitating a severe polarization between the wealthy and the poor.[9] While corporate elites and the
top echelon of America's wealthy have enjoyed enormous leaps in income
and profitability over the last few decades, social safety nets and public
goods, namely "welfare as we knew it," health care, and public education
have been eviscerated.[10] As scholars have noted, neoliberalism, with its
subordination of social needs to the mandates of a free market, has compromised the public sphere, democracy, and social citizenship.[11]

The weakening of the public sphere plays out in public schooling in
the United States. In Portland, Oregon, white, middle-class students faced
unprecedented cuts to their education as a result of larger neoliberal projects that have starved public schooling. Oregon ranks fortieth in the
nation in per capita revenue raised for public education, spending per
pupil has declined since 2000, and Oregon ranks forty-eighth in the
nation in student/teacher ratio in the classroom (Education State
Rankings 2004). Even in schools located in middle-class communities, per-
manently nonfunctional and broken drinking fountains line the hallways
while students' options for hydration whittle down to bringing water from
home or buying bottled water or soda from the vending machines of corporations like Coca-Cola. The middle-class students in Portland represented in this study have spent the last decade attending schools equipped
with Channel One and have grown accustomed to fast-food chains setting
up shop in their cafeterias.[12] Because public monies are dwindling, schools
must rely more and more on corporate charity to keep a float. These
schools become branded by corporate logos: soda and candy companies
line the hallways with their advertisements and vending machines, school
buses are painted with huge corporate advertisements, sports teams play
soccer and baseball in uniforms branded by corporate sponsors. Even

school curriculums are infiltrated by corporate advertisements. These practices constitute the corporatization and commercialization of public schooling (Saltman and Goodman 2003; Saltman 2000; Molnar 1996).

In Portland, students were facing the early summer closure of their schools due to budget shortfalls. While some commentators on the schooling closures anticipated that students would celebrate these closures as an early summer vacation, many students surprised adults with their worry and anger. Some students felt that a shortened school year would make them less competitive for college. Concerned about the lost school days, SRU held a community meeting at a local public university to discuss what students could do to continue their education. After reading about the civil rights legacy of SNCC's (Student Nonviolent Coordinating Committee) liberation schools, youth SRU organizers became inspired to use this opportunity to initiate a liberation school for Portland students during the furlough period. This school would be taught by both adults and other youth with knowledge to share and represented to SRU students an unprecedented opportunity to create a new model of noncorporate education rooted in local community expertise and student needs. Because the school budget crisis was temporarily solved through donations from local business owners, the liberation school never came to fruition. However, it provided SRU organizers with an opportunity to develop a critique of corporatized education and a vision for a grassroots model of schooling.

While white, middle-class youth faced education cuts and corporatized schooling in Portland, working-class and poor youth of color in Oakland faced a much more pronounced militarization of public schooling, which is also consistent with a neoliberal ideology.[13] Kenneth Saltman rightly notes that the militarization of public schooling is connected to the larger militarization of civil society "exemplified by the rise of militarized policing, increased police powers for search and seizure, antipublic gathering laws, 'zero tolerance' policies, and the transformation of welfare into punishing workfare programs" that "accompany the increasing corporate control of daily life" (2003, 2). It is no exaggeration to say that Oakland's Patterson and Kendall high schools, both located in deep East Oakland, look and feel like prisons. This is not lost on Patterson and Kendall YP students. On one of my first visits to Patterson High, I found YP organizer Guillermo at the front door engaged in serious debate with two burly security guards dressed in full uniform. As I walked up to the door, Guillermo recognized me and the security guards asked, "Is he with you?" I answered, "Yes," and they opened the door for us so that we could proceed down several bare corridors lined with security cameras to the classroom designated for YP's summer program. I asked Guillermo if this happens a lot: "Do they always harass you like that?" Guillermo shrugged, "Yeah, I try to tell them I'm with YP, but a lot of times they don't let me in the school, since I'm not taking summer classes." "Then how do you make it to YP meetings?" He responded, "I sometimes have to jump the fence," pointing to a tall, wrought iron fence that surrounds the campus. I marveled at the fact that Guillermo, a student at this school, had to jump a tall iron fence to participate in organizing work. Although I was a complete stranger who had never been to Patterson High before, I was an "older-looking, white woman" (as YP students phrased it) and thus legitimized Guillermo's presence at his own school.

This incident was the first of many during this research that underscored for me how militarization plays out for low-income students of color in their everyday lives. The security cameras, the locked front doors, the bars on the windows, and the many intimidating guards stationed throughout the school's hallways communicated a constant message of distrust of students. There is a disturbing blur between these students' experiences of schooling and California's growing prison industrial complex, which is now the largest industry in the state.[14] In Portland and Oakland, student activists have become conscious of where new money is being spent in their schools. They have seen it in their everyday experiences of schooling. They have become aware of an increased corporate presence on school grounds (Portland) and increasingly sophisticated penal systems—for example, security cameras and security guards (Oakland)—being instituted in their schools. They have noted these spending trends while contending with old textbooks held together with duct tape and rats in the lunchrooms (Oakland) and the prospect of early school closures and cuts to extracurricular activities due to educational budget cuts (Portland). Both SRU and YP have argued for a restructuring of education that confronts the neoliberal ideology of privatization and militarization, one that recognizes education as a public good and a democratic right.

In Oakland, youth of color contend with more than the gutting and militarization of their public schools. Their families are being hit the hardest by welfare retrenchment, and their lives are profoundly shaped by the deindustrialization of Oakland and intensified urban poverty. Census data from 2000 reveals that in Oakland poverty rates among whites hover around 7.7 percent, while among blacks, Asians, and Latinos poverty rates are 24.9 percent, 21.9 percent, and 21.7 percent respectively. In California, 30.4 percent of black children and 27.2 percent of Latino children live below the poverty line, compared to 8.9 percent of white children (CCSRE 2002). In 2002 the National Center for Children in Poverty in conjunction with Children Now in Oakland reported that the number of California's poor children has doubled in the last twenty years. Nationally, children represent 36 percent of the official poor (California Institute for Federal Policy Research 2002).

Global corporate and industrial restructuring has impacted middle-class as well as working-class and poor communities, producing stark economic polarization between the haves and the have-nots.[15] However, because globalization has engendered economic devastation in both manufacturing and government sectors in the United States, it has hit urban communities of color particularly hard. More people of color than whites have been concentrated in these economic sectors, sectors that had provided relatively high paying jobs to relatively low-skilled workers (Dawson 1999). Most of the recent economic growth in the United States has occurred in suburban areas, while urban areas have been hit particularly hard by white flight, deindustrialization, and social divestment. Because student expenditure correlates with social class (schools are funded according to local property taxes), schools in impoverished communities of color lack crucial facilities, materials, and human resources compared to whiter, wealthier communities (Kozol 1991). The processes of deindustrialization in urban Oakland have exacerbated these inequalities in school funding and have intensified community and school poverty in communities of color.

Bert, an Asian American YP intern, painted this bleak picture: "In the United States of America, poor people of color are living on reservations today. Because they feel trapped within their communities, they feel like there is no hope. . . . That's why a lot of times when people who do get the benefit to move, they move somewhere *far*, 'cause they understand the cycle within this reservation." Bert became involved in YP as a high school sophomore and had just graduated from Patterson High, located deep within East Oakland. East Oakland is an impoverished area that is nearly devoid of white residents. During my first visit to this area of Oakland, I could count on five different bus routes servicing a busy stop in front of a small grocery store located forty blocks nearer to the city center. These buses would take me to the eastern edge of Oakland where the school is located. By my third visit, three of these routes had been marked "Discontinued," and, by my fourth visit to Oakland, only one route to Patterson remained. I wondered how I was ever going to be able to reach Patterson High on future visits if trends continued this way. If I could not get to Patterson on public transportation, how can residents living near Patterson get out?

Although youth in East Oakland live in "the Bay Area"—what is considered by many to be one of the most vibrant and progressive urban regions in the United States—many of these youth rarely had the opportunity to leave their neighborhoods. Public transportation is becoming more scarce and expensive: most youth in East Oakland don't ride the BART regularly. As a relatively privileged white, middle-class visitor, I crisscrossed the Bay Area by Muni, bus, BART, and bus again.[16] On many days my transportation costs alone added up to ten dollars or more. Most of the Oakland youth I came to know during my research could not afford this high cost of transportation, and several had never once been to San Francisco.

Douglas Massey and Nancy Denton emphasize the important role of racial segregation in the making of urban poverty in the United States.[17] They argue that persistent policies of racial segregation are key factors in the political and social isolation of communities of color: "Barriers to spatial mobility are barriers to social mobility, and by confining blacks to a small set of relatively disadvantaged neighborhoods, segregation constitutes a very powerful impediment to black socioeconomic progress" (1993, 14). According to 2000 census data, blacks experience the highest level of residential segregation in California's major metropolitan areas. This suggests that in Oakland nearly 65 percent of blacks would have to move to be evenly distributed among Oakland's white residents.

Bert's analogy of a reservation rings true as a description of many of these young people's neighborhoods. Neighborhoods are becoming more bounded and isolated: spatially, politically, economically, and socially. As in many formerly industry-dependent regions that have undergone a transformation to a service sector economy, in Oakland many employed adults—the parents of these youth—find work in jobs that provide little or no benefits. Some of these parents cannot find work at all. YP adult allies and student organizers spoke with me at length about the difficulty of organizing a student population reeling from the effects of parental unemployment and economic insecurity at home. They pointed to parents' unemployment as a major contributor to students' overall stress, cynicism, and hopelessness. Oakland youth contend with sick parents at home, and they themselves are also often sick. Sometimes a school nurse is the only health care provider available to Oakland youth, and cuts to education in California has meant that many impoverished schools such as Patterson have eliminated nurses from their schools. A serious health crisis faces many Oakland youth, and the health care of students had become a major politicized issue in YP organizing. YP youth decried the lack of recreation centers and public parks in their neighborhoods, and the unhealthy foods served in their schools. By contrast, the mostly middle-class, white SRU youth in Portland did not politicize student health care at all.

The antitax rhetoric of the post-Reagan era has compounded the crisis of social divestment and has played a key role in fueling school budget crises. In the face of disappearing funds for public schools in Portland, for example, a largely white, middle- and working-class electorate has been left to shoulder the costs of public education. Fueled by resentment (a resentment fomented by a particularly strong antitax movement in Oregon), the mostly white voting electorate refused to increase local taxes to keep schools open in the face of school closures. This refusal has been fed by a larger neoliberal discourse that views government regulation and social provisions as the real enemy of free-market capitalism. Much of SRU's struggle in Portland focused on rallying adult voters to vote on local tax measures that would save schools.

War in Iraq and School Defunding

Rather than teaching a whole generation of youth to be fearful of terrorists, the attacks on the World Trade Center and the Pentagon led some youth (and adults) to question the United States' foreign policy in the Middle East and elsewhere and to examine deeper crises within Western society. Sixteen-year-old Jazmin, who emigrated with her Mayan family from Mexico to the East Bay, explained her interpretation of the "war on terrorism":

> The fact that we are calling these people terrorists because they came in and blew up the Twin Towers . . . the reason that they blew up the Twin Towers is what we're doing over there. But they are not going to say what we are doing over there; they are just going to say what they did over here and make our people angry at those people, so then we can get an "okay" to do something even bigger over there. And then we can take over their country so that we can control their economy and their money, their people.

For many immigrant activists and activists of color, the war on terror did not represent a new development in U.S. history. Rather, it represented a new and intensified chapter of a much older story of European conquest and imperialism that stretches back roughly five hundred years. For white, middle-class student activists in Portland, the attacks signaled a deep crisis in Western notions of progress. These teens began to question the growth of the United States into a worldwide empire. However, unlike YP student organizers, SRU students rarely discussed this crisis in the context of an older European imperialism.

While 9–11 fomented intensified patriotism and xenophobia among many adults and youth alike, the attacks also prompted some youth to ask, "Why did they attack us?" Dissatisfied with the Bush administration's oft-repeated explanation, "They attacked us because they hate our freedom," the youth activists I met began to investigate other sources of the politics behind the attacks. Youth in Oakland and Portland talked with their parents, attended early antiwar meetings and rallies in their communities, researched information on the Internet, read articles, and gleaned some information on U.S. foreign policy from Michael Moore's popular documentary *Bowling for Columbine*.

Central to youth movements in both Portland and Oakland has been the politicization of the link between school budget crises and the war. The events of 9–11 ushered in and legitimized a host of new political developments across the United States and globally, including the U.S. wars in Afghanistan and Iraq. In both Oakland and Portland, youth began to recognize that just as needed resources were flowing out of their schools, enormous resources were being channeled into two simultaneous wars in the Middle East. Student activists not only *worried* about school defunding. They became *outraged* that their futures were being sacrificed for a two-fronted "war on terror."

Sixteen-year-old Sheng attended Kendall High School. His parents emigrated to the United States from China and have settled in the Oakland flatlands near Kendall High. Sheng had been at the forefront of YP organizing over the past year. He explained the connections he sees between the war in Iraq, the prison industrial complex, and the crises in his school and larger community:

> The government puts more importance on taking over a country than on our education. And the reason they are spending so much money and, like, creating more prisons, that's why we are having cutoffs and that is why a lot of students are having subs [substitute teachers] all through the year. That's the reason why we have these crappy teachers; that's the reason why we have a school system where our curriculum is so unrelated to our lives. That's the reason why so many students drop out. . . . That's the reason why a lot of students are incarcerated.

Like Sheng, many other youth activists in both Portland and Oakland questioned the existence of a school budget crisis or shortfall, when so much money has been flowing into funding the war in Iraq. On a dreary March day in 2003, eighteen-year-old SRU organizer Joni, a student about to graduate from the relatively affluent Rose Valley High in Portland, stood before a crowd of nearly thirty thousand people gathered in downtown Portland to protest the impending war on Iraq. Joni was the last speaker to address the crowd before the antiwar march through Portland's streets began. She stood on a stage and shouted into a bullhorn, "How can we even think about entering a billion dollar war in Iraq when we can't even keep our schools open?!" Her indignant voice carried across the crowd and elicited a roar of applause from the thousands of protesters. Collective student voices like SRU and YP have been instrumental in bringing the concerns of school budget crises to larger antiwar coalitions and gatherings such as these.

Besides the effects of the budget crises, students felt other aftershocks of 9–11 reverberate through their education. After 9–11 and during the bombing of Iraq, dissent was quickly labeled by national mainstream media as "unpatriotic" and student organizers noticed new campaigns within their schools to quiet student dissent and foment patriotism. Some of these campaigns were instituted by groups like the Parent Teacher Student Association, who in the East Bay proposed that school administrators establish a new educational policy that would require the whole school to take a few minutes out of each day to meditate on a patriotic quote and look at the U.S. flag. YP student organizer Naomi explained how this played out at her high school: "They brought all these American flags, like, boxes of flags. And each teacher had to take one and put one up in their classrooms. . . . So they started taking two or three minutes out of second period to do a quote, and we had to just, like, stop the entire school and look at the flag." Student activists talked about some of these campaigns as more ubiquitous, not so much instigated through official educational policies but rather enforced, symbolically, by other students. Seventeen-year-old Portland activist Scott described the alienation he felt in school as a result of this pressure to support the war:

> I definitely feel like there's some force that's trying to influence me, especially at school. You know, I see people wearing T-shirts, advocating, supporting the troops, and American flags. And, you know, people talk about it. And I just feel like they look at it like, "This is what our country is doing and I need to stand behind it because it's my country." And they don't really think about it. You see these messages so much and you see it as your culture and you just can't escape it. And you feel bad. You feel like you're not part of your society.

Dissenting students found some relief from this alienation as they formed politicized student networks like YP or SRU, peer groups that fostered a collective critique of patriotism during wartime.

Compounding the effects of global developments like war, deindustrialization, and the ascendancy of neoliberalism are also the erosions of the movement gains of the 1960s. Especially in Oakland, the cultural backlash against previous civil rights and antipoverty programs fueled racial and ethnic violence between youth in their schools and in their larger

communities. While YP and SRU youth organizers held a global consciousness about U.S. foreign policy and war, their orientation to social problems
was also profoundly local. This was especially true for the spatially and
socially isolated YP youth in Oakland, who through their organizing
learned how the seismic shifts in California's political landscape over the
last few decades structured the reality of their everyday lives.

Race and Class Politics in Post–Civil Rights Oakland

Civil Rights and Antipoverty Backlash

Deindustrialization, widespread unemployment, and the trend toward
poorly paid, service-sector employment are major developments within
the last few decades that partly contribute to the subordination of youth of
color in urban areas. However, also important is what many communities
of color consider to be a racist, anti-immigrant backlash against the gains
made during the civil rights and black insurgency movements.[18] This backlash has found expression in a spate of legislation that has been proposed
and passed in California since the early 1990s. Most notable is California's
"Save Our State" Initiative, or Proposition 187, which voters endorsed in
1994. This legislation prohibited undocumented immigrants from receiving state social services, medical care, or education for their children.
Proposition 187's campaign relied on highly publicized gendered and
racialized images of pregnant, brown-skinned women from Mexico living
illegally in the United States and draining social services. Pierrette
Hondagneu-Sotelo notes that the anti-immigrant backlash in California at
the turn of the millennium differs somewhat from the xenophobia and
racism in nativist movements during the Reagan administration: "The
xenophobia of the early 1980s focused on labor, while the more recent
backlash against immigrants focuses on reproduction, or everything it
takes to bring a new generation into the labor force" (1994, 26).

The vilification of a new generation of Californians of color is centered
not only on the women who settle and build new communities but also on
young people themselves: those who represent the new multiracial generation and a United States that is becoming less white.[19] Following
Proposition 187, California voters passed Proposition 209 in 1996 (the
"Civil Rights Initiative"), which dismantled affirmative action policies in

higher education, and Proposition 227, which eliminated bilingual education in California public schools. The effects of Proposition 21, which expanded the number of youths under age eighteen who could be tried as adults, and of Proposition 184, or California's "three strikes" law, have resulted in the imposition of harsh measures on youth of color, subjecting them to trials in adult courts, incarceration in adult prisons, and harsher and longer sentences (Giroux 2003b; Males 1996). Proposition 21 has made it easier for police to classify young people of color in public spaces (gathered in groups as few as three people) as "gangs." Passed in 1994, Proposition 184 counts many juvenile offenses as strikes, allowing for juveniles with three strikes to face life imprisonment. According to Scott Ehlers and others, blacks and Latinos have been sentenced to life imprisonment in far greater numbers as a result of Proposition 184 than their white counterparts. Blacks make up 45 percent of third-strikers and Latinos make up 32.6 percent (2004). As Aihwa Ong (1999) and Patricia Zavella (2001) observe, this spate of legislation in California has been fueled by rapid demographic shifts and white people's perceived loss of power in the face of a swelling Asian and Latino population in the state.

According to YP young adult allies, this backlash during the 1990s (the backlash that had galvanized their political consciousness during their own adolescence) had set the stage for the newer crises in education spending and the boom in the prison industry during the first few years of the new millennium. Twenty-nine-year-old YP adult ally Estella explained,

> All those laws, those were all precursors to set it up so now people will not get riled up around the budget cuts that are happening now. Because it is something that has been happening, and something that voters have endorsed. So nobody is going to come out and support more funding for education, more funding for students of color, because they have been fed the politics and the conservative ideology for ten years.

Indeed, both California and Oregon, like many other states in the United States, are facing landmark budget cuts to public education. Activist youth in both Portland and Oakland interpreted these cuts as evidence that older generations cared little about their future. However, while Portland youth interpreted these crises through mostly a lens of generational neglect, urban youth of color in Oakland interpreted the simultaneous cuts to education and growth of the prison industry in California as a generational and racist backlash. According to 2003 Bureau of Justice statistics, 455 of every 100,000 people in California is in prison, and California's imprisonment rate jumped 14 percent between 1995 and 2003. California spends $400 million each year on the California Youth Authority System, which has a 90 percent recidivism rate (Anderson et al. 2005). Compared to white youth, California youth of color are 2.8 times more likely to be charged with violent crimes, 6.2 times more likely to be tried as adults, and 7 times more likely to be sentenced to prison if tried as adults (Males and Macallair 2000). Not only are resources to education being cut most severely in poor communities and communities of color, but students are being held to new and harsher standardized testing schemes in the wake of NCLB.[20] These new standardized tests, such as the California High School Exit Exam, adds one more barrier for students who are already lacking sufficient resources in their schools to prepare them for these tests.[21] Seventeen-year-old Naomi explained,

> The cuts to public education, and just the state political climate, and just backlash against everyone . . . I think things are becoming more and more clear for us, for students of color at least, that there is a track. And it's a track to either prison or to being cheap labor. Because it is just so obvious how we are being shut out of education, right, with the high school exit exam. So there is just the struggle of leaving high school. Not to mention what comes after high school.

Issues such as the high school exit exam and cuts to education in both impoverished communities and relatively affluent, middle-class, white communities such as Portland are new developments that are pushing students to create school-change and school-funding campaigns. The crisis of educational budget cuts alarmed many Portland students, who feared that cuts to their high school education would compromise their ability to get into college by making them less attractive candidates. In Oakland, activist youth of color and the school-change movements they organized were also connected to larger social justice campaigns against California's expanding prison system and the increasing criminalization of youth of color.

The Cycle of Violence in Oakland

Violence thrives in postindustrial Oakland: it is threaded through the very experience of growing up. As Salvador noted in the beginning of this chapter, his letter to the president was prompted by concern about drug dealing and violence in his East Oakland neighborhood. The effect of everyday violence on young people's lives hit me particularly hard as I listened to young people talk about violence at a YP organizing retreat. I sat with about thirty YP student organizers—black, Latino, and Asian—in a large circle on a cabin floor. Each student was asked to make a "weather map" that describes the "weather" in different parts of their lives: family, school, racial/ethnic identity, and organizing. We took swaths of butcher paper and began to draw rough pictures of hurricanes, sunshine, wind, rain, earthquakes. When we finished, we took turns explaining why we assigned certain weather patterns as symbols to describe different areas of our lives. Overshadowing all the students' lives was violence, and violence is what students talked about the most. Their weather maps were full of tornados and hurricanes. I listened as one student after another described the fear of never making it to age twenty, of never living to see adulthood. Even as they voiced these fears, not one student broke down. They each said this so softly that at times I had to strain to hear them. At Patterson and Kendall high schools, there had been recent shootings of students on school grounds. Kendall High is located right in the middle of gang territory.

Patterson High and the surrounding community are not so much torn by gang warfare as they are by turf warfare. Where residents live and the turf they claim (rather than gang affiliation) are important markers of supremacy over and differentiation from other people, a development more pronounced in areas like those around Patterson High, where few residents actually own anything. The lack of actual property ownership intensifies the politics of claiming ownership and claiming space in these neighborhoods. Sixteen-year-old Shandra and I met for our interview at the YP office in downtown Oakland. She told me about her tense bus ride to downtown Oakland: "These students were all in the back of the bus. And some guys got on the bus and they were like, 'You get off the bus!' And they were all talking hella turf stuff. Naming a whole bunch of turfs, talking like, 'so-and-so's from this turf,' and I was like 'damn,' you know. It was all the way down here. And it was just really frustrating, to the point where I had to move." Turf wars are often expressed through racial and ethnic conflict, as turfs are often racially and ethnically segregated (Massey and Denton 1993). YP student organizer Tevin, seventeen years old, explained turf wars as race wars:

> It's like, "I am from here, but this person is from over there. And I don't like that turf. And if he comes on my turf I am going to kill him." And turfs are about stereotypes, you know. So people have their stereotypes and everything; it's like, "Oh, he's Mexican; he ain't no nigger," you know. Like, this dude almost got jumped; he was a Latino guy; he was like, "Hey, what's up nigger"; and this dude was like, "You ain't black." And he was like, "Oh, my bad, my bad, I wasn't trying to say it in that way." And I'm thinking to myself, we are all people of color. We're all going through the same thing. It's just so stupid.

Although immigration has not caused the displacement of low-skilled workers among blacks or other ethnic groups (Dawson 1999), media panics about immigration and racist political rhetoric have generated significant resentment of immigrant workers in working-class and poor communities and have fueled racial and ethnic violence.

Many YP students have lost friends and family members to violence. Driving through impoverished Oakland neighborhoods, one can see teddy bears and candles set up on street corners and shoes thrown over telephone wires every few blocks or so. I hadn't really noticed them until James, a YP student organizer, pointed them out to me. He and Jazmin explained to me that these are markers of where someone was allegedly shot, hurt, or killed in Oakland shoot-outs. In the wake of California's civil rights backlash in the 1990s, racial and ethnic violence on school grounds across the East Bay intensified, prompting the formation of YP in the 1990s. Both students and adults in the community recognized the immediate need for some kind of youth empowerment campaign coupled with ethnic studies and multiracial movement development on campuses. This would be one measure toward stemming the violence erupting in California's working-class and poor communities of color.

Tevin attended the more affluent Brookline High School, which is on a hillside overlooking the flatlands where Patterson High and Kendall High sit. However, like many YP students who attend Brookline High, Tevin did not live in the relatively affluent neighborhoods that surround it. Instead, Tevin took the bus each morning from his family's small home in the flatlands. Tevin described the tension and division in his community: "I know in my community, it's really divided. And nobody really knows anybody. I don't think any of the neighbors talk to each other. Like, I try to talk to all my neighbors. Some of them look at me; some of them don't speak. Some of them just give a real crappy wave."

Although dominant media images of youth of color portray them as "violent superpredators" and heartless thugs, YP youth developed a more humanizing view of violence among youth of color, shifting the focus from vilifying youth to the social conditions that breed violence.[22] In YP's Cycle of Violence workshop (which all YP student organizers learned to teach to new high school freshmen), the cycle is seen to start at birth. YP organizers note that children are not born violent; they are not born hating; they are not born bitter; they are not born racist. As they come of age in impoverished and violent neighborhoods, youth develop survival strategies to deal with living in these conditions. Some of these survival strategies are healthy (making art, getting agitated to the point of making social change, organizing, writing poetry), some are disempowering (taking drugs, joining gangs, carrying guns, becoming pregnant). In this workshop, students learn that outsiders such as social scientists, policy makers, and those that carry the power to define social problems are often unable (or refuse) to see the larger structural and historical conditions of urban violence and racial segregation. Outsiders can see only what is left hypervisible: young people's survival strategies, especially the disempowering strategies. Outsiders then blame young people themselves and their survival strategies for creating poverty and violence, rather than blaming social and historical processes of racial isolation and wealth inequality, or noticing that young people's behaviors are responses to larger injustices. These outsiders give youth of color strong labels like "superpredators" and demonize gang members, high school dropouts, and teenage mothers in public discourses on social problems. According to this YP worldview, once these powerful labels are conferred on youth of color, youth internalize these messages and become even more disempowered, bitter, and violent.

This YP political framework shifts the dominant focus on violence from young offenders to structural inequalities. Eighteen-year-old YP organizer Gayle illustrated the cycle of violence as it played out at her school, Patterson High:

> I mean, the school is so tore up. We need health services at school. And we need mental health services. But we don't have them. So kids are all screwed up. They come from their home where their mom just got laid off; you got all these problems that are being forced upon students, and they have to go to school and deal with all this. And then somebody steps on your shoe and you are already pissed, and that's it! You are going to fight. You are going to hurt somebody. Something is going to go down.

Gayle's narrative highlighted the problems of school violence without demonizing young people themselves. This shift in focus to the structural roots of violence was crucial in building an Oakland youth movement against community and school violence, one that worked to empower and humanize youth rather than vilify them.

For youth in Oakland, violence was the great divider: it prevented youth and their communities from uniting to fight the underlying structural and cultural crises that fomented their neighborhood tensions. However, Oakland youth and Portland youth were also concerned about the less obvious but more insidious white noise of consumerism, which they saw as distracting their peers from thinking, speaking, or acting politically to address the many social problems threatening their well-being.

Cultural Numbness and Youth Political Inaction

Consumerism

> One thing I have been thinking about lately is, why do we need so many screens? Television screens, computer screens, why do we need screens all the time? What happened to our humanity? Are we becoming this omnipowerful race of screens? We are just animals. We need to remember that we are just a part of our culture, our schools, our world. (Hayden, fifteen-year-old Portland SRU organizer)

One of the charges that has been made of this emerging generation is that it is the most materialistic one we have ever seen and that this is one reason for teenagers' apathy, self-centeredness, and supposed lack of vision.[23] I asked teenage activists if they agreed with this assessment of their generation. To my surprise, many of them did, although not without critiquing consumerism first. While many of these politically conscious teens agreed with critics from older generations about the devastating effect that consumerism has on youth in the United States, they did not fault their peers for this development. Rather, these youth developed complex critiques of consumer capitalism, technology, and the power of advertising and noted that these developments have been set in motion by wealthy [adult] profiteers. Eighteen-year-old SRU activist Megan considered my question about her generation as overly materialistic and emphasized the socially constructed aspect of youth materialism:

> I would say that my generation is materialistic, just because we have been trained to be that way in general. Kids are told not to say anything, and to sit down in front of the TV and watch TV, so the TV will tell you what you need to know. So the TV tells us that we are materialistic. Well then, we are going to be materialistic. And so I think, in general, kids can get lost in that mindset. But I think some kids can see what is going on is not cool, and they will be there to say, "This is not going to work." I think there is an unconscious responsibility that kids have when it comes to taking care of what is going on in society.

Although the income discrepancies between Portland SRU youth and Oakland YP youth were large, both YP and SRU activists talked at length about the damage that consumer culture has wrought on their generation and also on the adults they know. Seventeen-year-old YP organizer James discussed the extent to which consumer culture dictates young people's relationships to each other:

> Everyone is so much into material stuff. And it's just like the way people socialize, and everything has to do with material things. And that's just benefiting the corporations; that's all you see on television. That's all you see: television. You can ask youth about any TV show, any commercial, and they will be able to have a full conversation with you about it. And they are so into it.

As James pointed out, students have learned to bond over consumer culture. Observing this social dimension of consumption, Amy Best (2006a) argues that, among many things, consumer culture can provide a means for youth to participate in public and community life. In Best's study of youth and their cars, cars represent not only mobility, freedom, and individualism for youth but also a way to break free from isolation, to gain membership into certain status groups, and to participate in wider communities, such as San Jose, which sport a culture of wealth and consumption. According to politicized YP and SRU youth, consumption can cultivate communal and social bonds, but these bonds are not innocent, nor are they without their consequences. The way that youth are encouraged to relate to each other within a larger context of consumerism means that their relationships are influenced by consumer tastes and preferences and ultimately translate into profit for corporations. Both YP and SRU youth were building youth movements that encouraged young people to bond and find solidarity with each other outside of this consumer context. This shift by itself required that these youth activists, through their movement ideologies, redefine what it means to be young in the United States. YP youth emphasized that instead of connecting through consumption, young people should bond with each other over shared experiences of oppression: police harassment, poor public schooling, and histories of colonization, as well as common visions for multiracial youth resistance. SRU activists, more overtly anticorporate and antiauthoritarian than YP youth, encouraged each other to take an explicit anticonsumerist stance, participating in Food Not Bombs weekly communal feedings in Portland, engaging in periodic dumpster diving ventures, and discouraging peers from bringing fast food to meetings.[24]

Corporate profit is one consequence of constructing youth as consumers. Fifteen-year-old SRU activist Tory pointed out that violence is another consequence of teen consumerism. Tory feared that young people's lives are so saturated with violence-as-entertainment that they lose the ability to fully comprehend the violence of the war in Iraq, for example. Slick new army commercials are indistinguishable from commercials for violent video games. As Tory noted, this integration of violence into entertainment leads teens to pursue a fantasy life in the armed forces without understanding the real costs of killing and dying:

We're just young, frustrated animals that are stuck in front of TVs and video games. I mean they have those video games where you kill each other, but when you actually kill somebody it's really traumatic and people don't seem to understand that. Like, they were recruiting at the mall, and kids were, like, joking with each other: "Go sign up, man; go sign up," and I was sickened because they don't understand what comes with that price.... You just become a killing machine for our government. And once you get out, they don't help you out. You are just a lost veteran with diseases.... Students are so sucked into their media and TV that they don't want to learn and understand the reality of it.

Most importantly, while student organizers recognized the extent to which their generation has been constructed as silent, apathetic consumers rather than engaged and responsible beings, they also argued that this is not necessarily a discrete youth issue but is a larger societal issue that spans the generations. As fifteen-year-old SRU activist Josh mused about his generation's obsession with consumption, he took issue with the claim that there is something inherently consumer-oriented and solipsistic about his generation. He emphasized that "youth apathy" is something that is shared with other generations, a social process rather than an innate, generational characteristic: "I don't really think there's such a thing as *youth* apathy. But in our culture especially, everybody is bombarded with so much media, just so much crap, that they become numb. But that's *everybody*, not just the youth."

Apathy and Hopelessness: The Difficulties of Organizing Youth at the Turn of the Millennium

Both YP and SRU students cited consumer culture as a major roadblock to organizing youth into political movements. As noted earlier, student organizers viewed consumerism as a force that distorts young people's understanding of their social worlds, makes them numb to social problems, and warps their relationships to each other. As Josh noted before, consumerism is one cause of youth apathy and of a cross-generational apathy to social problems in general. Henry Giroux writes, "In the eyes of many young people, politics as a sphere of concrete possibility appears to have given way to an unregulated and all-powerful market that models all dreams around the narcissistic, privatized, and self-indulgent needs of consumer culture" (2003b, 3).

Even though many of my interviewees noted the numbing effect that consumer culture had on their peers, I would like to point out here that not all students in this study spoke of the inaction and numbness of their peers in terms of apathy. In fact, while white, middle-class SRU students in Portland spoke at length about the widespread apathy of their peers, working-class and poor YP students of color discussed the numbness and inaction of their peers in terms of internalized hopelessness and cynicism rather than apathy. The distinction between apathy and internalized hopelessness and cynicism reflects the major differences between the life conditions of white, middle-class youth and working-class and poor youth of color at the turn of the millennium. This distinction is also indicative of the different ways in which middle-class, white youth and working-class and poor youth make sense of local, regional, national, and global problems, and also the ways in which they envision youth liberation more generally.

In the following exchange, sixteen-year-old SRU activists Sara and Kristin spoke about their peers' apathy as rooted in middle-class comfort and obliviousness:

KRISTIN: There are a lot of people that are like. . . . I don't know what to say. . . .

SARA: They just don't understand.

KRISTIN: Like, everything is just kind of going on *around* them.

SARA: Everything is confusing about politics, so they just say, "Oh, whatever, it's the government," and they don't really get involved. If they just sat down and thought about things, they'd realize that a lot of things they support are bad. But they don't think about it, so it doesn't affect them.

KRISTIN: Well, there are so many people living in their comfort zone. They have everything that they want, so they can't imagine having problems in their country. And they can't imagine what that would be like for someone else. I mean, some kids pretty much have everything they want; they've never had to struggle for anything. I mean, do you see that, Sara?

SARA: Yeah, totally. A lot of kids are just so sheltered.

In this exchange, Sara and Kristin agreed that it is difficult to organize their peers into movements for social change because their peers don't feel the immediate effects of social problems. Thus, social problems are going on "around them" rather than directly affecting them. They are able to insulate themselves from the rest of the world, and often times they use material comforts and consumer culture to do this. But social problems like school budget crises can penetrate white, middle-class student apathy. Once the problems ceased to go on around them and came knocking on their doors, many students became concerned, critical, and, with the help of SRU, organized and politically active.

For SRU student organizers, the most important first step in their political project was to "wake students up." As fifteen-year-old Alana exclaimed, "We want education! We want people to wake up! You know, get out of that business as usual, school as usual, TV and media. . . . We're trying to change this." SRU organizers aimed to jar their peers out of their comfortable routines "and wake them up so they realize everything isn't all happy and nice. There are really bad, serious problems going on" (Shae, eighteen-year-old SRU organizer). Although SRU activists viewed their peers' inaction as consumerist-induced numbness and an outcome of material privilege, Tyrone Forman (2004) points out that this kind of apathy among whites can also have a racist edge. As "racial apathy," white people's apathy can be a widespread but insidious expression of racism that works to uphold the racial status quo. Forman notes that racial apathy can comfortably coexist with deeper and persistent negative views of people of color. For SRU youth, however, this racial dimension of their peers' political apathy went unnoticed.

YP organizers in Oakland also aimed to shift their peers' political consciousness. However, their major goal was not necessarily to wake up their peers to social problems going on around them. Working-class and poor students of color already know firsthand the social problems of poverty and violence that come with living in impoverished, racially isolated conditions. They are not operating under the illusion that everything is "happy and nice." Eighteen-year-old YP organizer Gayle explained this as she reflected on being a student organizer at Patterson High:

> High school is too hard. 'Cause when you walk in the door, it's like
> something bad is going to happen. You can feel it. You walk up there

and you just feel like something is going to happen. Somebody is going to get hurt; somebody is going to get kicked out of class; somebody is going to miss out on an education. And it's not supposed to be like that.

I mean, everyday it's a new teacher. Every year it's a new principal. Every minute it's some more mess. And it makes you want to give up. It makes you want to say, "to hell with it." I don't ever remember the Brady Bunch going through drama like this! Everybody just wants that rose-colored beautiful high school . . . but it's never like that.

As Gayle indicated, the major problem is not insulation, comfort, and apathy but rather an internalized hopelessness and cynicism among youth that comes with living in impoverished, violent, and racially isolated conditions. Elaine Bell Kaplan, in her study of teenage mothers in Oakland, observes, "These schools, plagued by violence, drugs, and gangs, reflect the drama in the world right outside the school door" (1997, 31). YP organizers talked at length about the extent to which a deep-seated cynicism prevents many youth from becoming hopeful enough to pursue social change. As sixteen-year-old Guillermo said, "What would I change about my school? I would change the way people's attitudes are. How, like, most of their attitudes are so negative toward everything. Everything is always like 'Fuck this' and 'I am going to beat somebody up' or 'We're going to jump them' or something like that. I would just wish for everybody to have a positive attitude and be down to make change." Sixteen-year-old Alisha told me that when she goes on to college, she plans to major in psychology because she sees this as one way to undo internalized hopelessness:

I've learned this from being an organizer . . . people are so messed up. Their energy comes off of what's forced onto them. As long as situations are screwed up, people aren't going to get any better; situations aren't going to get any better. Stuff is still going to be bad. The way you feel, the way you think . . . it can piss you off to the point where you are ready to change. And that is what organizing is about. You have to get to that point where you light that fire in yourself and you are ready to say, "Screw this; let's change this!"

Many YP organizers told me over and over again that the project of undoing internalized hopelessness and cynicism among their peers was one of the biggest challenges that came with youth organizing.

The problems of white, middle-class apathy and the internalized hopelessness and cynicism among working-class and poor people of color are not unique to the youth of these populations. Carl Boggs notes that in the last decade U.S. society "has become more depoliticized, more lacking in the spirit of civic engagement and public obligation, than at any time in recent history, with the vast majority of the population increasingly alienated from a political system that is commonly viewed as corrupt, authoritarian, and simply irrelevant" (2000, vii).[25] At the same time however, other scholars have noticed a hopeful exception to this increasing alienation: an actual spike in youth civic engagement. Robert Putnam (2008) states that there is now a clear "9–11 generation," a generation of youth who were high school and college students at the time of the 9–11 attacks. He notes that for the first time in several decades, surveys of youth interest in civic engagement indicate increasing youth interest in politics, public policy, and social issues—perhaps as a result of this unifying national crisis. While this may very well be true, Jessica Taft and Hava Gordon (2009) argue that most scholarly discussions of youth civic engagement (both those that argue that youth civic engagement is sorely lacking or that it is on the rise) are overwhelmingly focused on normative forms of civic engagement that prepare youth for participation in institutional and electoral politics as adults.[26] For YP and SRU activist youth, these forms of youth civic engagement are much less critical, dissident, or accessible to teens than the social movement politics represented by their groups. This might help to explain why youth activists in SRU and YP did not necessarily view their peers as meaningfully engaged in politics, despite service learning programs or volunteerism in their schools that might have been explicitly designed to socialize youth into becoming civically engaged adults (see chapter 2).

Instead, charged with mobilizing their peers, YP and SRU youth confronted daily the challenges that apathy and cynicism posed to their efforts to mobilize other youth into social justice campaigns. In many ways, apathy and hopelessness are compounded by teens' subordinated status as people without any immediate institutional channels for political

participation. Youth are conditioned to understand themselves as passive
social actors who do not participate in political processes, social decision
making, or larger political projects before adulthood. They are constructed
as passive objects to be seen and not heard and to express agency only in
terms of consumption. They are socialized to see themselves as unable to
make change until they become "real" adult citizens, if ever. The first challenge for youth activists is to counter this hegemonic construction of
young people's political and social passivity. Their task is to first show
their peers that social movement is one avenue open to youth where
they can make social change in their communities. Only then can youth
organizers tackle the larger problems of student apathy and internalized
hopelessness: two of the biggest forces that stand in the way of their movements' success.

Youth Political Power

If apathy and cynicism construct youth political powerlessness and inaction, then youth who transform into social movement participants find
their political power through both political *action* and political *transformation.* These paradigms of political subjectivity took on different meanings
for SRU and YP youth. For SRU youth who were steeped in a larger antiauthoritarian culture, political action was the goal and took precedence over
longer-term political transformations of the self and the larger community. SRU's insignia was a fist in the air, and their slogan was "ACTY-
OURAGE!"—which cleverly parodied and subverted the adult power in the
condescending phrase "act your age" while emphasizing an empowering
youth "action" and "rage." These symbols of student rage proved to be a
successful organizing tool within the high schools and also aligned the
adolescent movement with radical direct action movement groups in
Portland. As I will demonstrate in the following chapters, high visibility
direct actions were key to SRU's vision of political power. For these youth,
action was the ultimate antidote to the curse of generational *apathy.*

In contrast, YP youth underwent a much deeper political transformation of the self. These youth recognized that if the biggest barrier to youth
mobilization was a deep-seated cynicism and hopelessness, then the first
task was to undo this by politicizing almost every aspect of their lives.

Through YP political frameworks, students' health, school engagement, and familial and community relations became politicized as important social justice issues. In this sense, the politicized terrain of youth activism in Oakland included the inner spaces of the self. As Alberto Melucci (1989) argues, the self has become an important form of property that new social movements try to capture from those in power through the creation of new politicized identities. This was especially true for YP youth. As YP organizer Salvador put it, "You gotta clean up your own house before you can go out and clean up the block." As a result, the counterweight to widespread student cynicism and hopelessness among low-income youth of color was self and community transformation, strong enough to sustain long-term social justice campaigns and withstand short-term defeats. As I will elaborate in chapter 3, accessing the histories of multiracial social movements became essential to YP students' ability to transform their cynicism into hope. For YP youth, this paradigm of transformative political power took precedence over short-term direct actions. SRU's emphasis on short-term direct action and YP's emphasis on long-term political transformation represented paradigms that differed sharply from adults' conception of young people's political subjectivity as becoming but not yet actualized.

Conclusion

Essential to the project of denaturalizing adolescence is to make visible the many historical, geographical, and cultural threads that come together to produce young people's lived experiences of subordination, as well as their opportunities for claiming political power. The issues examined in this chapter are not limited to youth or adolescence alone; they are social problems that shape adults' lives as well. However, when I asked youth to discuss why they became politically active, these social problems emerged as key issues in both their narratives and in their actual organizing work.

The subordination of youth involves processes that have been drawn from larger neoliberal developments at the turn of the millennium. The corporatization of schooling that middle-class, mostly white students experience aids in the construction of youth as consumers instead of as active social participants. This has further cemented their status as nonpolitical actors even as they engage in schooling practices that are supposed to prepare them for adult political responsibilities. Young people's marginalization from political action is exacerbated by the rise of consumerism in general, which shapes young people's experiences in many other realms of their lives besides schooling (e.g., watching television at home, hanging out at the mall).

Impoverished youth of color in Oakland are also constructed as a subordinate group through other processes associated with neoliberalism. Working-class and poor youth of color are increasingly subordinated, through schooling, as an imprisoned and criminal class of people rather than as important contributors to a democratic society. This follows a larger pattern, associated with neoliberalism and social divestment, of militarizing public spaces and institutions such as schools.

Both youth of color in Oakland and white youth in Portland are also experiencing their youth during a time when acute social divestment and the defunding of education are happening in concert with a massive and seemingly endless war in the Middle East. This double and simultaneous crisis has propelled the formation of YP and SRU as proeducation and antiwar youth movements (and, in the case of YP, also as an anti–prison industrial complex movement).

Importantly, these social and economic crises construct youth differently along racial and class lines. While neoliberalism, social divestment, school defunding, war in Iraq, and consumerism have been formative for constructing youth as a powerless group of people, there are specific historical and social processes that affect some youth more than others. In the context of deindustrialized urban Oakland, violence has become paramount in shaping the conditions for youth subordination. Importantly, young people's responses and adaptations to violence have also come under the microscope of outside commentators who have further demonized youth in particularly racialized ways. Thus, youth of color must contend with labels like superpredator in the construction of their adolescence-as-subordination, while middle-class, white youth do not. Undoing these distorted stereotypes of gang activity and violence, as part of workshops such as the Cycle of Violence, becomes an important mechanism to transform youth of color from passive objects into engaged activists. These nuanced discussions of violence were notably absent among white, middle-class students in Portland. Importantly, youth of color in Oakland are also struggling with their status as a subordinated group in the context of an historical backlash against the civil rights movement. White, middle-class students have not experienced this same racialized form of youth subordination.

Finally, while much is made of youth apathy in popular discourses that blame youth for social problems (Males 1996), I argue that apathy on the one hand and hopelessness and cynicism on the other are two different phenomena that compound young people's social subordination. These forms of constructed youth subordination are produced along lines of racial and class privilege and oppression. In different ways, they work to marginalize youth from collective political power in their daily lives. In a similar vein, young people's visions for collective social power, whether they be through taking concrete political action or achieving a deeper political transformation, are also developed out of these divergent realities.

2

Reading, Writing, and Radicalism

The Politics of Youth Activism on School Grounds

What happens when youth try to tackle social justice issues and organize other students on school territory? Before SRU and YP youth activists eventually coalesced with larger social movements in their communities, they first attempted to politicize the social and academic elements of their schools. Just as labor activists start organizing in their workplaces, youth begin their political projects where they are: in their schools. Student activists recounted to me their frustrating experiences with school clubs, student government, curriculums, and all the other activities that constitute the social and educational life of high schools. As I listened to their stories, I began to grasp the difficulty that youth activists face when organizing student movements on school grounds. The deeper question became clear: why do youth movements so often run into roadblocks inside the educational system, and what might this say about the role that schooling plays in constructing youth as citizens-in-the-making rather than as actualized political forces in their own right?

Youth activists in Oakland and Portland recounted story after story of the frustrations they had experienced trying to organize youth movements on school grounds. Their stories are instructive, for they reveal the role that schooling often plays in *thwarting* youth from claiming political power. Schools do foster a kind of social citizenship, but one that is most often dependent on a model of citizenship-in-the-making, which presumes an eventual social inclusion and engagement. In this model, the future adult self is the real political subject, the end product. Young people's school experiences as model UN members, student senators, or student body presidents are the means to this end: the training ground for the eventual adult political subjectivity. When youth insist on taking political action in their schools, as youth and not as adults-in-training, they often run into roadblocks and resistance from administrations, teachers, and even other students. This resistance is not uniform or total: there are the extraordinary teachers who are invaluable advocates to student movements on campus. There are the principals who support student organizing around particular educational justice goals. As indispensable to the successes of student movements as these key players are, however, their efforts do not add up to a larger and more sustained institutional support of student activism and youth political engagement. It is this institutional resistance to student political power, embedded in school practices, that is the subject of this chapter.

Sunnie's story is revealing. Sunnie was an eighteen-year-old suburban Portland student affiliated with SRU. She had just graduated from high school and couldn't be more relieved. Sunnie's high school was far removed from the urban center of Portland, located in a peaceful, wooded area. In the far reaches of the Portland suburbs, this area had also been a stronghold of the conservative Oregon Citizens Alliance over the last decade.[1] In high school, Sunnie's gay best friend was constantly harassed by students in the hallways, classrooms, and lunchrooms of their school. Sunnie also suffered this harassment from peers because of her association with him. Between her friend's parents' fierce rejection of their son (his parents burned his clothes and kicked him out of the house when he came out to them) and his peers' harassment and threats of violence, Sunnie's friend soon began to contemplate suicide. That's when Sunnie, along with her circle of friends, initiated the formation of a Gay/Straight Alliance at her school. The proposal to establish a Gay/Straight Alliance as a sanctioned school club met with resistance from the administration at her school. Sunnie explained this resistance as stemming from the administration's wishes to keep the school "safe" from political conflict or confrontation:

> The school doesn't want . . . like if it is going to create conflict, they
> don't want it. So that was definitely the message that I got. They

wanted to keep things civil; they didn't want anyone to try to protest or do anything of that sort, because they wanted a very quiet school. Which is understandable. But at the same time kids are being harassed. Like we had to sit through science class one time with a kid waiting outside to beat my friend up; he just stood there waiting. And no one was going to do anything about it. Like, what are you supposed to do?

Although her school administration at the time was unwilling to admit it, the school was already a political battleground, as students were embattled by the same gender and sexual politics that rocked the quiet wooded neighborhoods of their parents' world. Oakland and Portland student activists who tried to foment social movement activity in their schools and who drew their schools into larger social movements began their work by publicly acknowledging that their schools were not isolated institutions, separate from their communities. They insisted that schools are living battlegrounds for local, regional, national, and even global struggles. They argued that violence engendered by sexual politics, class struggles, and racial tensions in the wider society also played out on school territory.

Sunnie joined the Human Relations club: a group of high school students at her school that went from class to class to discuss relationships among students. The group was designed to reach across cliques and build good friendships among different types of high school students. Sunnie thought this might give her an opportunity to speak openly to students about homophobia in her school. Her experience was disappointing:

We would go around and give presentations on acceptance, and you would talk about that. But it was never really as direct as I thought it should be. . . . It should have been focused on the problems our school really does have. I mean, the problems get so overlooked. Like, we mentioned homosexuality, but we never got to really talk about it. I kept saying, "How come I have to keep walking around the edges on certain issues here? Like, some people are gay, some people are straight. Why can't I talk about the reality of the issues here?" And the administration thought about it, but they didn't want the kids to go home and talk to their parents about homosexuality, and then have the parents call the school.

In the end, Sunnie and her friends successfully organized a new club that could discuss, within certain limits, the effects of homophobia in her school. But to get a teacher to sponsor the club (a requirement for all official student clubs) and to get the administration's consent, they had to name the club Students Against Hate rather than the more overt and direct title they originally wanted: the Gay/Straight Student Alliance. The veiled name was a signal to the administration, teachers, and community that the students were working toward eliminating a vague and general scourge of hate in their schools, rather than publicly aligning students with a national and even international gay rights movement. It also represented the concession students had to make to create a truly safe space, in regard to homophobia, in their schools.

Through Students Against Hate, Sunnie and her friends organized a Day of Silence to coincide with a national gay rights campaign to get schools to raise student consciousness about homophobia. Although her school administration forbade students to name their club in any way that would stir controversy in the school (or among parents), the principal did approve their Day of Silence, much to Sunnie's relief. Apparently, the prospect of students protesting homophobia for one day, through their collective silence, did not strike the administration as overly threatening or disruptive to the smooth functioning of the school. Nationally, the Day of Silence is followed by a Night of Noise, often in community spaces like the town square in downtown Portland, where students, parents, teachers, activists from various human rights and gay rights organizations, and even legislators and political representatives gather to speak out against homophobia and hate crimes. The Day of Silence is designed to connect student bodies with a national gay rights campaign, at least for one day. Sunnie described how the event turned sour at her school:

> We would do a Day of Silence, where we would go to our classes and have a piece of paper that said we were silently protesting the mistreatment of homosexuals. So we would not speak all day, and we would go in and hand the teacher the slip. And we also had ribbons on our backpacks and stuff. It was really cool that the school let us do that.

But it turned out really terrible. We put up posters, and, at the same time, the posters would be ripped down, so we would put up another little piece of paper under it if someone did rip it down that said, "You just committed a hate crime." But eventually, a couple of weeks later, there was another group that came through and had a piece of paper that said, "I am silent because I believe that homo-sexuality is wrong and immoral." And they got to do it, too, 'cause we got to do our thing. So there was arguing about it at school, and the principal said that they have the right to do it.

But it's like, we are supporting people, and they are saying they're immoral. Come on! I ended up leaving class; I was almost crying. It was terrible. So we really couldn't do much outside of our club. Like, we could operate in our own club, but whenever we went outside of that, they [students] would protest back.

Citing a vague notion of fairness, the school administration allowed a silent counterdemonstration, which was in concert with the larger community's antigay values. This points to the presence of politics even in supposedly safe and nonpoliticized spaces, such as the classroom or other school spaces. As hooks (1994) points out, "safety" often means reproducing racist, sexist, and heterosexist values and paradigms within the curriculum, and, in this case, within the political and social life of the hallways.

Of the thirteen schools that students in this study attended, none were located in a more overtly politically conservative area than Sunnie's school. Counterdemonstrations such as the one organized by students at Sunnie's school were notably absent in the other schools of this study. Rarely did the student activists in Oakland or Portland encounter politi-cally conservative students who organized in reaction to YP or SRU orga-nizing. This may be, as Sara in Portland and Jazmin in Oakland explained in almost similar phrasing, "because most students don't know how to organize," regardless of their political leanings.

Indeed, my first contact with Oakland and Portland student organizers occurred outside of their schools—where they did most of their networking with other students and obtained most of their political training. I found SRU students on a fall afternoon of 2002 in downtown Portland, gathered with a few thousand other Portlanders at one of the early antiwar rallies before the invasion of Iraq. In a sea of adults with kids on their shoulders or in strollers, the SRU youth stood under one of the largest and unmistakable banners in the crowd: "Students Rise Up." The following spring, I met my first Youth Power organizers as I sat with them at a long table at their downtown Oakland office for a weekly coalition meeting with other pro-education, anti-incarceration youth activists. I wondered: Why were high school students connecting with each other over educational and social justice issues outside of their high schools? What opportunities did they have for political organizing within their schools, and how did these compare with those that they found outside their school territories?

The particular reasons for student movement setbacks on school grounds are many. Some of these reasons have to do with crumbling infrastructure: low-income schools in Oakland, for example, have school clubs that are either inactive or nonexistent due to lack of resources, lack of space, lack of available teachers to sponsor the clubs, and an institutionalized hopelessness among students that comes with living in oppressed and impoverished communities. In wealthier schools there are more clubs and extracurricular activities available to youth and, theoretically, more opportunities to galvanize student movements on campus. However, student activists in this study argued that even these clubs are not ideal structures that work to engage students as political actors in social movement work, because subtle and overt pressures—both institutional and cultural—work to keep political talk and action out of school spaces. Undoubtedly, these pressures have intensified after 9–11 and federal mandates to gear education toward standardized testing.[2] Importantly, the budget cuts that are eviscerating poorer schools and whittling away resources at wealthier schools impact the extent to which school clubs can provide high school students with opportunities to become political actors and community organizers. These forces combined help to explain how schooling can often gear students away from taking meaningful political action and why students in this study recognized the need to forge new spaces for youth political involvement outside of their schools.

How Schools Create Citizens-in-the-Making

Progressive educators in the early decades of the twentieth century and again in the 1960s envisioned public schooling as the mechanism to transform children into socially and politically responsible adults.[3] According to this model, public schooling serves as a training ground for the real thing: adult citizenship and participation in a democratic society: "schooling [becomes] a broad preparation for life . . . an effective means to reproduce the kind of society and individual consistent with Western Humanist traditions" (Aronowitz and Giroux 1986, 5). Thus, schooling instigates a process of human and citizen development, both of which ought to be fully realized in adulthood. In this view, schooling is central to the reproduction of a democratic society.

Critics of public schooling's role in creating "good citizens" have argued that rather than fostering democratic citizenship, schooling's major role in a capitalist society has been to reproduce capitalist social relations.[4] Thus, schooling has been a major focus of social reproduction theories. Marxist theories of schooling and social reproduction differ sharply from the earlier humanist theories of public education as a democratizing institution. They draw attention to the power dynamics between teacher and students, the role of obedience and authority in the classroom, the hierarchical nature of the institution, and schooling practices dictated by the value systems and interests of the middle classes that lean toward the reproduction of larger social inequalities.

According to Michelle Fine, public high schools are far from democratizing institutions, as they represent "a moment of hegemony," particularly for low-income, urban youth of color. In Fine's analysis, public schools

> seduce students away from the recognition of social inequity, power asymmetries, and social diversity and toward identification with individual mobility out of their communities; nurture participation, democracy, and critique largely in students who demonstrate that they are unlikely to rebel or act on anything that is unsafe to name; and discourage parent, community, and/or advocacy involvement in critical, creative, and transformative ways. (1991, 199)

Indeed, schools not only reproduce social inequalities. They also *produce* mechanisms of disengagement and political powerlessness among students. This is a double production: the production of larger social inequalities and the production of a political powerlessness among students that ensures that the continued reproduction of social inequalities proceeds undisturbed. The experiences of student activists who attempt to claim collective, political power on school grounds reveal that central to schooling's role in perpetuating larger social inequalities is the simultaneous construction of students as passive, compliant social actors. This construction of youth as passive beings disconnected from social movements and estranged from political power happens through schooling processes that can take on race- and class-specific forms. Despite the claims that schooling is central to producing an engaged, active adult citizenry, and despite its potential to do this, the struggles of students to organize their peers and to create new social movement spaces on campus reveal the limits to which schools function as actual democratic institutions.

Keeping School Spaces "Safe" from Politics: The Structures of Schooling That Already Exist

The Depoliticization of Official School Clubs

It is important to note that the formation of Gay/Straight Alliances (GSAs) in schools do not always engender the kind of resistance from school administrations that Sunnie experienced, nor do they always elicit a great deal of controversy from parents and other adults in the community. Many students in both SRU and YP were active members of their GSAs and attended schools where a Gay/Straight Student Alliance was as much a part of the established student landscape as was the school newspaper. These activists strongly believed that GSAs held great potential to be centers for gender and sexual justice on their campuses. At the same time, these YP and SRU students had strong critiques of their GSAs. YP student organizer Jazmin explained why she felt her GSA was not necessarily a politically conscious or active student organization: "There is GSA, which right now I am organizing with my consciousness that I have gained from YP. I mean, the GSA existed before, but it didn't do much. And definitely, it was a space to talk about harassment, but not any kind of action. It was not very conscious."

According to Jazmin, her school's GSA was not a place to critically analyze systems of oppression such as sexism or heterosexism. There was no overarching political framework that guided the group, nor any kind of direction for political action around gay rights issues. Tory, a fifteen-year-old SRU transgendered student, attended a suburban Portland school that she talked about as "isolated," though just a short bus ride from Portland's city center. Tory echoed Jazmin's critique of her school's GSA:

> The GSA kids at Vista aren't very activist-minded like I am. Most of them don't want to get into it—because they have a skewed view of what activism is. They don't realize that having a GSA is activist in itself! I feel that the people in the GSA don't think the way I do. They're more conservative. And they might be because they might not know any other gay people in Portland. And most of them have never been to the queer youth groups in Portland. Our school is just different that way. It's in the suburbs; I mean, how much more isolated can you get!

Tory, a suburban Portland student, and Jazmin, an urban Oakland student, both criticized their GSAs for not being "conscious" or "activist-minded." Tory attributed this lack of consciousness in the GSA to a geographically isolated student body and community. Frustrated with other students in the GSA, Tory finally left the club and devoted time to both SRU and the youth branch of a gay rights organization (one of the few adult-dominated social justice organizations that have carved out a space for young people's involvement). Jazmin, on the other hand, decided to stay in the GSA at her Oakland school and tried to infuse it with her newly learned political consciousness. She introduced discussions of homophobia, sexism, and oppression into a school club that she felt had no overarching political consciousness.

While Sunnie battled to establish a GSA in her school, Jazmin and Tory already had GSAs waiting for them as incoming freshmen in their high schools. Yet a recurring motif throughout these students' narratives was a frustration with their schools' tendency toward keeping school spaces divorced from politics. Teachers, principals, parents in the communities, and even other students themselves exerted subtle and overt pressures to keep the school severed from social movements and the talk that would bring those movements into being. Jacob, a sophomore at a different suburban school close to Portland, took full advantage of his school's affluence. Enrolled in such classes as Independent Publishing and Visual Photography—classes that did not even exist in many of the urban Oakland and Portland schools—Jacob submitted his photo essay on local Portland activism and created a zine devoted entirely to issues of environmental destruction and the negative effects of advertising and media. "My teachers get sick of me sometimes. They're always telling me, 'Stop trying to make this all political.' And I am like, 'How is it not political?' especially since this is a place of education. This is our school. I guess a lot of people are just closed-minded to realize it's all political . . . and to say school is not a part of politics is just dead wrong."

When I asked about the opportunities for social justice activism within already established school infrastructures, YP students described ACLU clubs in relatively wealthier Oakland schools that "don't do anything" because the students in the club had never learned tools for organizing sustained student campaigns. SRU students discussed Amnesty International chapters that were somewhat political but were disconnected from area community organizations and local issues that hit students the hardest: issues such as school budget crises or the war in Iraq. Both YP and SRU students described service learning and volunteer opportunities that lacked a clear political education about social inequalities or the need for active social change, as one seventeen-year-old SRU activist explained, "At my school, there is a lot of volunteering and what not, but there isn't, like, you know, activism, or mentioning *why* this isn't right, or something. You know?" Other students discussed the limits of their environmental clubs: "They mostly do cleanups and plantings. But they don't really do political stuff."[5]

The disconnection between larger social movements and secondary schools works to politically sanitize the many student clubs and extracurricular activities at schools that have the resources to host them. This sanitizing effect is more overt at certain schools than at others, but nearly every student I spoke with expressed frustration with the degree to which their school clubs limited political action because they lacked a social movement framework, a political consciousness, or a clear connection to larger movement networks outside of the school itself. More noticeable in wealthier schools like the suburban schools of Portland and the relatively wealthier urban schools of Oakland, this sanitizing effect was not as evident at poorer urban schools in Oakland. Instead of a multitude of school clubs that engaged in talk that skirted potentially explosive community and school political issues, poorer urban schools often had no clubs at all, or had clubs in name only that were in practice completely inactive.

In comparison to the active YP presence on the impoverished campus of Patterson High in Oakland, the other Patterson clubs were ghosts. Ethnic-specific clubs at Patterson that had been active decades ago, such as the Black Student Alliance, were now nearly defunct. This was striking in a school that was over 50 percent black. This club inactivity was not just a result of the widespread cynicism and hopelessness among students: in poor schools like Patterson, club advisors are teachers whose time and resources are already stretched too thin. If these clubs are functioning at all, it is because generous teachers are willing to spend their only major break in their work day, the lunch break, to advise a student organization.

While many commentators have decried the ways in which school budget cuts are threatening arts, physical education, and music curriculums in schools, less recognized is the extent to which the concentration of urban poverty and school budget cuts are also devastating school clubs in postindustrial cities like Oakland. Although school clubs are often seen as peripheral to student and school success compared to the centrality of the formal curriculum, school clubs have the potential to galvanize students into active social change campaigns that may ultimately work to improve both their experiences of education and their schools as institutions. Teacher layoffs and the slashing of school programs curtail the potential viability of student activist infrastructure within the schools.

Beyond schools' budgetary constraints, there are also enduring institutional barriers to student movements within adult-dominated and hierarchical institutions like high schools. In trying to establish a GSA club to tackle homophobia at her school, Sunnie had to search for a willing teacher to sponsor the group to make it an "official," and thus an unshakeable and enduring, part of school infrastructure. Because homosexuality was such a politically charged issue in her community and in her school, Sunnie could not find any teachers willing to associate themselves with such a controversial issue. To find a willing teacher sponsor, Sunnie and her friends were forced to change the name and even the nature of their organization. The institutional requirements for teacher sponsors and club charters make the creation of politicized student clubs a difficult task. One fifteen-year-old SRU activist who helped to establish an activist club at his Portland high school cited these institutional constraints as reasons for eventually leaving the club and organizing students outside of school spaces:

> The thing at Vista was, it was an official club and we were supposed to have a club charter and all that crap. But it also meant that we really couldn't do that much. We were totally controlled by the administration. And I think things have changed at Vista, but in SRU, we can do basically whatever we want. . . . Whatever we want to do in SRU, we can do it.

YP adult ally Yesenia observed deeper problems with the institutional requirement for teacher sponsors of student clubs, namely that teacher sponsors are not required by the institution to develop student leadership or organizing skills: "The way the clubs are structured right now, is that a teacher sponsors it. And that teacher pretty much doesn't have to provide any information, doesn't have to administer to them through troubleshooting." In many cases, teacher sponsors do help students develop leadership and organizing skills and serve as important catalysts for student movements. But teacher sponsors are not required by the institution to conference individually with students about their progress in the club, nor are they required to educate them, nor to mentor them. Some responsibilities teachers have in the classroom, namely to educate and evaluate the progress of students, do not necessarily extend to the clubs. In this sense, teacher sponsors are mostly needed to give an adult face of legitimacy to student clubs. Other responsibilities, such as surveilling students and maintaining discipline, remain ubiquitous throughout official school spaces. Teachers are required to sponsor school clubs because the possibility of students inhabiting official school spaces without adult supervision would be anathema to the requirement that youth fall under the watchful eye of responsible adults.

In turn, students feel constrained by adults in power within their schools, as fifteen-year-old SRU activist Hayden observed of her peers: "It also seems since they are high school students, they are kind of nervous to be disobedient, especially in school and everything, where there are set rules and stuff. They get really nervous about that." In this sense, the institutional hierarchy of the school, which is marked by adult domination, is maintained within both the classroom setting and the student club setting. Student leadership and organizing skills can be encouraged out-right in schools through the individual efforts of willing and dedicated teacher-mentors. In all cases, however, the development of student organizing and leadership skills is not an established mission or requirement of the high school institution.

The Limitations of Student Government

Student government is definitely not a place for student voice. It is a popularity contest. The popular students get into this club and into this group, or whatever, and they plan rallies, plan dances, school dances. And they are really school spirited. That's it. So it's non-political. It doesn't connect with the community. All they do is, like, campus cleanups. They try to bring a school spirit to the students. And I don't think school spirit is important at all. I mean, um, like, it's cool to have activities at times; it's like a break from reality trying to pretend your school is all fine and dandy. But it's not. (Pilar, sixteen years old, Youth Power)

The institutional infrastructure of public high school includes student governments and student councils. The design of student government adheres to the citizen-in-the-making model, where schools serve as practice runs for the real thing: eventual adult citizenship. Student government is a space for students to engage in social decision making and to take a certain measure of control over school-sponsored activities.

However, students in both YP and SRU did not recognize student government as a viable means for galvanizing student voice on issues such as school budget cuts; racial tensions at school; and local, regional, national, or global issues such as the war in Iraq or corporate-led globalization. Indeed, Pilar and other student organizers viewed student government as promoting a "school spirit" divorced from community and school politics. Penelope Eckert, in her ethnography of schooling and the reproduction of class inequalities, argues that student government is designed to align with adult (and middle-class) values and hierarchical systems of order within the school.[6] Explaining the Burnouts' (working-class students) hatred of student government, Eckert writes, "student government inherently involves participation in a student hierarchy. Furthermore, because student government does not have the power to affect the running of the school in any significant way, the Burnouts view it as a hierarchy that exists for its own sake" (1989, 165). Most YP and SRU students, like Eckert's Burnouts, were critical of student government as a school structure. They noted the impotence of student government in solving real school and community problems. These organizers conceptualized a sharp distinction between real student leadership and student government. According to youth activists in both cities, student government primarily functioned as a route to popularity rather than as a real representation of the student body, or as a method of tackling student issues. In many ways, the formation of YP and SRU has been a conscious and direct reaction to this institutionalized format for student input and thus to the adult construction of youth as citizens-in-the-making.

In some schools, mock elections determine student government representatives and are designed to run students through the motions of electoral politics. In other schools, elections are bypassed and the students who teachers or the administration identify as "natural leaders" are simply appointed to student government. In low-income schools like Kendall High in Oakland, student government is hardly active at all. Yesenia, a YP adult ally who worked as an advisor to YP on the Kendall High campus, explained,

> I mean, student government is *defunct*. Well, not really, they have an election. Well, not really elections, like, there's not campaigning; there isn't debating; there isn't putting out issues. One year the administration just picked: "Hey, I think you'd be a good president." I mean, that's how people were selected. They don't do anything that sort of . . . they do prom, or whatever. So YP students hate student government. They're critical of it. They wouldn't join that.

For student organizers and activists in YP and SRU, student government, like most extracurricular clubs, was not in itself a sufficient avenue for developing a student voice in real-world community issues.

Miseducation and the Missing Social Justice Curriculum

The prohibition of social justice talk in the classroom and the absence of a larger context for social activism in their curricula is a major source of frustration for student organizers. This frustration is an added motivation for students to find a safe space to talk and enact politics away from school. YP student organizer Jazmin described her frustration with having too few teachers in her large Oakland high school who actually took the time to educate students about real-world issues, social inequalities, and social movements:

> There is very few teachers who will actually take the time of day to talk about race, class, sexist oppression. First of all, there is very few teachers who are conscious. And the teachers that are conscious—not many are willing to take the time of day to educate their students about something. I have had two teachers so far who have been somewhat conscious and took that time of day to educate students. And one, she taught a lot, and sometimes kids would look at her like, "Oh, here she goes again!" preaching-type thing.
>
> Or, a lot of times it's not that they tried to ignore her. It's like they are all "fuck, shit is so fucked up. I don't even want to hear this anymore, it's depressing me." You know, 'cause they don't want to take any type of action. It's just too much for them, you know. And then I had a history teacher and he took the time. He taught by the book, but then on the side he was like "and this and that happened," you know what I am saying? But all that, it's not enough. I mean, two teachers out of the whole school is not going to do anything. We're thousands of students!

Jazmin articulated an important relationship between the missing movement context of the classroom, the missing movement context of other school spaces such as clubs and student government, and the lack of opportunities for youth to get involved in the many adult-led social justice organizations in their communities. Jazmin echoed other student organizers I spoke with who observed that very few teachers will bring social justice talk or movement histories into their lessons. But for those few that do, their efforts to teach "on the side" instead of teaching "by the book" are often not enough to create a safe zone for developing sustained student political consciousness. As Jazmin observed, it can be defeating for students to learn about the political context of social inequalities if they have no opportunities in their schools or communities for political agency and collective action.

In most secondary schools, the opportunities for students to talk politics in the classroom are sparse and uneven. Scott, a seventeen-year-old SRU activist from an urban Portland high school, remarked that he felt safer expressing his political views in certain classes more than others: "Like in my government class, I feel a lot safer expressing my views because it's sort of like, you know, it's government and that's what we are going to talk about. And so I feel like it's sort of more of a forum, where people have that in mind and, you know, they're like, 'Well, that's how you feel, so now you can argue it.' But, like, in other classes people are not in that state of mind, and they are a lot more hostile to talk and ideas." Thus, political talk can be bounded within certain "appropriate" classroom spaces such as government class, but may be stifled, both by teachers and students, in other classes. This poses a problem for the political development of younger high school students, who may not even take a discussion-oriented class like government where the setting is "more of a forum," until they are older. Zoe, a freshman SRU activist, traced the small proportion of younger students in SRU to the lack of political education available in freshmen classes within the schools:

> The freshmen don't know that much, because you don't get taught politics when you're a freshman. I learned most of my stuff from my family; that's why I participate. And even I don't know that much. I don't know positions, like secretary of state, and other stuff like that. And I don't know who our senators are of Oregon, and our house members and congress members. It's kind of annoying 'cause there are so many names and so many people. And its like, the freshmen don't know. When you don't know it's hard to get into it, because it's, like, confusing.

The lack of opportunities to discuss politics (whether electoral or social justice oriented) for younger students makes joining a social justice organization or getting involved in political action especially intimidating.

Sixteen-year-old SRU activist Amanda pointed to the lack of political education in the classroom as a major source of a wider student ignorance and apathy: "A lot of people, specifically students, don't realize what's going on politically because that information is not out there, that you can talk about in seminars. Like, *seminar* really doesn't take place."[7] Even as student organizers venture into spaces outside of schools to establish a foundation for student organizing, this lack of political education in the classroom lends to a political ignorance among students. This makes political mobilization among youth, inside or outside of school, particularly challenging.

In Portland, SRU activists lamented the absence of a political education in their classrooms, noting this political void as a factor promoting student apathy. Even as they fought to save their school systems, they deemed much of what they were learning in school as "irrelevant." Kristin, a sixteen-year-old Portland high school student who had been active in organizing sit-ins and protests against school budget cuts, was the first to discuss the seeming irrelevance of her English class: "Yeah, my English teacher, we don't even bother to read the books that he tells us to read. I mean, this book we're supposed to be reading now, it's, like, about robots on another planet. It's just . . . I don't want to read about that [laughs]. I don't see why I need to. I don't know. I mean, it's school, and it's important, but there are so many other important things going on in the world."

Meanwhile, YP organizers in Oakland saw their education as colonizing and racist, reproducing white supremacy. Thus, not only was education irrelevant for YP kids, it was also seen as part of a larger system of violence that could be traced back hundreds of years to European conquest of peoples of color all over the globe.[8] Like SRU students, YP students organized against sweeping school budget cuts. But unlike SRU youth, they also called for the establishment of ethnic studies in their classrooms, which they envisioned would help to undermine the ravages of white supremacy in their schools. When they spoke of the difficulty in politically mobilizing their peers, they did not speak so much of student apathy as they did of internalized hopelessness among students, one that, according to YP organizers, is fed by a white supremacist education in the classroom. As Christine Sleeter writes, "Schools are an instrument of the maintenance of colonial relationships in that they constitute an arm of the state through which belief systems and cultural relationships are taught" (1999, xvii). This was the major thrust behind YP's Five Hundred Years of Miseducation workshop, which seasoned YP student organizers taught to new incoming YP mentees. This workshop detailed the historical role that education has played in both maintaining colonial relationships and fostering social justice and liberation—especially for people of color. This workshop helped to present youth with a political critique of their schooling as white supremacist, while also providing them with a vision of education that could be relevant and liberating.

Since the advent of the Reagan era, a concerted backlash against the gains of the civil rights movement has infused classroom curricula. Backlash against multicultural approaches to education and a trend toward the dismantling of affirmative action admissions policies in higher education have fueled the institution of classroom curricula that resemble racial assimilationist models of education during the early twentieth century.[9] Although recent decades have been marked by a major influx of immigrants to the United States, many school systems are still largely unfamiliar with and unresponsive to the needs of immigrant students. Most school systems lack basic information about these students' countries of origin, cultural practices, or understandings and expectations of schooling (Aronowitz and Giroux 1994). Angela Valenzuela (1999) argues that the development of new social movements such as the Chicano student movement, demands for bilingual education, and demographic shifts precipitated by new waves of immigration have all combined in recent decades to destabilize the racial social order in the United States. At these moments we see the emergence of new conservative schooling efforts to undermine these developments and restore Eurocentric social order. Valenzuela calls these efforts to recapture Anglo supremacy and assimilate non-Anglo students "subtractive schooling."

While the development of multicultural curricula has made some impact on the culture of urban schools and has buffered the processes of subtractive schooling, YP students found fault even with these developments. Although some YP students had taken "ethnic studies" classes at their schools, they were highly critical of the ethnic studies they had received. Gayle, a YP organizer and recent graduate from Patterson High, recalled her experience with ethnic studies:

> Yeah, I mean to be honest. I took a class that was ethnic studies. It was called ethnic studies. And I'm like, there was nothing ethnic about the studies; it was ethnic studies from the Eurocentric view. It just seemed like, "Africa, that's where black people are from," you know; it was just so obvious. But what about the struggles? What about the slavery? There is more to it.

I don't remember learning about Polynesian history and struggles and alliances. I don't remember hearing about any of that in high school. I don't remember learning about any of the Raza studies. I don't remember in detail. They are all mentioned, "Oh, Polynesians, they live here." They are all mentioned, but not in detail. Like, Polynesians went through this; their homes were burned, imperialism; where are those stories? It's like, so much more to it. It's taught in, like, no way for me to understand.

As Gayle illustrated, what was missing from her ethnic studies experience was a relevant framework for understanding the history of political oppression and struggle. The kind of ethnic studies she described is reminiscent of the multiculturalism that stresses only the surface elements of cultural difference—a melting pot of ethnic foods, music, clothing—but not a solid framework for understanding oppression, power, and racial and ethnic differences and alliances in movements.[10] In the end, the sanitized version of ethnic studies that Gayle received in high school felt irrelevant to her, distant, "taught in, like, no way for me to understand."

While these opportunities to learn even limited multicultural studies are very important, students noted that they were insufficient in providing a fruitful context for the development of student political consciousness and action. What was missing in their schooling was a social movement context that stressed not only the histories of oppression, imperialism, and racial violence but also the histories of social movement struggles and alliances. From a student organizer's perspective, education in the classroom does not spur student empowerment if it is without reference to a larger social movement context of race relations in the United States. This disempowerment in the classroom is compounded by the lack of political development opportunities for students in other school spaces and in the communities in which they live. As Louis Miron argues, historically classroom teachers and professional educators have been taught to view the curriculum as "depoliticized texts" (1999, 84). A depoliticized curriculum cannot foster a politically engaged student body. As student organizers have noted, it does the opposite.

This ruptured link between education and social movement politics does not simply foster a sense of political ignorance, powerlessness, and inaction among students of color. It also inadvertently feeds racial and ethnic violence on school grounds. Seventeen-year-old YP organizer Guillermo explained how well-intentioned, depoliticized "celebrations of diversity" on campus actually intensified already existing racial and ethnic conflicts at Patterson High:

> Like, every year you got the assemblies; you have the Latino assembly, the Polynesian assembly, the Asian assembly, and I always feel we need an ethnic . . . something that represents all cultures in one assembly, not separating them, you know? Patterson has two or three Black History assemblies. And the Latino students are like, "Oh, how come we only get one?" And then you have the Polynesian students, "Oh, how come we only get one, why not two?"
>
> And it feeds into everything. You got all these students walking around feeling unfair, and it separates students. Like, at lunch you see the Polynesians sitting over here, you can't go over there because you are not Polynesian. You got the black people sitting here over by the tree. And if you ain't black you can't sit over there. You got the Latinos over there. And if you ain't from [a specific turf] you can't go over there anyway. There is just so much separation.

Even supposedly wholesome school activities like Spirit Week have become lightning rods for racial tensions in schools like Patterson and Kendall, located in racially segregated and impoverished areas of Oakland.[11] I asked Salvador and Alisha what happens during Spirit Week, and Alisha explained, with a sly smile, "Yeah, Spirit Week is when all the seniors pick on the freshmen!" Alisha and Salvador told me about their own and their friends' experiences with this ritual. Salvador added, "But the rule is, you don't pick on freshmen of your own race; you always pick on freshmen of another race." When I asked him why, he shrugged. They both grew quiet for a moment and then Alisha said, "Yeah, it was really crazy a few years ago, like, people started bringing guns to school during Spirit Week, and all these people were coming to campus who didn't even go here. It was hella violent."

Student activists and organizers in YP and SRU spoke of the injuries of school education that estrange students from themselves, from their learning processes, from each other, from their communities, and from opportunities for political agency. When Sunnie spoke of her educational injuries, she pointed to all that she *didn't* learn in the classroom. She contrasted her otherwise privileged life with her high school educational experience:

> I've had a pretty good childhood; my parents are great. I got a wonderful family. And the thing that really screwed me up was school. And it's so wrong. It should be the thing that helps you most in life; it's your education! Everything was so, "This is how it is," you know? And I missed out on so much. Like, thinking about taking ethnic studies or women's studies at college, like, I would never have been able to even comprehend being able to have a chance to do something like that. We never talked about Native Americans and stuff, even though Native Americans lived in our community thousands of years before us. Those things were not discussed in any of my classes, ever.

Although many students felt disempowered and defeated by the lack of opportunities in their schools to engage in movements for social change, it is important to remember that students are both aware and critical of these missed opportunities. They also try to transform their student spaces and create new politicized spaces within their schools. Many times these efforts fail or never come to fruition. Sometimes these efforts enjoy a degree of success. For many organizers in both YP and SRU, attempts to transform school spaces into politicized spaces were formative experiences toward their development as community organizers. They were also instructive to students in exploring the political climate of their schools, learning about their peers, and discovering the limits of organizing on school grounds without connecting their work to larger social movements in their communities.

Taking Back the School: The Structures That Youth Activists Create

People say you should treat your school like your second home. I mean, we are here, like, hella hours. So, like, why not? Why wouldn't you want to be able to walk into the bathroom and not step in piss? Or you don't want to wash your hands because you don't want to touch the knob. Like, that don't make no sense. People are like, "I don't use the bathroom. I hold mine until I get home." I don't want to have to do that. That works on my whole little system and it hurts. It doesn't make any sense, you know? (Shandra, sixteen-year-old YP organizer)

For low-income Oakland students, student-led bathroom campaigns—those efforts to clean up trashed, dirty, and often locked and unusable school bathrooms—symbolized just the beginning of student-led efforts to reclaim their school spaces to make them more comfortable and usable. These bathroom campaigns became part of larger educational justice campaigns. For student organizers like Shandra, the goal was to spark a shift in students' thinking about their school territory. When students adapt to dirty and unusable bathrooms and resign themselves to the injustice of not being able to attend to their basic bodily needs as part of their daily schooling experience, they are likely to resign themselves to other educational injustices as well. YP student organizers found that when students took steps to reclaim their bathrooms, they began to understand that their school territory and their education were *theirs*. In some of Oakland's poorest schools, bathroom campaigns have been watersheds for further student activism.

In addition to initiating bathroom campaigns (Oakland), politicizing existing school clubs such as GSAs (Oakland and Portland), rallying for ethnic studies curriculums (Oakland), and even handing out student-produced alternative school newspapers or zines in high school hallways (Portland), SRU and YP students attempted to create new activist infra-structure within schools that later became especially central to their social change efforts both on and off campus.[12]

Youth Centers in Oakland

In Oakland YP student organizers fought to establish badly needed youth centers at their schools. They argued that in their communities and schools, where there were few safe places for young people to hang out and interact, youth centers were essential for giving students a comfortable and positive space to connect with each other. YP organizers argued to their administrations that the lack of comfortable student spaces on campus fed into school violence. Students envisioned that youth centers, operating much like student lounges, would transform uninviting, tense, and even violent school spaces into comfortable and politically relevant student spaces. Schools like Brookline High School, through the efforts of youth organizations like the Brookline YP chapter, now have youth centers painted with colorful murals. Inside, students have posted political posters and movement art, and banners that YP students have created for summer programs, protests, and rallies in previous years. Some youth centers even have a few torn but well-loved couches where students can relax and comfortably interact with each other between classes.

Before the U.S. bombing of Iraq began in March of 2003, youth centers provided more than just comfortable student spaces. YP students used their schools' youth centers to host antiwar teach-ins. Packing the center full with ninety students at a time at Brookline High, Brookline YP students led antiwar workshops and discussions and even invited guest speakers from other Oakland social justice groups to talk to the students about militarism, imperialism, and the costs of war for communities of color. Much of the antiwar organizing in East Bay schools began in, but then moved beyond, youth centers on campuses. Armed with new organizing skills and political education, YP students began organizing their peers in classrooms, hallways, and cafeterias. YP student organizer Tevin explained the way in which YP organizing began in youth centers and then became ubiquitous throughout formal and informal school spaces: "We did workshops in the youth centers, and, of course, wherever there were conversations, like in the classroom or whatever; we were doing our own thing, in our own classrooms, speaking to our friends, you know what I'm saying? People that we knew. All the YP youth always, we always educate on our own, anytime we get the chance." These youth centers, created and instituted by youth, became unusual politicized spaces on high school campuses and were instrumental in developing student activism among Oakland youth.

Student Unions in Portland

Well, last year, there were some students, mostly seniors, that started the Student Union at Rose Valley High School. And basically, our goal was to make people's voices heard. It actually started as a voice, having a voice in Rose Valley High School. Letting the students say what they want to say to the administration. Because, student government, you know, they're great and they have lots of fun and it's a way to make friends and stuff like that. But really they mainly deal with dances and various things like that, and socials. And, you know, that is important in the high school experience, but it's not everything. (Michelle, seventeen-year-old SRU activist)

Notably absent from the enduring infrastructure of the high school and unlike student government structures, student unions are politicized spaces that students develop anew. Student unions disappear for a few years and then are recreated again by a new crop of students. Many SRU students said that the student unions they created were spaces to cultivate a real student voice, as opposed to the student government.

Student unions swelled in Portland at the turn of the millennium, and in most cases preceded the creation of the SRU student movement. Before the advent of SRU in Portland, students concerned about school budget crises and the threats to their education began organizing separate student unions, unbeknownst to each other, all over Portland area high schools during the beginning of the school year in 2003. Student unions began as an effort to establish communication within the school, mainly between students and the administration. Members active in the student unions surveyed the student body about their concerns, collected data, and presented data to the administration. Students also noted that the initial goals of student unions in their schools included educating the students about the funding crisis, local ballot measures, and governmental policies like the No Child Left Behind Act. Thus, local and national political and economic crises sparked the simultaneous emergence of many student unions across Portland high schools. These student unions provided at least an ideological connection between local political issues and students, and, like youth centers at Oakland high schools, provided a flow of information to students about these crises that they might not get in their classrooms or in other school spaces.

Although in Michelle's school, where the administration "basically didn't do anything" with student input, student unions in other schools brought teachers and students closer together during the budget crisis in schools where teachers' unions were strong. As SRU activist Stephen

explains, student unions became the student version of worker and
teacher unions:

> I think the part that started the student union was the funding
> crisis. And it was a part of giving the students the solidarity with the
> teachers, especially at Cleaver, because the teachers were more
> organized and unified than in the other public schools, and they
> were really into, like, getting the students involved with that and
> everything. That was really important for us. There were some
> other clubs like, um, the environmental club and some other clubs
> like that, but not anything that really focused on getting together
> and being informed about political things, getting involved and
> interacting.

In fact, several Cleaver SRU students recounted that it was Cleaver teachers
who held the institutional memory of past student unions at Cleaver.
These teachers informed students that Cleaver used to have a student
union many years ago and suggested to students that they should form one
again to get involved in the local school budget crisis. At other schools,
older siblings or friends held this institutional memory of student unions,
providing students with a template for creating a new, potentially empowering student space within the school.

Because student unions are not part of the enduring structure of the
school, and because they emerge and then disappear again according to
political climate, student unions are spaces within the high school that are
unlike any other. SRU students who were also members of their high
school student unions did not always know whether or not their student
unions were officially recognized by the administration. Because student
unions are not always set up as school clubs, they are not necessarily held
to the same institutional requirements (teacher sponsors, club charter).
Many student unions in Portland operated under semisecrecy, during
lunches, if they could find an empty room at school. Often, these students
met without any adult supervision. With their nebulous stance as a more
informal and nonenduring space within the school landscape, students
found they had less constraints on them imposed by the administration
and more potential to take on not only real political school issues but also
the larger community politics that fed these school issues.

Struggles to Sustain Youth Movement in Schools

Impoverished Schools and Shifting Power Players:
Youth Centers in Oakland

YP students at impoverished Patterson and Kendall high schools found that the terrain of administrative power within these schools was constantly shifting. Teacher and administration retention rates are relatively low at schools in low-income areas, and high turnover rates in school employment inevitably affects the ability of students to secure new politicized spaces on campus. With a different principal each year, students found that even when they successfully negotiated with school administrators over the creation of new student spaces like youth centers, they could not hold these administrators accountable to their promises if these administrators ultimately left for a better job somewhere else. A negotiation with one year's principal over the creation of a youth center, for example, has to be repeated again and again with each new principal. YP student organizer Alisha expressed her exhaustion, disappointment, and defeat in having to negotiate with school power over and over: "Wow, how are we going to get something done if we can't even keep someone, you know, we can't keep someone of power there for long enough? How are we going to do it?" In impoverished school systems where the power structure itself doesn't change but the players always do, negotiating with the school administration can be a defeating prospect.

At Patterson High, YP student organizer Gayle led an effort to negotiate with the administration over the creation of a youth center on campus. She and other YP students, in a series of meetings with the principal, made impassioned arguments about the necessity of having a safe, positive space on campus for youth. The student organizers argued that having this center would not only diffuse school violence and promote good relationships between students but would ultimately improve scholastic achievement because the youth center could also be a space where students could get tutoring and mentorship from peer educators and student mentors. YP student organizers envisioned the youth center to be a liberating space, with political posters, empowering social justice slogans painted on the walls, even a graffiti wall for students to add their own messages and express themselves. They envisioned this space as one for liberatory peer education, one very different from the education they received in their overcrowded classrooms. YP students were thrilled when the Patterson principal, Mr. Roberts, agreed to allow them to organize a youth center. Convinced by the students' arguments, he promised they could have a room of their own on campus for the center the following school year, and eventually Patterson would allow YP students to move their center to an even larger space, a portable classroom, a year or two down the road.

Elated by their win and emboldened to organize new student campaigns, YP students left hopeful for summer vacation, making their plans to claim their temporary classroom space for their youth center at the beginning of the next school year. At the end of the school year, Mr. Roberts announced that he was leaving for another job and would not be returning in the fall. YP students figured that because a promise was a promise, they would simply explain the deal they had made with Mr. Roberts to the incoming principal.

The new principal, Mr. Connors, agreed that students needed a youth center. However, he decided to give away the youth center space to a mentorship program run by the district, instead of giving it to YP. Mr. Connors assumed that the district mentoring program would serve the same function of the proposed YP youth center. From the perspective of YP student organizers, however, the two programs and visions for the center were vastly different. YP students envisioned the youth center as a youth-run school space that would cultivate academic achievement, social justice, and youth empowerment. The district mentoring program represented a vision for adult-run education that would strive for academic achievement but that missed the crucial ways in which social justice and youth empowerment could contribute to academic achievement. Stung by Mr. Connors's betrayal, Gayle bitterly remembered,

> The person that the district chose to be their senior mentor, he was not at all into politics, into the politics of YP. He was an adult who was working for the district. He didn't agree with a student voice. He believed that the students should do what the adults tell them. He had this whole adultism: "Youth don't know what they want unless adults tell them. How can a student know what they need unless a teacher tells them?"

And it's like, what? How can students know they don't have an education, unless a teacher tells them so? Students aren't dumb. You can't just take an education away from a student. An education shouldn't be taken away, and that's something that a lot of adults who are in the district, who are supposedly the "educators," just don't get.

James, a YP student organizer, identified a similar process happening a few miles away at Kendall High School:

> We fought for the student center, and now it's gonna be taken away. . . .You know, that is so disempowering. 'Cause I mean, the new administration's plans, they want to make it [the student center] into a workstation. So there's going to be computers in there. It won't be our lounge area; there won't be the "free speech" wall that we wanted. I mean, we had such great plans and we put so much time into them. And then we sat through meetings with people . . . and, you know, now for our visions to just be taken away. . . . It's just so disempowering.

In the case of Patterson and Kendall students, the rapid turnover of powerful players within the school system created a shaky basis upon which to build new and lasting politicized student activities and spaces. For YP students at Patterson and Kendall high schools, the need for a stable youth movement rooted in communities outside of schools became vitally important for leveraging the uphill battles to create activist spaces at their individual schools. School and neighborhood impoverishment, in many respects, influences the degree to which students are able to successfully create new and lasting activist spaces at their schools.

Age-Graded and Isolated: Student Unions in Portland

While student unions were crucial in mobilizing the first wave of student activists in Portland during 2002, and were later vital in connecting students from Portland schools to SRU, student unions in themselves were not enough to sustain a student movement in Portland. Because student unions were based in individual schools, they mostly operated within their own schools and could not easily provide connecting points to other students across the city to build a bigger student movement.

Importantly, most student unions were formed almost exclusively by senior high school students. Seniors in high schools are more familiar with the sociopolitical dynamics of their schools than are freshmen or sophomore students. Usually they have more connections to other students and to other readily identifiable student leaders, who are also mostly seniors. Seniors hold more status within the age-graded hierarchical structure of the school, which mirrors age-graded hierarchies in the larger society.[13] It takes a somewhat empowered student to be able to carve out a new space in the school landscape and to lead and organize other students. Seniors are most often these empowered figures who spearhead the creation of new student spaces.

The downside of this, however, is that student unions can take on the age-graded hierarchical system of the institutions that house them. Because student leadership is concentrated in the hands of seniors, student unions weaken when senior leaders graduate. This is partly why student unions disappear, reappear, and disappear again over a span of a few years. As the 2003–2004 school year came to a close, many student unions that had been active during the Portland school budget crisis receded. SRU activist Michelle explained that her student union at Rose Valley High "fizzled out" at the end of the school year because it was organized by "mainly seniors" about to graduate and leave high school behind. SRU activist Zoe explained that at her Portland school, the student union was not very strong. As she put it, "It kind of falls apart really easily." This was also the downside of creating a student organization that was not necessarily officially part of school-sanctioned infrastructure. Because these unions were sometimes semisecret, informal spaces, they escaped the constraints of formal club requirements. At the same time, unlike youth centers, student unions were not necessarily designed to be enduring pieces of the institution. They did not have their own formal spaces to meet, nor did they have official club charters. Thus, their institutional staying power was limited.

Student unions are not waiting for students as they enter high school. They must be created anew. Although the student union as a school space provides opportunities for students to develop organizing skills, these opportunities are limited because the student union itself is a highly unstable space. Michelle explained to me how she learned to facilitate meetings in SRU, a learning opportunity that did not exist in her high school student union: "Yeah, I really, really enjoy that [facilitating meetings in SRU] because the student union just wasn't around enough to get to this point, so I really can't say. I might have stepped up to the plate more for student union, but it just wasn't around long enough for me to even get there."

Perhaps the most limiting aspect of student unions in developing students as community organizers and political actors is that they are still firmly housed within their individual schools. As Eckert explains, high schools can serve to isolate adolescents from their larger communities:

> At a time in the history of the world when human beings need the broadest possible understanding, the school focuses adolescents inward. The school mediates relations not only within the local community, but also with adjacent communities. School attendance carves a coherent geographic continuum into separate units. Where adjacent population segments are demographically similar, this separation creates artificial divisions; where they are not, their differences become emphasized, obfuscated, and institutionalized. Thus schools create boundaries where there is similarity, and impose uniformity where there is dissimilarity. The effects of social polarization are carried out across school boundaries as well as within the school itself. (1989, 177)

Although the informal nature of student unions made them good connecting points to outside movements once an external, citywide student movement was established (as will be discussed in the next chapter), student unions, as isolated student collectives, do not have the capability to organize a mass student movement. SRU activist Megan explained this missing link between her school's student union and local movement activity in the Portland area:

> Well, we do have a student union. I typically don't go to that anymore because I don't feel like a lot happens and I don't feel like the people there know what is going on around town. And one of the best things I like about SRU, because I don't know a lot of activists yet, that SRU helps me find out what is going on. Because all those people there have a bigger perspective; they know what is happening here and other places.

Given student critiques of missing political opportunities in school spaces as varied as student clubs, student government, classrooms, and even student unions, it is no wonder why students eventually venture into urban spaces outside of schools to find opportunities for political development, mobilization, and action. Students like Sunnie have tried to forge new political spaces within their schools, but always with great struggle. Looking back on her experience in high school, Sunnie sounded more embittered than emboldened by her struggles to establish Students Against Hate as an official school club:

> The administration should be able to start these things. It shouldn't be the job of the students to start these clubs. They should just be able to go to them, just like any other club. They should be able to just have it there and waiting for them. I feel like I had to build my own place for myself at school. It wasn't waiting for me. And I don't think I should have had to. I think they should have made it available for anyone, and they didn't.

Sunnie's critique revealed a particular sense of entitlement to an institution that would actively encourage her and her friends' safety, comfort, and political consciousness. This sense of entitlement differed greatly from that of low-income students of color in Oakland, few of whom walked into their schools with this same expectation. In fact, YP organizers tried to actively foster this sense of entitlement among their peers, perceiving them as too quickly resigning themselves to substandard, degrading, and even violent experiences of schooling.

The Instability of Teacher Alliances

The potential for student political development on school territory is also hampered by adults' struggles over student dissent. These struggles, in the end, work to curb student organizing. At a Vista High activist club meeting in suburban Portland, students gathered in Mr. Mesner's classroom after school on a rainy day in February of 2003. Some sat quietly in desks at the back of the room, some sat on top of the desks in the front of the classroom, swinging their legs and looking expectantly at Alana, Sara, and Curt, who walked up to the front of the classroom to begin the meeting. Mr. Mesner's classroom was lined with posters. There was a huge poster of

Martin Luther King Jr., a poster for the film *The Take* about labor movements in Argentina, and even a small picture of Che Guevara.

Mr. Mesner, a young teacher in his mid- to-late thirties, walked into the room quietly as Alana, Sara, and Curt started the meeting. He gathered up his things from his desk and politely interrupted them before leaving the room: "Okay, like always, just make sure to lock up after your meeting is over. And if you use the VCR, make sure to turn it off when you are done, okay? Have a good meeting." The students thanked Mr. Mesner and continued their meeting as he left the room. Their meeting on this day lasted nearly two hours, and afterward students gathered around the TV to view a videotape of animals being slaughtered. In an effort to politicize otherwise neutral school spirit activities, the students were trying to decide on which clips to show the student body during Spirit Week, as part of a presentation on ecology movements and vegetarianism. Mr. Mesner was, by far, the biggest teacher ally to student activists in this entire study. There was no other teacher that had become this important to student organizers either in Portland or in Oakland. Not only were his values aligned with student activists, but, more importantly, Mr. Mesner provided student activists with a crucial necessity: a space to meet. Even though Mr. Mesner officially sponsored the activist club, he firmly believed in the importance of student autonomy. He wanted to foster student ownership of the club, which meant that he preferred to let students have the room to themselves, without adult supervision.

Both SRU and YP students were very grateful to influential teachers who taught them, in Jazmin's words, politics "on the side." These were teachers who supplemented their formal lessons based on official school textbooks with more explicit political commentary about social justice issues. Many of these teachers were hands-off allies, sponsors of clubs, and supporters of student organizing. However, students also noted the limitations of what teacher allies could do for student movements. The politics of teacher support is very tricky, because ultimately teachers are *en loco parentis* during school hours and are thus liable for student behavior. Although supportive teachers can mean the world to student activists and organizers, there is only so much teachers can do before they themselves are subject to the review (and even censure) of parents and school administrators. SRU activist Josh qualified the support he received from his progressive teachers: "Generally I feel like I get support from my teachers. Some of them are involved in social movements themselves. But, also, teachers are worried about compromising their teaching, because parents will start to complain. So they pull back a little; they have to be careful. Because ultimately what we do might come down on them. For the most part, parents will mostly direct their complaints toward the teachers, not toward us."

Mr. Mesner's support of student activism in Portland did not go unnoticed by the Vista High administration or parents of Vista High students. As SRU students became more visibly involved in the direct action antiwar protests in Portland's streets during the spring of 2003, local media, teachers, and parents began to withdraw their support for student activism. Josh's analysis of how adult power works (i.e., fallout from student activism will come down on teachers) certainly proved to be true in the case of Mr. Mesner. Parents began to complain to the Vista High principal about Mr. Mesner and the school's activist club. They began to question the relationship between the activist club and the increasingly confrontational SRU network. By April of 2003, Alana stood in front of the Vista High's activist club meeting and made this brief announcement: "From this point onward, we cannot mention SRU in this club. If you want to know what happened in a SRU meeting that you missed, we can talk about it later, but not in this club. Mr. Mesner is getting in trouble because of SRU, and he could lose his job. So no mention of SRU here, okay?"

Thus, teacher allies often take great risks to align with student movements. The adultist assumption that it is they who are driving student movements while students mindlessly follow their charismatic leadership means that teacher allies are often under the microscope of administrators and concerned parents.[14] Student voice and political agency is undermined and often erased altogether within the power struggles between teachers, parents, and administrators over the "proper" expressions of student activism and dissent. Remembering her schooling experience, Sunnie criticized the ways in which she felt that her dissenting voice had to be filtered through her parents: "It's amazing that now that I'm graduating, I can get a voice. Like, I don't get how that should make a difference. Like, they [teachers] listened to my parents, but, you know, they wouldn't listen to me. . . .And I don't think that's the way education should be." Sunnie's critique of the parent-teacher power structure mirrors Josh's observation of how student organizing sparks debate between parents and teachers, not necessarily between parents and the students themselves, because both parents and teachers are the parental figures, ultimately held accountable for student action.

Because teachers are often held responsible for student organizing, they must develop their own strategies for navigating other powerful adults (concerned parents and potentially punitive administrators) if they are to align with students. Gayle echoed many students' observations about the range of supportive and nonsupportive roles that teachers play in encouraging or opposing student organizing. She described a complex landscape of teacher support and opposition at Patterson:

> We have teachers who are allies. You have the silent allies, the teachers who are allies but if something goes wrong, they don't want to say. . . . They just want to be hush-hush with their friendship with us. But they are all in all still helpful. But we have a few teachers who stand out, who are down for the workshops in their classrooms, down for the students being educated on their rights. All kinds of teachers. Then you have the teachers who were flat out opposing us, especially when it came down to the war on Iraq; there was actually a walkout here. And you had all these teachers who were like, "What are students walking out for? What are they going to do? How is that going to help anything?"

Because there is such a wide range of teacher support and opposition, students must carefully assess when and how they can utilize teacher support. In both Portland and Oakland, the politics of teacher support intensified and became more polarized after the beginning of the war on Iraq—when new media campaigns demonized protesters and direct action in the streets; dissent was immediately broadcasted as "unpatriotic"; and students took direct action and walked out of their schools to join larger community demonstrations in San Francisco, Oakland, and Portland.

In the case of Vista High School in Portland, teacher support for student antiwar activism was increasingly seen as dangerous and punishable by parents and the administration. With his job on the line, Mr. Mesner had to insist that the activism club cut its ties to SRU and its antiwar activism. This contributed to a rupture between school activism and community activism, a connection that student organizers had worked so hard to build. For student activists, consistent adult allies to youth movement within the school system are hard to find. Clearly, student organizing can be dangerous endeavors not only for students but also for the teachers who support them. The power struggles between parents, administrators, and teachers over the boundaries of what is permissible student dissent and what is not are windows into the web of adult politics that ultimately work to steer youth away from social movement activism at school. These struggles reveal the extent to which youth are ultimately conceptualized by all adult parties as citizens-in-the-making, not developed enough as political beings to be held fully accountable for their collective actions.

Conclusion

The structures of schooling, rather than producing a responsible, engaged, and democratic adult citizenry, often serve to reproduce youth subordination and political powerlessness by encouraging youth to both avoid politics and define politics narrowly, as something that they should practice for until they are responsible adult citizens ready to engage in the real thing. As the struggles of student activists reveal, this political avoidance is actively constructed through various schooling practices, as well as through the watchful eye of adults who hold the power to intervene in youth organizing when it becomes perceived as dangerous and out-of-bounds of proper youth behavior.[15]

Extracurricular infrastructure designed and approved by adults to facilitate youth voice and models of student governance on school grounds are not necessarily designed to foster meaningful leadership, engagement, and actual political power among students. They are designed to prepare students for future leadership as adults in a very ambiguous way, introducing them to the superficial forms of adult political and civic participation, but depriving them of the substance of this participation. The enduring extracurricular infrastructure of schools, such as student government, runs students through the motions of electoral political decision making without according youth any real decision-making power in their schools or communities. Club charter and teacher-sponsor requirements also structure adult power and youth subordination into student extracurricular activities on campus, making it nearly impossible for students to have an autonomous space of their own on school grounds—unless they can operate with some measure of secrecy.

In wealthier schools, the institutional pressures for youth to avoid political talk on school grounds can sanitize student clubs of their potential political power and can sever students from social movements in their communities. In acutely impoverished schools such as Kendall and Patterson High, school budget cuts have all but eviscerated the school clubs, and potential teacher-sponsors are already overworked and are often unable to devote the time necessary to sponsor new clubs. Thus, school impoverishment exacerbates the processes that sever students from political movements in their communities, as it leaves students with no extracurricular infrastructure at all.

Also telling are the prohibitions on social justice talk or even political talk within school classroom discussions and the near absence of ethnic studies in public schooling.[16] The prohibition on talk in the classroom that would bring social movements into being inevitably leaves white supremacy undisturbed in educational curricula, disempowering students of color most of all. Students in this study criticized their curricula, even their multicultural curricula, for eliminating information about relevant social issues, histories of oppression, and histories of collective insurgencies. According to these activist youth, theirs were not curricula that prepared them to take their place as active agents in a struggle for a better world.

Student activists create new institutional infrastructure in reaction to these extracurricular and curricular aspects of schooling that produce student political inaction. In some Oakland schools, YP youth led the creation of youth centers: autonomous and politicized spaces where youth could connect with each other, develop ties to community social movements, and organize their fellow students into social justice campaigns on school grounds. In Portland schools, students began their political work by creating student unions: student-led organizations more closely resembling labor unions or worker collectives than the electoral politics represented by student government. For these students, student unions could do what student government could not: represent a collective student voice to school administrators and tackle issues of concern to the student body.

The instability of structures such as youth centers and student unions reveals the tenuous nature of student-created politicized spaces within the institutional setting of the school. There is the challenge of poverty and high turnover rates among power players in Oakland, which requires that students in particularly impoverished schools must continually negotiate their demands with every new administrator. Underneath this frustrating process are the hazards of negotiating with administrators and trying to secure their cooperation. After all, these adult players hold significant power to break agreements and betray students *without reprisal.* This speaks to the institutional hierarchy of the schools, where administrators ultimately hold the most power and students hold the least power. In Portland schools, student unions became ways to politicize the student body around the school budget crisis and became an avenue for articulating a student voice to the administration. At the same time, these were highly unstable student organizations and took on the age-graded character of the school system itself. Organized by seniors, the student unions collapsed in sync with the rhythm of the school year. On the edge of summer and graduation, seniors who organized student unions left their institutions and took their organizing skills with them. And, without any official presence on high school campuses, these politicized spaces fell apart easily. Although these student unions were instrumental in organizing students into active campaigns for educational justice issues, they were limited to political activity on their individual campuses.

Finally, there are the tricky politics of teacher alliances. The fact that student organizing can endanger teachers says a great deal about how youth are conceptualized in school systems as citizens-in-the-making rather than as purposeful, actualized, and strategic actors who can be held accountable for their own political action. Student activism comes under the scrutiny of parents, administrators, and teachers—and ultimately teachers become accountable for student organizing on school grounds. This makes it difficult for student organizers to form alliances with supportive teachers. Even in the most supportive cases, such as Mr. Mesner, institutional pressures influence the extent to how far teachers can support students' political development. Without adult allies in the school system, it becomes difficult for students to sustain activism on school grounds.

Schooling, as a major orienting institution for youth, constructs the citizen-in-the-making by turning teenagers inward (Eckert 1989) rather than by connecting them to community politics. According to this model, adolescent political activism is often interpreted as a kind of precocity (Lesko 2001), one that requires adults to intervene and steer students on the "right" course of youth behavior, away from politics. Although young people's efforts to transform themselves into social movement actors on school grounds do not always succeed, it is important to recognize their efforts in building social movement spaces on campus. As evidenced in this chapter, adolescents are aware of the ways in which their schools promote their development as politically passive and powerless, and they notice the missing social movement elements of their schooling. They struggle to politicize their Spirit Weeks and school clubs. They create youth centers and student unions and spearhead campaigns to institute ethnic studies into their classrooms. These efforts stand as evidence of young people's capacities to subvert the many prescriptions for their political passivity, even if these efforts take place at individual schools and ultimately do not come to fruition.

The periodic failures of these efforts reveal more than just students' tactical choices: they also reveal the institutional limits of schooling in promoting more active models of youth civic and political participation. It is no wonder why students begin to look outward, even as their schools turn them inward. Extending their student movements into their larger communities, they connect to each other beyond their school walls and establish multischool youth networks in the midst of larger social movements in their cities. In many ways, the world outside of the school offers new opportunities for students to develop into full-fledged social movement participants. As SRU organizer Alana put it, "That's where the picture opens up."

3

Allies Within and Without

Navigating the Terrain of Adult-Dominated Community Politics

I think one of the things that society does is say, "Well, teenagers are just rebellious; that's just the way it always has been and that's always how it will be." Like, it's some natural thing about nature that kids are just rebellious; that's the way they are. Like, there is no actual reason for why kids are doing it. And it's, like, I could have easily believed that myself before I got into activism. I could have just believed that "yeah, kids are just rebellious; that's what they do; kids go steal stuff. Some kids are so crazy and rebellious that they go shoot people in their school, and that's really insane."

But I think it's more to show the problem with society. Like, kids are saying, "Yeah, you're right, we are rebellious, but for this reason. And we are going to march up there and tell you what we think about it, and tell you why we think about it." And I can't think of any other situation where a bunch of radical youth could demand that the mayor come down and talk to them. That couldn't have happened unless it was us, the youth, doing it. (Stephen, seventeen years old, Students Rise Up)

When students begin to organize beyond their schools and in their larger communities, they struggle to find their place in local social movements. In doing so, they reflect on their unique position as youth in adult-dominated community politics and develop politicized frameworks for understanding ageism. Both YP and SRU organized outside of schools because, first and foremost, that's where young people could mobilize as a larger base. Of

the many barriers to youth political participation inside of the school system examined in the previous chapter, the biggest barrier is that there
exists no mechanism that can sustain the organization of youth across
schools. Because there is often a disconnect between schools and community politics, there is a related disconnect between schools themselves.
Thus, social movement organizing within the high school alone is ultimately limited to the organizing base within each particular school. When
students are able to devise ways to link their school bases together, they
find new student power, agency, visibility, and voice that extend within
and beyond their schools.

However, students venturing outside of their high schools to organize
student movements cannot just walk in to any public space and find liberation and voice. In fact, public civic spaces that are usually reserved for
adult participation can be difficult territory for students to break into.
While one of my primary research questions asked why students are compelled to go outside of their schools to organize student movements,
another question nagged at me: why don't students simply walk out of their
schools and into the diverse array of local social justice organizations that
already exist in their cities?

A major barrier to adolescent participation in local community organizations is adult power. Of course, youth under eighteen are officially
banned from participating directly in electoral politics simply because of
their age. But the organizational and cultural dimensions of adult domination in social movement circles can seem to adolescents as real a barrier to
political participation as are state-imposed age restrictions on voting.
Seventeen-year-old SRU activist Megan viewed this as a barrier to participating in adult organizations and made her case for creating a youth-led
space: "Youth have a part in society. Even though twelve-year-olds or high
school kids may not be ready to take full responsibility of what needs to go
on in the normal adult life, they can still have a place to be active. 'Cause
there are just so many restrictions. Like, all these organizations are, like,
eighteen and up. I mean, what are we supposed to do?" Many young people
in this study had tried to join already established adult groups. However,
youth found themselves faced with a great deal of disregard from adults in
their communities as they tried to join their organizations. SRU activist
Josh, who had participated in a largely adult peace organization in his

community, shared his perception of adult power in these organizations: "I think in adult movements . . . for adults it's a lot easier to blow off kids than to blow off other adults. They feel that youth have less of a contribution to make. Youth lack the resources, connections, friends already in the movement." The perceptions of adolescents that are widespread throughout society at large are also at play in adult social justice organizations. Many adults involved in social justice activism—even those who recognize racism, sexism, and heterosexism as systems of oppression that are alive and well—still may not recognize ageism as a legitimate oppression. Nor might they think about how they themselves perpetuate ageism and ageist stereotypes. In turn, young people have learned to internalize ageist oppression as well, so that they may devalue their own voices when in the presence of adults.

Indeed, networks like YP and SRU have been able to organize hundreds, and even thousands, of youth because they have found and created spaces outside of their high schools to strategize with each other and have returned to their individual schools with collective movement goals. More profound, however, is that YP and SRU organizers credited the formation of this external youth space for cultivating a collective student voice that they could neither develop within their individual high schools nor within already existing community organizations. When I asked Zoe to imagine student life without SRU, she talked about the loss of a collective voice: "We wouldn't have a voice. Well, not that good of a voice. We'd just be the whispers behind the CEOs of businesses." Thus, when both YP and SRU students talked about finding a voice, they talked about finding this voice within specific youth-run spaces that they themselves created outside of their schools in the public sphere. Importantly, a space where youth voice is cultivated does not only signify a space of expression or resistance. It is also a space firmly rooted in civic activist networks, where one's words can be listened to and one's actions can be recognized. This kind of youth empowerment is gained in a different kind of space than the spaces that youth subcultures typically inhabit, a far cry from Donna Gaines's (1991) abandoned buildings and public margins where youth subcultures find their own social liberation in an age-segregated environment. Youth organizers and activists seek out spaces in public, civic life where they can speak to, with, and among other civic participants and political actors. As

SRU activist Megan said, "I think right now SRU is the only high school student–run activist group in the whole city. This is a place you can come and be heard."

The visibility and voice that develop in these youth-led spaces stem from the connections that these spaces maintain to adult allies in community social movements. It is when students venture outside of their schools and access new forms of knowledge in movement communities that they can develop into full-fledged social movement organizers. Among YP youth in Oakland, these new forms of knowledge included how to successfully put together a meeting agenda, how to facilitate a meeting and mediate conflict, how to identify and mobilize other student leaders, how to create coalitions with other social justice organizations, how to develop public speaking skills, and how to give political workshops.

In Portland, new forms of knowledge gained among SRU youth included learning how to facilitate meetings to maximize group consensus, how to develop a security culture, how to put out press releases, how to contact media and distribute "propaganda," how to prepare for arrest and jail, how to ensure protests remain safe, how to administer first aid, and how to manage and coordinate working groups and affinity groups. These types of knowledge are not part of formal curriculums in the school and are accessible only within movement networks. As SRU activist Jacob remarked, it was only within an external youth space like SRU that students could access the knowledge and skills needed to develop into organizers rather than mere activists: "If we didn't have a larger SRU, it would just be, like, a lot of young activists just kind of out there doing activism instead of organizing. And I know SRU is just a chance to, like, get people to organize. Like, 'Hey man, you want to be an organizer? You can even do it at your school in the suburbs, on Friday nights. Start an activist club.'"

In Portland, even though students did not learn to give their own political workshops, they contacted others who routinely gave these workshops and invited them as guest speakers to their SRU meetings. Guests were almost always young, twenty-something, white adults who usually represented more radical groups that had specific knowledge about street protests, police surveillance and infiltration, jail support, and even the dangers of unexamined white privilege. The founders of SRU—mostly boys with connections to older siblings, friends, or even roommates involved in radical direct action groups—attained information and passed it along to the students in SRU, thus importing organizational knowledge into the group. As SRU participants learned about other political groups in the community, they also attended their meetings and then brought back their newfound knowledge to other students.[1]

While somewhat plentiful in Portland, these adult sources of new knowledge were not necessarily stable forces in SRU as an organization. Select boys in SRU had sustained relationships with these younger adult resources in the radical community. However, these young adults were often unknown to most members of SRU, and particularly to SRU girls.[2] Young adult contacts showed up to make announcements, give workshops, or connect with students at periodic SRU meetings and sometimes at protests. However, they were not part of the SRU network and did not provide ongoing mentorship to most students in SRU. Despite the lack of ongoing adult mentorship to most SRU participants, the workshop presentations, announcements, information and practices that were imported from radical movement networks into SRU provided all participants with at least some new knowledge and opportunity to develop as student leaders and organizers.

Even as high school student movements in the East Bay of California and in Portland, Oregon, have been similarly facilitated in part by the mentorship of young adult organizers in the urban environment, YP and SRU sharply diverged in the structure of their organizations—specifically in regard to how closely they integrated young adult mentors into their networks. While YP youth in Oakland strategically integrated adult allies into their network, SRU youth established their citywide network as youth only. These structural differences regarding young adult mentors stemmed from different conceptions of ageism and adult power, and the availability of other resources for youth empowerment that were rooted in privileged class and racial social locations. In each youth activist network, young people had to engage with an adult-dominated social movement scene in their cities while protecting themselves from adultism and social marginalization based on their age. In doing so, SRU and YP developed their own unique political critiques of ageism. This political consciousness about age inequality guided their relationships to adult allies in their communities and eventually helped to structure their city- and region-wide movements in vastly different ways.

The story of how young people break into community politics is ultimately the story of how they wrestle with the adultism that so often exists in established social movement networks. It is also the story of their collective, political, and organizational responses to ageism. Whether youth activists reach out to adult allies or keep them at bay, young people make these key decisions as a result of their understandings of ageism, their critiques of adult power, and their positions in other systems of power and privilege.

Adult Allies Within: Youth Power in Oakland

Ageism as a Systematic Oppression

Sixteen-year-old Jazmin, who had attended adult social justice meetings on community violence and school reform in Oakland, echoed many other Oakland and Portland teenage interviewees' perceptions of ageism among adult activists: "At adult meetings, they tokenize your ideas a lot of the times. Like, they come in with an agenda and they ask you for input, knowing that they are already going to do what they're going to do. So, it's just like, a lot of times it is pointless for you to even be in there with the adults." For YP participants in the East Bay, however, there was a space between youth subordination and adult power where students and adult allies could work together and subvert ageism in the same organization. Sixteen-year-old Shandra explained this simultaneity:

> There is Teens on the Move, or Youth Arts, but they are not about fighting against oppression; they are dealing with just straight-on violence. Not fighting for youth justice, not fighting for this and not going on, like, "This prop. came out; we are going to march with the rest of the people," you know. Like, I feel what they do, but, to me, I am more comfortable within YP. It's more diverse, it's more youth-led most of the time, and there are a lot more adult allies in YP than there is in TOM.
>
> Like, there it was more, "You guys sit down, we give you some curriculum, you go over it, and then you go teach the main players." And

I wasn't really feelin' that. I was like, "How come we can't facilitate meetings sometimes?" or "How come we can't get more involved? How come we just have to listen to what you say?" Like, they give you a choice to voice your opinions, but in the end they just kind of knock them down.

This in-between space where adult mentorship met student empowerment existed only because YP adult allies and students politicized and openly claimed adult power to be a systematic oppression. This interpretation of ageism and specifically adultism was the key to why YP as a movement organization could remain youth-led while integrating adult mentorship. Because ageism was not conceived of as a characteristic of specific groups of adults but rather as a systematic oppression (one that, as YP organizers taught in their workshops on ageism, exists on institutional, interpersonal, and individual/internalized levels), then any adult was capable of reinforcing ageism through their behavior or assertion of power. This included YP young adult allies.

YP adult allies spent a great deal of time reflecting on the ways they themselves perpetuated ageism and tried to become conscious of how adultism affected their relationships with student organizers. Yesenia, a twenty-five-year-old YP ally, reflected on how sometimes she tended to slip into adultist behavior: "You know, sometimes you just act on instinct. And then I have to stop myself, and I'm, like, 'Huh, I just shut that kid down because he is younger than me' or 'I just told him his idea is a bad one without me really going into it.' It was just me, dictating."

While YP adult allies reflected on their own tendencies toward adultism and tried to catch themselves, YP student organizers were quick to take ownership of the organization and called adults on their ageism if they perceived that adults were stepping over the line. I witnessed several instances when YP student organizers called YP adult allies on behavior that they interpreted as adultist. For example, high school organizers Guillermo, Pilar, and Salvador had prepared a workshop on Raza studies for incoming freshmen. During the workshop, a YP adult intern became very active, offering answers to questions that student organizers were actually posing to the freshmen students. After the workshop was over, the other adult intern and I convened with the presenters to go over what went well with the workshop and what should be changed for next time. Pilar offered that the adult intern stepped up too much and stifled discussion among freshmen students. Guillermo echoed this and lectured the intern about her proper role as an adult ally in YP: "See, you are there to support us. To catch our backs. You step up if what we're saying is off base or wrong. But let us do this work. I mean, we were just talking about ageism yesterday, and this right here is an example of it." From there, the adult intern expressed that she felt hurt by their criticism but understood and apologized for her overparticipation. This interaction was one window into the ways YP adolescent organizers and adult allies collectively interpreted, defined, and negotiated adult power. Through these types of interactions they built a collective understanding of youth empowerment that rested upon youth leadership with the support of adult allies, rather than youth autonomy from adult allies. YP students and adult allies used the understanding of ageism as a social oppression for a tool to interrupt tendencies toward adult power within the group. In this way, adolescent organizers felt that they could access adult mentorship without succumbing to adult power.

It is significant that YP collective identity was more youth than it was high school student. And who exactly constitutes youth (whether just adolescents or adolescents and young adults) was openly negotiated and contested within the organization. YP students and adult allies were constantly engaging in discussions about who are the youth, when are adult allies too old to be functional mentors to high school student movements, and which actions constitute ageism. As Mary Bucholtz observes, the concept of youth "foregrounds age not as trajectory, but as identity, where identity is . . . agentive, flexible, and ever-changing" (2002, 532). In this sense, youth in YP had multiple fluid meanings. Sometimes it meant just the high school students (when youth autonomy from older adult allies was emphasized, an important part of youth leadership development). Sometimes it encompassed all student activists, including college students. This was especially important during discussions of ethnic studies and educational change, because high school and college students' fights for ethnic studies in the Bay Area have happened, often in concert with each other, as part of a larger multiracial civil rights struggle. When seventeen-year-old YP organizer Alisha showed video clips of UC Berkeley college students' fight for ethnic studies to an audience of nearly two hundred YP high school students, she reminded them, "This is youth movement too, y'all! It's not just the high school students that are fighting for these changes." YP activists' political framing of ageism as a systematic oppression, and their ever-changing definition of who occupies the category of youth, proved to be essential in maintaining a delicate balance of adult mentorship and youth empowerment. In the next section, I discuss how this delicate balance of maintaining adult allies within YP was especially crucial for low-income youth of color, who tried to claim political power from a particularly disadvantaged intersection of age, race, and class subordination.

Adult Allies Within: Facilitating Youth Movement in Oakland

Adult allies within YP, as key interfaces to institutions outside the movement, were vital to furthering youth movement objectives for a particularly devalued student population lacking many basic resources of their own. Not only did adult allies provide a safe space for YP students to meet (as they did the actual fund-raising and grant writing to financially maintain the organization's space), they also provided crucial links to social services. When Bert, a twenty-year-old YP intern, explained the importance of YP for working-class and poor youth of color, he noted, "And for them, you know . . . there isn't anybody or any organization that they can really join up to, to just not get caught up in all the stuff that they get caught up in." Bert and other YP participants explained this "other stuff" as the drug trade, gangs, prostitution rings in schools, alcoholism, homelessness, incarceration, and innumerable other forms of violence engendered by poverty and social divestment. In East Oakland's more impoverished schools such as Patterson and Kendall, school links to social service providers such as counselors had been eliminated due to budget cuts. There were neither school nurses, nor any easy access to health care for the students. Because these students and their larger communities were lacking basic mental/physical health, economic, and other social services, YP adult allies provided links to these services as best as they could. YP adult allies connected student organizers with homeless shelters, rape crisis centers, job corps, counseling services, anger management courses, food banks, and other services students needed. Mentors who aligned with working-class, urban youth of color and helped them to develop political empowerment felt that they could not disregard students' material, physical, and emotional needs. Twenty-seven-year-old Emily pointed to the importance of this adult role in developing youth leadership:

> A lot of the students here do need a lot of support. And a lot of it is not coming from their peers. It's not coming from their parents. It's not coming from their school. So we [adults] play that role also. . . . What's the point of us opening up a youth center or fighting against the exit exam, if one of the students that I'm working with is being physically assaulted at home and isn't empowered enough at home to change their own conditions? But we want to teach them how to change school conditions? They're in the same pool of work.

Thus, YP activists asserted that conditions of impoverishment among working-class and poor, urban youth of color sometimes necessitated that adult allies serve as key links to needed resources. In this sense, the potential for young people to develop political agency and voice in larger social decision-making processes is endangered by systematic racial oppression and economic instability. To develop as political actors vis-à-vis adult power, both adolescents and adult allies in YP argued that teens needed a basic measure of human security. Budget cuts to public education means that many schools are now poorly positioned to provide these basic services for their students.

Beyond providing needed links to social services, young adult allies in YP sometimes provided the legitimizing face of the student movement, one that strategically worked around other adults to facilitate student organizing. Although YP adult allies might have shared a generation with YP high school organizers, they still held some cultural capital (Bourdieu 1977) derived from their adult status. YP adult ally Yesenia, who started out as a teenage political organizer herself, noted the difference in adult reactions to her being a student organizer versus being an adult ally: "When I became an adult organizer I noticed the amount of respect from other adults in the community. It was different because now I wasn't speaking as a high school student; I was speaking as an adult. I was speaking as a college student, and now a college-educated woman. You know, the accountability to parents, the trust that was given, it was a change." Although

Yesenia was speaking of her transition from teenager to adult, she illustrated this transition as moving from high school student to "college-educated woman"—invoking educational advantage in her illustration of adult status. This demonstrates how adult cultural capital involves a dimension of economic advantage (here embodied in educational advantage). According to both YP students and adult allies, the adult trust that is given more freely to other college-educated adults than to adolescents means that a strategically placed adult presence in adolescent networks can facilitate student movements in important ways. It can be instrumental in gaining parental permission for student activities and can work like a passport into adult-dominated spaces such as schools, retreat centers, and even social justice networks.

As an ethnographer in YP, I was invited to volunteer in the organization in specific capacities that at first seemed to me to assert adult power. My presence as a researcher overlapped with my more official titles as a YP tutor, a YP adult intern, and even a YP "adult chaperone." Over time, however, I began to understand that some of these roles existed in name only and were often more for the benefit of parents, school administrations, and other adults external to YP than for the students themselves. For example, during the YP summer program when student organizers gave political workshops to incoming freshmen, I was expected as a YP adult intern to show up an hour before the program began each day so that I could meet with parents who were dropping off their freshmen kids and answer any questions they might have about the summer program or YP. Even though I was new to YP, as an adult (and perhaps as a white person), I helped to legitimize the summer program to parents in a way that other YP adolescents felt they could not. Sheng, a sixteen-year-old YP student at Kendall High explained the importance of this adult YP face to the project of youth mobilizing and contextualized this within a larger framework of youth subordination:

> By there being an adult face in YP, it brings students around. Like when there are meetings you can explain to your mom, "Oh, there's this adult who is going to be there; I am not just hanging out in the middle of the night." Which is something that a lot of parents are concerned about, especially in Oakland, because it's dangerous.

And as long as they know that there is someone responsible, because "youth aren't responsible," I guess, then it's cool. So in that way the adults help out a lot.

However, during the actual summer program, the YP adult allies and I would sit at the back of the room quietly while the students led workshops that they themselves designed on ethnic studies, organizing strategies, movement histories, and the prison industrial complex (among many other workshops); mediated conflicts between students during the workshops; and led YP freshmen mentees in fun and energizing icebreakers, which broke up the long six- to eight-hour days of intense political discussion among the students. We would participate when student organizers asked us to or would offer answers to student organizers' questions when they would get stuck. However, in this YP youth-led space, the students themselves held the real power. The contrast between the labeling of adults-as-chaperones or even leaders in the presence of other adults and their marginality during actual student organizing work spoke to the strategic use of adults as faces of student movements rather than as true directors or leaders.

YP young adult allies were an especially important legitimizing face of student movements vis-à-vis school administrations. While several YP students and adult allies recognized that students are much better equipped than adults to negotiate with teachers over school-change issues (because students had a closer relationship to teachers than did most YP adult allies), many agreed on the importance of adults ultimately being the face of YP when negotiating with school administrations, who had a much more distant relationship with the students. Although YP students learned how to negotiate with adult power—and even with the school principal—on their own, sometimes YP adult allies would have to follow up these meetings to hold the administration accountable to promises they had made to the students or to rearticulate students' visions for school change.

I witnessed several moments when gifted YP student organizers, who could easily inspire a roomful of their peers, would say with frustration: "I can't speak to them [the school administration] that way. I don't know how to speak like that. I can't speak." Middle-class, white SRU youth in

Portland rarely expressed this same frustration. Although they too were periodically betrayed by their school administrations, they still made substantial headway in negotiating their school-change visions without relying on adult allies to mediate these discussions between youth and adult administrators. SRU youth had confidence in their abilities to speak eloquently to adults in power: indeed, to speak like well-educated adults. Underlying this difference between youth is the crucial role that class advantage plays in supplying young people with the verbal resources to speak, unmediated, to adults in power. Aligning with youth who lacked this specific kind of cultural capital, YP college-educated young adults often acted as translators of student movements to school administrations to further, rather than hinder, student wins on campus. Twenty-three-year-old YP adult ally Ephram observed,

> I am really the adult face for the administration, and even some-times the teachers, because that is what they relate to and that is what they need. . . . It's kind of going around their adultism. Their ageism is just a reality. . . . I don't think they [students] have the ability to hold the administration accountable unless they involve a parent or they involve a teacher or they involve a community per-son to hold them accountable. 'Cause that is who the principal is accountable to. They should be accountable to the students, but they're not.

It is important to recognize here that in Ephram's reflection on his own position as an adult face of a student movement, he did not invoke ageist stereotypes about youth as inherently lacking in maturity or skills. Instead, he drew attention to poor school resources and a flawed school power structure for reasons why student movements need adult faces, especially when negotiating with administrations. This power imbalance in the school system and lack of educational resources that would give students the cultural capital (such as "more adult" vocabularies) to negotiate with school power was something that YP students and adult allies openly dis-cussed and politicized in their interactions with one another. In this way, YP students and adult allies both recognized that the adult face was only a face, one used to leverage specific negotiating power in the face of other powerful adults. Consider the following exchange between seventeen-year-old James and me:

JAMES: It's to the point where students are like, "Oh, the principal is not going to listen to us," and it's like, "Okay, well, they are going to listen to an adult, so we need an adult."

HAVA: What if YP was all youth? Do you think . . .

JAMES: Um, I don't think that would progress. Because, you know, how the government and the principal only listen to adults.

HAVA: So you feel, like, if you guys got together, just yourselves, no adults . . .

JAMES: No, it wouldn't work. Yeah, 'cause it's like, they don't listen to us. We have to have an adult.

Despite YP student and adult ally interpretations of the way in which adult power often works, YP adult allies were careful to not present this same face to the students within the organization. While they claimed that ageism, as a system of oppression (in conjunction with racism and classism), organizes institutions like schools, they consciously worked to undermine ageism within the organization and in their relations with YP student organizers. Sixteen-year-old Salvador reflected on his relationship with YP adult allies: "I like that adults listen to us. The adults in YP, all of them . . . they listen to us, and they take adult consideration second. And it's always about us. It's never about themselves." In this way, perceived adult power was delegitimized within organizational activities (such as YP student summer programs, for example) while YP young adult allies, as adult faces, were able to facilitate the student movement as it moved through adult-dominated worlds.

Adult Allies and Social Movement Continuity

In YP, past movement histories proved to be crucial sources for student empowerment and political perspective. Because of the social movement histories that adult allies brought to the organization, YP understood itself to be a continuation of the civil rights struggles from the 1960s and 1970s. YP also positioned itself as a continuation of a much older legacy of resistance among people of color, globally, in the face of European colonization. Not only was the relatively recent history of Oakland's Black Panthers,

New York's Young Lords, Malcolm X, and California farmworker movements invoked throughout YP's workshops and practices, but an older history of slave rebellions in the United States and Latin American indigenous uprisings, for example, were also interwoven into YP.

During a YP summer workshop on social movement histories (designed by students but researched by both students and adult allies alike), five YP student organizers from Glendale High taught twenty high school freshmen about famous organizers and social movement leaders of movements around the world. Some of these organizers, such as Haunani Kay Trask and Arundhati Roy, represented contemporary movements. Some, such as Fred Hampton, Bayard Rustin, Fannie Lou Hamer, and Che Guevara, were major leaders of twentieth-century insurgencies. Others, such as Tupac Amaru, were leaders of much older struggles against European conquest.[3] To reinforce the information in a more interactive way, YP student organizers made a large name tag for each revolutionary figure they had introduced in the workshop. They taped the name tag to the back of a new YP mentee (without the mentee seeing which name was on her back). As she walked around the room, students shouted out clues to her so she could guess which revolutionary she was. YP adult allies reinforced this new movement education to students by showing documentary footage of civil rights struggles in Oakland, ethnic studies struggles at Bay Area universities in the early 1990s, and even organized resistance among impoverished communities against police brutality in Brazilian favelas. Twenty-five-year-old YP adult ally Javier reflected on his work as an adult ally to youth in a larger movement for social justice:

> It's about understanding our role in the overall social justice movement, and just the legacy of the civil rights movement, the legacy of resistance of the different colonization of our ancestors, and the different countries. It's just a continuum in that legacy and I think that is the seed we really try to plant in our students. So we are focused on school change but then also planting that seed so they can continue to be resisters, to continue to build this movement.

Because of YP adult allies' active work in linking new student movements to past struggles, YP student organizers began to see their resistance as continuations of older struggles. These histories of struggle, especially their multiracial and multicultural dimensions, were notably absent from school curriculums. Adult allies in YP became vital bearers of these histories, and students began to understand their struggles for educational and racial justice in new ways: as linked to past generations. Sixteen-year-old Jazmin explained the dual character of YP's struggle in terms of generational alliance and difference: "Like, there is always different struggles to fight, a different culture we're fighting to struggle in; you know what I'm saying? It's always going to change when the generation changes, but it will still be the same fight."

When students were able to connect to past generations' struggles, they gained a new sense of purpose and empowerment, one they felt was not possible if their generation was isolated in its fight. YP student organizer Pilar explained the strength these historical struggles gave her, especially when she was feeling particularly hopeless:

> It's hard to get wins. And a lot of people get frustrated, you know. But what I always think about when, like—sometimes I get disempowered by, like, a campaign not going our way or something like that—I always think about if our people wouldn't have did it in the past, then maybe we would still be in slavery or be getting our heads chopped off for ten cents, you know. So, like, looking at what is done in the past and having a vision of what you want things to be like and work for that. And to see that they were able to do it, then you can eventually do it too.

Linking students to their ancestors' histories of struggle, change, and wins was part of a broader strategy of YP adult allies to help develop student empowerment and political perspective. YP adult allies and YP student organizers spoke at length about the internalized hopelessness that racism and poverty engenders among youth living in the East Bay, and the danger it poses for youth mobilizing. Eighteen-year-old Gayle lamented this hopelessness among her peers as she described her "tore up" and violent high school:

> They [students] internalize all of that. And it's like, once you internalize it, that's it. You're going to see something bad happen at Patterson High, and you are going to be like, "Huh, that's Patterson;

that's just how it is. Get used to it" or "What? You're new at Patterson? Get used to it; you are going to see it everyday." Instead of trying to change it and say, "Hey, that's not right; it's not supposed to go down like that." They don't see it like that. And that's not a way to grow up.

White, middle-class SRU youth in Portland began the process of their political transformation differently than did students in YP. SRU students did not have to undo the same internalized hopelessness wrought by racism and poverty to become empowered political agents in their communities. Although they too occupied a socially subordinate position as adolescents, SRU teens began their political journeys already feeling somewhat empowered to speak, act, and organize in ways that poor and working-class students of color did not. In Oakland, many YP adult allies and student organizers argued that the first step toward building an empowered youth base was to undo the internalized hopelessness that comes with living in conditions of poverty and racial violence. A powerful way for youth to undo this hopelessness is to gain historical perspective through connecting to social movement histories. In the absence of ethnic studies curriculums in their schools or other potential sources for accessing this history, adult allies within YP became the vital links to these movement legacies.

YP's framing of adultism as a systematic oppression enabled youth to understand, analyze, and politicize age inequality within their everyday lives. Inside the organization, this framing also became the key mechanism through which youth could hold adult allies close, while at the same time develop and maintain their own political leadership within the organization. Moreover, this cross-generational mechanism within YP enabled organizational continuity. Because the organization integrated adult allies, it could sustain long-term political projects and campaigns, absorbing high school student leaders who would eventually transition out of high school and serve as seasoned YP young adult mentors to new high school student organizers. Because of this enduring organizational structure, YP organizers' worldview of social change politics was fundamentally about working toward long-term gains and building momentum. This perspective included an understanding of historical social justice legacies, of transforming oneself and one's internalized oppressions into collective movement momentum and power, and setting one's goals far ahead to withstand the successes and defeats of year-long and even multiyear social justice campaigns. Their focus was on making long-term self, institutional, and cultural change.

At a YP organizing retreat, students brainstormed the qualities of a warrior as another student wrote them all on a big piece of butcher paper: outspoken; strategic; courageous; faithful; positive; aware of what one is up against; willing to leave one's comfort zone; understanding one's own and other people's struggles; nourishing oneself and taking care of one's body; giving and receiving respect; having endurance; willing to be humbled; willing to be a leader but also knowing when to step down and create other leaders; willing to learn; surrounding oneself with other warriors. Students then discussed concrete ways they would integrate these qualities into their lives as student organizers. This signifies a long-term political project and a long-term integration, one made possible only by a lasting organizational structure that could support such a radical and deep transformation of the self and community.

SRU activists, on the other hand, felt compelled to keep adult allies at the fringes of their network to protect themselves from adultism. Largely because of this, their organizational focus was on quick-change, direct action politics. Their "struggle sessions" were usually cut short, and brainstorming sessions about personal and social transformation like those I witnessed in YP were virtually nonexistent.[4] SRU youth were keenly aware that they had a limited amount of time to achieve social transformation through their movement. They knew that because they could not return to the group once they "aged out" and became young adults, they had to make the most out of the time they had in SRU, in the present moment, while the citywide network they had built from the foundations of their individual high school initiatives still remained visible and viable.

Adult Allies Without: Students Rise Up in Portland

Ageism and the Importance of Youth Autonomy

The youth-only character of the SRU network became an important facet of the political power they developed in the course of building student movements in Portland. Claiming a meeting space on the lawn of a Portland alternative school, for example, where students could control the flow of adult guest speakers and patrol the perimeters of their space proved to be an especially important source of collective agency for the group. Of course, SRU youth's ability to appropriate this kind of space without adult supervision stemmed largely from their race and class privilege. Jens Qvortrup (1994), Spencer Cahill (1990), and Gill Valentine (1996) have rightly noted that groups of adolescents in public spaces without adult supervision are often read as dangerous by adult publics. However, the extent to which these groups of adolescents appear to adult publics as dangerous, and also the kind of danger they pose, varies largely by race and class. In the time that SRU youth appropriated the alternative school lawn for their weekly meetings, they never once encountered a security guard or police harassment, or experienced significant disruption of their meetings by adults. In contrast, working-class and poor youth of color would not have been able to appropriate public space and transform it into a politicized youth space with such ease in Oakland, as there are few such urban spaces for black, Latino, and Asian youth that are accessible, safe, and free from police harassment. In the process of forming youth-led spaces in Portland and Oakland, this racial and class difference proved to be significant and meant that white, middle-class youth in Portland did not have to depend on adults for a safe space to meet while YP students in Oakland ultimately did.

This was not necessarily a problem for YP youth, only because YP students and their young adult allies in the organization engaged in a constant process of negotiation and conflict, openly discussed youth subordination, and consciously worked to subvert age hierarchies in their relations with each other. Because of these conscious and ongoing efforts, the funded meeting spaces of youth-centered organizations such as YP in Oakland still achieved the character of truly youth-led spaces, although not autonomous from adults. The whiteness and middle-class status of SRU activists, on the other hand, combined with the availability of "livable" (read: white, middle-class) neighborhoods in Portland, exempted young activists from engaging in this sustained struggle and negotiation with older activists and enabled SRU members to appropriate safe, public spaces for themselves.

Despite the unacknowledged racial and class privilege that afforded them their autonomy from adults, there was a special kind of empowerment that SRU youth derived from becoming visible to the public as a completely youth-led movement. As SRU activist Jacob remarked, "It's really beautiful . . . kids who don't even depend on adults. Who have accomplished so much." SRU's youth-only character proved to be a key part of the students' ability to become visible to the media as social and political actors, and thus visible to a wider Portland population. Many of the SRU organizers anticipated that their visions for their own education, independent of parents and teachers, might have been eclipsed had they allowed adults to become faces of their movement. Sixteen-year-old Hayden recalled, "We thought that we ourselves could work on it without help. We were organized enough, and we cared enough about the issue to do it ourselves. We didn't want help from adults, because we thought we'd be pushed into the background, and that adults would do everything." Seventeen-year-old Michelle explained the deliberate strategy of SRU to remain youth-only to undo ageist stereotypes that the students saw as constitutive of adolescent powerlessness:

> We didn't want anyone saying, "Oh, they're just puppets for the teachers" or "Oh, their parents are putting them up to this," even though people said stuff like that already. I mean, even though no one was helping us . . . I think it's really important that all different ages, and all different everything get together and help, with whatever form of activism. But for this one it was so important that we express how much we care about our education. Because it's really easy for people to say, "They're just little; they don't really know what they are talking about."

While student organizers in YP derived political and personal empowerment partly from the mentorship and past movement histories that YP young adults provided, SRU students derived their empowerment from the fact that they built their movement without any sustained adult participation. Students discussed the experience of creating a new movement as formative and life changing, a lesson in self-reliance, innovation, and resourcefulness. SRU activists felt that what they had created in this youth-only space would empower them even beyond adolescence.

Seventeen-year-old Scott explained the lessons he learned through building SRU: "I mean even if you don't know what you are doing, try to get advice, try to find resources; there is always something around. There's always a way to accomplish a goal. Really, it comes down to only two words: keep brainstorming." Many SRU participants also credited SRU for giving them new skills to become leaders and organizers, as the organization helped to plug them into a loose coalition of young adult radical activist groups with organizing knowledge, yet gave them a relatively safe space away from adults, who even as activists can often be intimidating.

Politicizing Ageism: Liberals versus Radicals

In Portland, SRU students made sense of generational divides and alliances in the way they positioned themselves within a dichotomy of liberal versus radical social movement tactics. Liberal tactics, for SRU, meant such things as obtaining permits for citywide antiwar marches, securing principals' permission for student sit-ins against school budget cuts, and seeking teacher alliances that would help sanction student walkouts against early school closures. In short, to SRU youth liberal tactics were less risky: they involved some kind of cooperation and negotiation with adults in power to ensure that youth could express their dissent. Radical tactics, on the other hand, did not rely on the cooperation or permission of powerful adults. Radical tactics included unpermitted school sit-ins, walkouts, and the blocking of traffic during the antiwar protests in Portland. Many SRU students, in their interviews and weekly meetings, struggled with how they felt about civil disobedience and property destruction, and how they identified within the liberal/radical dichotomy of Portland's progressive activist scene.[5] SRU participants saw the value in liberal tactics—and used them in certain instances. For example, SRU students staged simultaneous school sleep-ins across the city to demonstrate how much they cared about their education. These sleep-ins were approved by school administrations, lasted all night, and received widespread media attention. However, during the planning process the students braced for the possibility that their administrations would not allow the sleep-ins. In cases like these, SRU students had to make a difficult decision as to whether or not they would continue with their actions if they were unable to secure adult permission. In the case of the student sleep-in, many SRU youth decided that if need be, they would prepare to take radical, direct action and would occupy their schools overnight, even if the action was unpermitted. Thus, radicalism in SRU made it possible for the students to work around adult authority and to be more autonomous from adults. If negotiation or other liberal tactics did not go their way, then students could still take action in case adult allies backed out, betrayed them, or messed things up. As Troy observed, "I think that's one of the coolest things about the youth movement. We can take radical direct action and be totally accountable for it. Because if they are not giving us a voice, then fuck them. If we are not going to be able to participate in the system, then we are outside of the system, and there it is." For SRU adolescents, radicalism and direct action were means toward youth autonomy and political action.

This liberal/radical split, according to SRU participants, was very much a generational split within Portland activist networks. In their interviews and in meetings, SRU participants repeatedly identified adult liberal organizations as more adultist than radical organizations. One of these liberal organizations was the Portland Network for World Justice (PNWJ). PNWJ became the prominent group in Portland to organize large-scale peaceful marches in response to the bombing of Iraq. In SRU meetings, the critique of liberal tactics/organizations focused largely on PNWJ's or other organizations' repudiation of a "diversity of tactics," which alienated SRU's direct action tactics in favor of gaining community popularity. According to SRU activists, these liberal organizations did not repudiate just SRU's age-specific tactics, they repudiated an entire younger generation's approach to activism. This liberal/radical generational split often manifests in the many split marches in Portland: sanctioned liberal marches in Portland's center (which includes the older, tamer crowd) and unpermitted feeder marches that draw a younger and more radical crowd. SRU's vilification of PNWJ in SRU meetings not only vilified liberals but also created a group critique of ageism, even if veiled. Jacob explained this link between ageism and liberal organizations' repudiation of a diversity of tactics:

Some larger liberal organizations . . . they are living this culture difference and this age difference. Like, these are people trying to remember stuff that happened from the sixties, and trying to do as they did. And we're just trying to find new ways to do stuff. And

some people don't like the way we march, or agree with the tactics
we use. So they shut us out. It's like a stab in the back. I mean, our
activist culture is just a little different from the adults.

What did not fit into SRU's collective paradigm of generation and politics
in Portland was the ageism of other young-adult radical organizations,
which was more often experienced by and known to SRU's radical male
leadership. In SRU, boys I interviewed were more likely to talk at length
about allies and conditional allies in the community and were more likely
to be keyed in to what they perceived to be the subtle and overt adultism
of even their more closely allied radical organizations. Troy, Curt, Jacob,
and Pete all shared with me their experiences with the ageism of three radical organizations in Portland. Troy remarked, "It's amazing, because a lot
of the radical activists we work with, the ones that are patronizing towards
us, usually haven't been organizing as long as we have." I asked Pete about
one area radical organization that SRU students spoke very highly of in
their meetings. He surprised me with this story:

> Actually, they have really screwed us. We were supposed to organize
> a demo [demonstration] with them, and, like, the day before they
> crapped out on us. They said, "We didn't realize that you guys are
> minors." And so because we were minors there was some law that
> they brought up. And we were like, "You guys are so full of shit!" They
> were like, "We didn't realize you were underage." And because we are
> underage, they'd be liable for all of it, which I don't think is an issue.
> I don't think there were any illegal things in working with us.

In contrast, SRU girls tended not to have this insight into the subtle or
overt betrayals of these allies, nor did they always know the names of these
organizations or what their acronyms stood for. This gendered dynamic
reflected how male privilege in the group garnered greater access to potential allies in the community, even if these allies at times betrayed the
group through wielding adult power. Collectively, SRU had strong critiques
of stable categories of ageist adults such as cops, school administrations,
corporate media, liberal organizations, and to a lesser extent teachers
and parents. During one meeting, Joni announced to the group, "Okay,
everyone, someone's here from a local news station and he's waiting right

outside. He's here to interview us for TV. Be careful what you say to him, since he'll probably twist it around because we're kids. Keep your message short and clear. Anyone uncomfortable with being on TV should leave the room before we let him in." At another meeting, SRU youth debriefed after an antiwar protest, swapping stories of how police had targeted them specifically because of their age and their perceived unruliness. Because ageism was collectively understood to be embodied by specific people or groups rather than as a more generalized social oppression, the ageism of radical organizations or young adult anarchists did not fit in with the group's collective understandings of adult power. This male knowledge of radical allies and their periodic ageist betrayals was often kept under wraps by male SRU organizers and hidden from the rest of the group. This secrecy had the effect of keeping the group as a whole under the impression that they had stable allies in the Portland activist scene and that they had achieved status among a network of adult radical activist groups.

The Crisis of Youth Autonomy and Movement Discontinuity

Despite the social visibility and the political and personal empowerment that SRU activists derived from their youth-only structure, SRU as an organization did run into problems that endangered it, problems that YP did not have because of the mentorship and resources that adult allies brought to student organizers. For example, after the antiwar protests waned and the school budget crisis was temporarily solved, SRU students began to see their own movement as largely reactive instead of proactive. Seventeen-year-old Shae observed,

> I know we do have some sort of mission statement; I am not sure what it is. And I am not sure anybody else knows either. But I think we need some sort of goals, and I think that's why we haven't gotten very much done. Because we don't know what we are trying to do. And that's probably something SRU should have. With the whole school budget thing we were successful, but that was mostly the reactionary part.

The budget cuts and the impending war sparked newfound outrage among many Portland students. However, once the budget cuts were temporarily fixed, and the bombing of Iraq commenced despite widespread social protest, the student movement in Portland lost some of its steam and SRU organizers became burned out. I interviewed sixteen-year-old Pete right before the summer break of 2003. He lamented the strength SRU had lost in the previous few months:

> I think we were doing the most when we had these budget cuts in our faces and we had to do something about it. And I would like to think it was partially because of us that we got the [school] days back from the city. And I think back then we were a powerful force, because we could get thousands of kids to walk out of school. And that is something to be reckoned with. I don't think we have that anymore.

As YP student organizer Pilar explained in the previous section, when she became disheartened and burned-out, especially when it is "hard to get wins," she thought about her ancestors and their fights. She then found renewed purpose for her continued social justice work. Indeed, it was hard for YP youth to forget the movements that inspired their own: the integration of older generations' struggles into their youth movement was often ritualized. For example, before or after almost every YP meeting and event, a different student would lead a circle of youth organizers in the classic United Farm Workers unity clap, developed in the late 1960s. Farmworkers from different nations, separated by language barriers, expressed solidarity and unity with each other through the unity clap. The clap starts off slowly and then picks up steam, becoming louder and faster. The unity clap symbolizes multiracial unity and the pace of struggle: first slow and steady and then a fast, powerful roar. Without a connection to this kind of historical memory, SRU students felt as though they were fighting alone, as a generation in isolation from other generations. Feeling lost and trying to find a connection to past generations, fifteen-year-old Alana researched student activism at the library and at bookstores, trying to find information from past movements that might help her understand the direction of her own activism. She found her search to be largely fruitless:

> I've tried to look for stuff about youth activism. . . . I found a little on college student movements of the sixties, but nothing younger than that. It's frustrating. There's no road map for this stuff. There's no

guidebook. There are so many times when we could really use some advice. So I guess that's also one of the biggest challenges about youth activism: lack of guidance.

I can't really think of anyone I can go to for this. I have my teacher, Mr. Mesner, who is great. But also, he's a teacher, so there's only so much I can involve him. There's legality issues, and things kind of come down on him. I don't want to get him in trouble. So, like, there's nobody to go to and say, "Hey, this is the problem we're facing in SRU" or "Hey, we're thinking of organizing this; how do we do this?" and "What should we watch out for?"

Despite the autonomy from older generations that gave SRU participants newfound political power, student organizers were seeking out, in times of crisis, adult mentorship. This lack of mentorship was telling and reflected a major generation gap and age gap between youth and adults in Portland, especially within its mostly white movement networks. These gaps between youth and adult activists were undoubtedly shaped by race and class privilege, which do not generate the kind of legacy of struggle that can bond a community at large. Although Portland students received moments of important mentorship from young adult radical activists, this mentorship was not sustained. Unlike the young adults in the East Bay, these mostly white young adult radicals did not hold a political framework that necessitated a commitment to actively developing a new generation of young leaders to continue a legacy of social movement. In fact, proactive adult mentorship of young people might have run counter to the tenets of the antiauthoritarian movement, which emphasized other avenues for marginalized groups (such as youth) to claim involvement in the movement, such as consensus models of decision making and more generalized critiques of authoritative power.

Also telling is the lack of connection that SRU students felt to the student movements or antiwar movements of earlier generations of white radicals, such as the antiwar and student protests during the 1960s and 1970s. Sara echoed Alana's search for adult mentorship and explained why she did not find inspiration in the Vietnam-era antiwar movement:

What I would like from adults would be to just to learn from their past experiences, and see what works, and what doesn't work. See how we can build a movement that actually accomplishes something. You know, the Vietnam antiwar movements really haven't done anything. But, I mean, I have hope. I still have hope that maybe this will be the one time when we can just make change and stop the war.

The globalization of corporate power, environmental crisis, the growing inequality between the rich and poor, the prevalence of war, and a host of other social and political developments within the past decades stood as evidence to some SRU activists that the movements of the 1960s and 1970s were ineffective in creating a more just society. This belief was reinforced by the lifestyles of some of the SRU students' own parents, who appeared to have sold out in exchange for material wealth and the comfort of middle-class, insulated lives. Amanda's analysis of her parents was instructive in understanding why some white, middle-class SRU students did not feel like they could learn a great deal from previous generations of progressive activists:

> Like my parents, they were pretty politically active in college. And then they became lawyers. . . . and now my dad, instead of being sort of liberal, he drives his little—well not little—his big Ford F1–50 gas guzzler. And he kind of criticizes protesters for being dumb. He's really lost a lot of integrity, and that scares me. People get so numbed by their little lives . . . and it's really sad, because there is so much leisure time, and so much comfort in our country, that nobody really needs to worry about any other problems. And so they exploit people without even knowing it. And when you criticize them for that, they don't even see it. They can't even see that the problem exists or know what's going on.

This lack of guidance and historical perspective, or what Alana termed a "road map" engendered some frustration for SRU activists, who expressed periodic feelings of hopelessness and loneliness in their struggle. Sixteen-year-old Tory articulated this loneliness in her reflection on what constituted some of the biggest challenges to youth activism:

> I mean, the problem is, like, sometimes when the media pays attention to us, we feel all mighty and strong. And other times we have to

take a step back and say, "Whoa, this is a huge world. We're just a bunch of kids sitting in a room, thinking big." And, like, that's kind of depressing, to think we're just a few kids . . . and we see that the majority of the people don't have our appetite.

When YP students in the East Bay felt this hopelessness set in, adult mentorship—and especially the continuous movement histories that adult mentors brought to the student movement—helped to reinvigorate their activism and renew their purpose. Largely insulated from the strength and political framework that past movement knowledge could have provided, SRU students began to lose their drive and direction. Their group identity crisis, expressed through Shae's observation "We don't know what we are trying to do," was one manifestation of their disconnection from movement history.

Although the youth-only character of SRU was a source for student political empowerment and public visibility, some SRU youth felt like their retreat into a peer network was also a strategy they had to adopt to insulate themselves from adult power and ageist oppression. After considering why SRU was youth-only, Michelle commented, "I think it's kind of bad that society forces us to not combine with other activist groups. Sometimes I really don't like that." Her statement was revealing: to actively combine with adult activist groups is also to invite the consequences of adult power. For SRU students, there really was no in-between. As evidenced earlier, SRU students missed out on links to past social movements—"road maps" and sustained mentorship that adults could have brought—in exchange for a peer-to-peer safety zone free from adult power. Troy's analysis of why SRU did not join forces with a local college student movement against school budget cuts and war is instructive in understanding how ageism, or, as he says, "putting the ages down," can limit the possibilities for adolescents to form coalitions with other activist groups:

That's the thing with putting the ages down, because we have to realize that we are actually a high school group. We are not a youth group; we are not a young person's group, whatever. We are specifically a high school thing going on. We are not trying to work with colleges. We are down with allies, 'cause there are some things that affect both of us, but we are specifically leadership in high schools working for social justice. If we did ally with people like that, our concerns would kind of be wiped away. If we lent ourselves to their leadership, their leadership would take over. . . . It would just be like someone talking down to us. And that's what happens.

As Troy pointed out very explicitly, SRU meant Students Rise Up. It did not mean youth in the larger sense, in that it did not encompass young adults in college. In contrast to YP student activists in the Bay Area, SRU high school students could not easily find older, stable young adult mentors in Portland because most adults they knew did not themselves experience being high school activists. They hadn't navigated, for example, powerful school administrations, media coverage, and adult-dominated social networks in the same way that the SRU movement had to do. SRU students found the admiration they received from adult activists to be double-edged: on the one hand, students felt uplifted when they heard, "Hey, you guys are amazing! When I was in high school all I did was smoke pot!" from adults. On the other hand, this type of praise reinforced for SRU organizers that these adults could not really mentor them in the way that they needed. Fifteen-year-old Hayden noted that sometimes this praise still smacked of an adultist patronizing: "You know, sometimes the adult praise is good. But, sometimes, it really sounds like what you would say to a toddler taking their first steps, like, 'Oh, good! Look at what you did! Good for you, you cute little kids!'"

Importantly, most adults with whom SRU interacted did not have an articulated awareness, interpretation, or critique of ageism or adultism, so they could not as easily be trusted by SRU organizers to support their leadership development and to not betray them or dismiss them because of their age. Across California, the early 1990s wave of anti-immigrant legislation and the advent of super-jails, expansion and intensification of a punitive juvenile justice system, and backlash against affirmative action all helped to galvanize high school youth of color into organized fights and groups (some that vanished and some that have persisted as infrastructure for ongoing youth activism). It gave birth to a whole new generation of high school students and young college students who became involved in organizing, who became politicized at a young age, and who also experienced everything that comes with social justice organizing as a minor: firsthand experience with ageist adult betrayers, powerful adults that hold and per-petuate what students perceive to be white and middle-class power struc-tures, key adult allies, and all types of adults in between.

Given the paucity of adult mentors specifically in white, middle-class activist networks that were committed to subverting ageism and develop-ing leadership skills among youth, SRU found that its greatest hope for political agency and empowerment resided in its youth-only structure. However, preserving this youth-only character also meant that skilled organizers like Troy or Shae, for example, could never return to the group, in any capacity, once they left high school. Troy explained this dilemma: "It's sad, but if I come back in a few years and it's still going on, I won't be part of their group. I would be all, you know, talking. I'd have no bearing on . . . I just wouldn't be relevant to the group anymore. I wouldn't share that experience." SRU students who had worked so hard to develop youth movement in Portland expressed vexation about this dilemma, not want-ing to see their efforts come to nothing. Eighteen-year-old Curt explained,

> I'm not interested in working towards something and then having it completely forgotten afterward. I'm not interested in kids having to go through the same mistakes that I had to go through, because I didn't know what to do, or had the experience. And that's what's going to happen. I mean we're going to get kids who are radical into our schools. And they will have no group to go to, so they will start a group. And they will have to deal with all the crap that we have to deal with already.

The discontinuity built in between the generations and thus between the students and the larger community endangered SRU's future and made passing on leadership and spearheading long-term, proactive campaigns difficult. In the East Bay, the integration of adults within YP, coupled with their fluid interpretations of youth, meant that high school students could return to the organization in other capacities: as interns, site organizers, mentors, and allies. They could continue to pass on their organizing knowledge to younger students and could help to sustain long-term stu-dent campaigns. In contrast, the crisis of SRU movement continuity was an unintended consequence of SRU's youth-only structure. This structure, initially designed to protect youth activists from the dangers of adult power, was developed within a larger social movement milieu where few adult activists recognized ageism to be a legitimate system of oppression. Therefore, SRU activists felt that even as they sought out adult alliances in community movements, they had to simultaneously keep adults at arms length—as they did not trust adults in local community movements to have any kind of consciousness about age inequality and generational differences.

Because long-term campaigns were difficult to initiate and sustain in this youth-only organizational context, short-term direct actions (over long-term political transformation and in-depth group discussions) became paramount. Often at weekly SRU meetings, students would stray from their meeting agenda and become embroiled in a discussion about group dynamics, alliances, and tactics. Inevitably, even after just a few minutes, a student would become exasperated and irritated and would break into the group discussion: "Okay, everyone. We're not doing anything. This is stupid. C'mon, we're trying to change the fucking world here and we're just talking and talking. Is that all we're doing? What are we gonna do?" Half the students at the meeting would throw up their hands and wiggle their fingers in agreement, trying to signal consensus.

There were times during or after meetings when SRU students would openly express to me their embarrassment that I had witnessed what I thought were provocative and important discussions. During one impassioned and tense discussion about the lack of racial diversity in SRU, Curt leaned over to me and whispered, "You can totally tell we're just high school students, huh?" A few weeks later, as I walked to the bus stop after another particularly charged SRU discussion on direct action tactics, Zoe, ready to bury her frustration into her earphones and unwind to music on her bus ride home, said, "Didn't you think that meeting was just pathetic? We're usually not that immature." When I told Zoe that from an outsider's perspective, I thought the discussion was really interesting and important and that a lot of activist groups have the same tough issues to sort out, she looked genuinely surprised at my response. For SRU students, just talking itself, absent physical action, brought to the surface a profound impatience with the pace of social change and an embarrassment that their internal disagreements and struggles signaled their immaturity as young political activists.

Thus, the calls for "doing" and pleas for ending what many SRU youth referred to in meetings as "pointless discussion" saved the group from an encroaching sense of futility. This futility threatened to slow the momentum of SRU, and planning and participating in physical direct actions in city streets helped to shore up student political power and reinvigorate the group. At the same time, cutting short these important discussions meant that these youth were unable to attend to serious group divisions and mediate conflicts. Their political process was shot through with a profound sense of urgency and an intuitive understanding that their organizational structure could neither sustain drawn-out discussions nor long-range projects. SRU activists' distance from adult allies, as compared to YP youth, also worked to estrange them from important social movement legacies and long-term strategizing. Ultimately, this estrangement contributed to a collective impatience that characterized SRU's orientation toward quick-change, high visibility, direct action politics.

Conclusion

When young people extend their political organizing work beyond their schools and into their communities, they connect to each other and to adult allies and begin to realize their political power as a larger youth movement. At the same moment that they interface with social movements and learn crucial organizing skills, they also encounter adultism within the vibrant activist scenes in their cities. In the course of understanding the landscape of adult allies in their communities, they begin to recognize and politicize age inequality and collectively develop frameworks for understanding ageism. By transgressing the boundary between citizens-in-the-making and actual political actors, young people in Oakland and Portland found themselves to be infringing upon what is usually considered "adult" territory. In so doing, these activists became acutely aware of their own social status as adolescents and developed frameworks for understanding the ways in which adult power posed challenges to their social movement aims.

These frameworks for understanding ageism guided their social movement tactics and organizational strategies. Whether these youth developed mechanisms for integrating adults into their networks or cultivated youth autonomy to foster political empowerment and visibility, their strategies flowed from their perceptions of adult power. Given that the terrain of youth political action is one that is dominated by adult political players, the ways in which youth interpret adult power and understand their own social status become important guides for organizing their movements.

Furthermore, young people's interpretations of ageism, and their strategies to undermine adult power, are deeply rooted in racial and class contexts. While YP political frameworks conceptualized ageism as a social oppression on par with racism, poverty, and sexism, SRU political frameworks recognized ageism to be mostly embodied in particular groups of adults and in liberal strategies and ideologies versus radical politics. Importantly, young people's positions in racial and class hierarchies engendered these different understandings of ageism and adult power, contributed to different definitions of youth as a social category, and resulted in different visions of youth political empowerment. In Oakland, students' social locations as racially subordinated, low-income youth resulted in the strategic integration of adult allies for specific purposes. Adult allies in YP served as links to social services and as adult faces for an especially devalued student population in ways that relatively privileged white, middle-class students did not require, as they transformed from citizens-in-the-making to actualized political actors. YP adult allies also helped to connect YP teens to a legacy of multiracial social justice activism, which was instrumental in combating the internalized hopelessness fostered by racial violence, segregation, and poverty. YP's understanding of ageism as a systematic oppression became an important tool for disrupting adult power within the organization. This tool enabled teens to keep adults in check and call them out on their adultist behavior, while utilizing adult privilege to facilitate the goals of the youth movement.

Because SRU was designed to be a youth-only organization, such a tool for disrupting adult power was less relevant to these Portland youth. Instead, they expressed their politicized critique of ageism as a general condemnation of adultist liberal ideologies and tactics. Their condemnation of liberals was instrumental in aligning SRU collective identity with radical adult activism in Portland. The relative class and race privilege of SRU organizers enabled them to maintain their youth-only structure and rendered the integration of adult allies less necessary. SRU youth were even able to find their own physical spaces to hold meetings in ways that YP students could not without the help of adult allies with material resources.

However, the same racial and class privilege that enabled SRU youth to establish autonomy from adults could not prevent their group identity crisis or sustain their movement momentum. Without adult allies as consistent mentors, SRU students found it difficult to position themselves as the inheritors of an activist history, one that could have given shape to a clearer direction for the movement's future. Moreover, SRU as a youth-only network lacked a mechanism for organizational continuity. When kids aged out of high school, they had to leave SRU. Without this mechanism for organizational continuity, important discussions about group disagreements, as well as long-term political projects, were difficult to sustain.

The crisis that the SRU participants encountered was not simply a result of their own perceptions of ageism and the choices they made to keep adults at the fringes of their network. They made these strategic choices in the larger context of an adult-dominated activist culture in their city. The adult allies they knew, those who were important in influencing their political leanings and in teaching them organizing skills in select moments, could not be trusted to seriously reflect on how ageism—along with sexism, classism, and racism—might also represent a real system of inequality. Without any discourse on ageism, these adult allies could not be trusted to actively promote young people's own capacity for political organizing and leadership. In short, teenagers' interpretations of ageism are not the only interpretations that influence youth movement strategies. Adult understandings of ageism also help to create the climate in which youth structure their movements.

This was as true in Oakland as it was in Portland, where young adult allies in YP recognized that age inequality posed an additional obstacle to the political development of working-class and poor teen organizers of color. These adults conceptualized ageism (and specifically adultism) as a legitimate system of oppression that they had to constantly confront while mentoring youth activists. In this sense, adults' recognition or denial of age as an axis of social inequality can also influence the ways in which youth conceptualize and respond to adult power. In the case of youth movements, adults' conceptions of age inequality can even impact the potential for youth movement organizations to sustain their social justice work into the future. Because adult allies in Oakland held a clear consciousness about age inequality, as well as about their own tendencies toward adultism, they were able to build much more productive and long-lasting alliances with youth activists than were adult allies in Portland. YP, as an organization, was able integrate these adults into their structure and organizational culture and to adhere to a definition of youth that was flexible enough to accommodate young organizers even after they transitioned out of high school and out of adolescence. SRU students envisioned a much sharper distinction between youth and adulthood, and considered adult allies to be so capable of betrayal that they even began to see their own future adult selves as fundamentally incompatible with participation in the youth movement.

Despite their successes and challenges in building alliances with adult allies in community movements, both SRU and YP youth used their city-wide youth movements, along with the many political organizing skills they learned from the larger movements in their urban environments, as newfound leverage for bringing social justice issues back into their schools. This time, their social justice efforts on school grounds would be anchored in their activist presence among a wider network of community social movements.

4

Toward Youth Political Power in Oakland

The Adult Gaze, Academic Achievement, and the Struggle for Political Legitimacy

So a lot of youth, when they go into the principal's office, they're scared. Unless they want to argue, or they're mad or frustrated, they don't want to speak to no adults. Because adults have their role in society, their so-called role in society, and youth have their so-called role in society, which is to shut up and listen, and you don't know nothin.' (Bert, twenty-year-old YP intern)

I am attending a YP weekend retreat in a large, log cabin in the woods about seventy miles outside of Oakland. We have been driving in vans for hours just to get here, crisscrossing freeways and negotiating the tangled mess of stop-and-go traffic rushing in and out of the Bay Area. Finally, the cityscapes give way to rolling hills, and we arrive. The students are giddy with excitement to be in the woods. They hardly ever get the chance to breathe clean air and stick their feet in an ice-cold river on a summer day. They hardly ever get the chance to leave the endless concrete of their Oakland neighborhoods. After spending an hour or so exploring the woods outside, the fifty YP teen activists converge in the main cabin to begin the retreat. It is in this log cabin where they will spend the next forty-eight hours mapping out their coordinated plans for political organizing at each of their Oakland high schools for the upcoming school year.

Tevin and Naomi, juniors at Brookline High School, have decided that we would begin the weekend retreat with a fun and energizing icebreaker. But like all YP games and icebreakers, this one also contains an important message that is designed to reinforce the students' political identity and commitments. Even with scheduled fun time, nothing is wasted. These kids are always doing politics. This icebreaker happens to be called the dance game. We split up into two teams and name them the Players and the Revolutionaries. I am on the Revolutionaries team. Tevin and Naomi hold out a small basket filled with pieces of folded paper. On each piece of paper is written the name of a popular dance. A student on the Players team goes first and picks a piece of paper out of the basket and covertly shows it to the rest of her teammates. All of them giggle and survey our team, trying to decide which one of us they will pick to perform the dance. The rule is that the chosen person must perform the dance for everybody. If the person performs the dance well, then that person's team will be able to guess the dance correctly and win a point. If the person performs poorly, then the other team gets the point.

The Players whisper among themselves and pick me to perform the dance, because they guess that I won't know the dance, or won't be able to perform it well enough for my team to guess it. I stand up and they show me what is written on the small piece of paper. It reads, "go stupid," and represents another defining moment that underscores the cultural distance—shaped by age, race, ethnicity, and class—between me and these kids. I whisper to Tevin and Naomi that I have no idea how to "go stupid." They shrug and give me no hints and whisper unhelpfully, "You have to do it. Just go for it." I stand in the middle of the room and the crowd counts down from three to zero. I struggle to come up with something. When they say, "go!" I do my version of going stupid, my arms and legs flailing, my eyes crossed, and my tongue sticking out. I feel like a complete idiot. But my team shouts in unison, "go stupid!" They guess the dance correctly and we win the point. I feel relieved that I didn't let my team down, and I wonder how one really goes stupid correctly, in style.

Naomi says, "Okay, now we pick the next dance and you all have to guess what dance it is." She and Tevin look through the basket and pick one specific paper out of the basket that nobody has picked yet. They read it and whisper to each other, and then when we all count down from three to zero and say, "go!" they begin to do their dance. They both groove to an imaginary beat, and while they dance they pantomime reading a book, turning the pages to the beat and occasionally licking their finger to turn an invisible page. Even though they are dancing, they act like they are entirely absorbed in their reading. Students on both teams yell, "go smart!" and guess the dance correctly, and both teams win the point. Everyone laughs, as there is not really a dance craze sweeping their neighborhoods called "going smart." One could hardly imagine that cool kids would be doing this dance at parties, or on the dance floor of some club. But here they do this dance, sometimes spontaneously, throughout the weekend. They had begun doing the dance at the last YP retreat, when they discussed the ways in which they felt adults in their communities held lowered academic expectations of them. Few adults they knew, and few of their peers, expected them to succeed academically and go on to college. They wondered if the well-known dance "go stupid" was a way this lowered expectation became inscribed into cultural practice. They decided to see what would happen if they countered this cultural practice with "go smart." Even though it made them laugh every time they did it, the dance reminded them of their academic potential and their intellectual power.

The oppositional culture thesis, popularized by Signithia Fordham and John Ogbu (1986), has theorized that youth of historically oppressed groups resist academic achievement as an expression of their antagonism toward dominant groups. Within this theoretical framework, academic disengagement has been conceptualized as resistance among low-income youth and youth of color. How does a social movement perspective shift these expressions of academic resistance among low-income youth of color? This chapter explores these issues of race, resistance, and schooling as they are refracted through the lens of teenage student activism.

Because adolescents are considered to be citizens-in-the-making but not yet real political actors, their battles to publicly weigh in on social and political issues require that they confront adultist stereotypes about their political capacities and develop strategies to engage powerful adults (such as school administrators) in negotiations over social change issues. As noted in chapter 2, much of students' political work takes place on school grounds, where students initiate and negotiate proposed changes to the school system itself. These proposed changes include the institution of ethnic studies curriculums; the creation of new activist clubs, youth centers, and student unions on campus; and the countering of military recruiters on campus, among many other school-based initiatives. Importantly, teen activists must employ tools that will disrupt adults' tendencies to dismiss them or minimize their demands based on their age (what I call "the adult gaze") and must develop strategies that will circumvent the adult gaze and lend them some leverage and legitimacy in their negotiating processes.

This chapter focuses on how and why some student movement groups politicize academic achievement as they battle over school-change issues, while other movement groups do not. I argue that a social movement perspective complicates the oppositional culture thesis, which has conceptualized academic disengagement as resistance. I demonstrate how politicized students of color in Oakland reframed academic achievement as *political resistance* against white supremacy in schooling. Furthermore, YP youth looked upon academic achievement as a central organizing strategy to gain leverage as political negotiators in the eyes of powerful adults. This politicization of academic achievement in student organizing, or the lack thereof, is inextricably tied to students' positions in racial and class systems of power and privilege. This is made particularly clear when we compare the politicization of academic achievement in YP with the striking absence of academic achievement as a political issue in SRU. This divergence in Oakland and Portland also reveals significant differences in the racial and class dimensions of the adult gaze in both regions, as adults' perception of youth is powerfully infused with racial and class meanings. Adultist stereotypes of low-income and poor black and brown Oakland youth as dangerous, degenerate, low-achieving, lazy, and impulsive were ubiquitous throughout all kinds of adult perspectives on these youth: from the relatively distant mainstream media coverage of Oakland city violence to the more proximate practices of police, school boards, school security guards, and various principals and teachers. White, middle-class youth in Portland struggled with a very different kind of adult gaze, one that did not require them to prove their humanity and political legitimacy in terms of their academic credentials.

Politicized Understandings of Schooling in Oakland and Portland

Politicizing the Link between Education and War

As discussed in chapter I, central to youth movements in both Portland and Oakland has been the politicization of the link between school budget crises and the war. Intensifying social divestment that has threatened urban youth's education most intensely in Oakland (but is also threaten-ing middle-class, white youth's education in Portland) became a source of deep resentment among youth in both regions, especially when coupled with the prospect of a never-ending, multibillion dollar war in the Middle East. For middle-class, white youth and working-class and poor youth of color, the orienting of the U.S. economy toward war (and, in California, also toward prison expansion) and away from social goods such as educa-tion exemplified the contempt that adults in power have for younger gen-erations. Youth activists in both Portland and Oakland viewed the war in Iraq as a literal and global war on youth. As SRU organizer Troy, sixteen years old, succinctly said, "We identified the fact that kids our age were going to go kill kids our age and get killed by kids our age." Young people's perceptions of social divestment in their futures went beyond criticizing the war or powerful adults such as the president, politicians who voted for the war, or officials in the California Department of Education who had authorized the California High School Exit Exam. At times, their critiques even extended to the adults in their communities. After viewing a segment of the video series *Eyes on the Prize*, in which black parents in late 1960s Brooklyn fought to take community control over their children's schools, one freshman YP student observed, "That really shows how much has changed between then and now. I mean, why aren't parents getting together to fight like that? I wish our parents would do that now." In instances like these, students contextualized war spending and school defunding as com-ponents of a larger generational abandonment.

For many activists, school budget cuts represented the final nail in the coffin for the emerging generation who must serve on the frontlines of war. In Portland, SRU students made this perception clear during their walkouts to protest local school budget cuts. Hundreds of students somberly marched through Portland's city streets, carrying black coffins they had made themselves and throwing their textbooks in the coffins. They held signs that read simply, "War Means the Death of Our Education." However, the connection between school budget cuts and war was most pronounced in Oakland's more impoverished schools, where the JROTC was the school club with the most resources. While other student clubs at Kendall High School struggled to obtain resources and gain the sponsorship of a teacher to help them organize a school dance, YP student organizers pointed out that the JROTC had the resources to put on these events for students. Students in YP argued that flashy JROTC-sponsored dances and events at their schools made joining the military even more attractive to youth with few other opportunities.

The politicized connection between war and schooling meant that student organizers in both Portland and Oakland viewed the fight for education as a radical political act, one consistent with antiwar and larger social justice values. However, even as students fought to save their education, both youth networks held strong critiques of the systems of schooling they were trying to save. As David Labaree notes, "Schools, it seems, occupy an awkward position at the intersection between what we hope society will become and what we think it really is, between political ideals and economic realities" (1997, 41). Student movements reflected this tension, as they fought to save their education and turn their schools into more liberating institutions, while sharply criticizing the kind of schooling they experienced in their everyday lives.

Irrelevant Education in Portland versus
White Supremacist Education in Oakland

> Youth not only face the consequences of economic downsizing, they often find themselves being educated and regulated within institutions that have little relevance for their lives. This is expressed most strongly in schools. Strongly tied to the technology of print, located within a largely Eurocentric curriculum, and often resistant to analyzing how racial, class and gender differences intersect in shaping that curriculum, schooling appears to many youth to be as irrelevant as it is boring. (Giroux 1996, 13)

As discussed in chapter 2, student activists in both Portland and Oakland collectively critiqued their school systems for their irrelevance to current political and social crises. Eighteen-year-old Portland activist Curt culled the lessons he had learned from the terrorist attacks of 9–11 to construct a larger critique of his education (much in line with Giroux's analysis):

> I think recent events show us, like when terrorists crash into skyscrapers with airplanes, there's a problem here. Building a country

is one thing, but building an empire is just completely wrong. In school, we are learning the same stuff that we have been learning since the industrial era. And this country doesn't need to be built anymore like it used to. We are learning how to build skyscrapers when we should be learning how to build sustainable things; we should be learning how to take apart things. How to reuse and recycle, and build gardens.

Youth activists in both regions began their social movement journeys in their schools. They formed criticisms of their schooling and turned these criticisms into visions for better education. For SRU youth, middle-class schooling was too often irrelevant, devoid of political content and sufficient opportunities to debate social issues and develop a political consciousness. Politically sanitized curriculums and school clubs not only estranged them from political power: these structures of schooling also fostered a widespread political apathy among their peers, which made student mobilization around social justice issues a challenge. For YP youth in Oakland, schooling went far beyond irrelevancy. Classroom lessons were also seen by these youth as white supremacist and Eurocentric. As Lisa Delpit (1995) and Prudence Carter (2005) note, most schools—even those with very few white students or teachers—still work to inculcate a "culture of power": a constellation of practices, rules, and styles of success that resonate with the dominant white culture that is the creator of these cultural codes. Through schooling, this culture of power legitimizes the practices and values of dominant groups, and estranges students from their education. YP students' criticism of their predominantly black and Latino schools as white supremacist fueled their call for ethnic studies: a movement goal absent from SRU's brand of political organizing.

The divergence in perception between "irrelevant" and "white supremacist" schooling was born from the wide disparities between the experiences of white, middle-class SRU students and low-income YP students of color. This divergence in young people's critiques of schooling resulted in more than just different goals for liberatory education; it also produced a particular ideology of resistance among YP youth that did not materialize among SRU youth. As a result, YP youth of color framed academic achievement as political resistance, an ideology that resonated with their larger critique of schooling as white supremacist. White, middle-class SRU youth did not develop such an ideology of political resistance, nor did they overtly politicize academic achievement at all in their movement. Importantly, YP's framing of academic achievement as political resistance held a double purpose. On one hand, it served as an *ideology* of resistance for YP youth, so that doing well in school and receiving good grades became a key piece of their political identities. On the other hand, academic achievement emerged as a major *strategy* that was especially effective in disrupting a particularly racist and classist adult gaze in Oakland, a strategy that gave them an added legitimacy for making political demands.

Academic Achievement as an Ideology of Resistance

Although all youth in this study struggled with an internalized sense of political powerlessness that threatened to break the momentum of their movements—and thus all youth had to find ways to undo this internalized ageism as part of their political development—YP students, as urban youth of color, have also internalized the ravages of racism and poverty. Thus, in YP the focus of political development was not only on political action, it was also on "being": on reclaiming one's body and mind and reasserting one's humanity to undo white supremacist colonization. Regardless of whether YP youth were black, Raza, or Asian, for example, these youth found common ground and multiracial linkages in the fact that they were all historical subjects of European colonization and current objects of what they perceived to be white supremacist programs.[1] In Portland, SRU's emphasis was on physical, high-visibility direct actions. Their dictum "ACTYOURAGE" not only poked fun at the adultism embedded in the saying "act your age." It also stressed the importance of political action motivated by political anger. SRU's emphasis on political direct action prompted some SRU participants to view SRU as a type of extracurricular activity almost outside of the self: a view that often took on a particularly middle-class orientation. As SRU activist Suzanne explained, "Like my dad always tells people: 'My daughter is on the varsity activist team'—it's like a sport, a hobby, a social thing—but it's *political.* It's a better use of my time." Although Suzanne's father's comment seemed to belittle her political activism—depoliticizing it by equating it with a "hobby" or a "social thing"—Suzanne did not see it this way. Instead, she was proud to view her activism through a lens of middle-class "concerted cultivation"—where she, with her father's approval, had managed to structure her extracurricular life in a way that could maximize both her leisure time and her institutional advantages (Lareau 2003). As Lareau points out, good parenting in middle-class families means "developing" children's talents through adult-initiated organized activities and eliciting children's thoughts and opinions as part of this development. Although SRU was not adult-initiated, SRU action-oriented activism at times resonated with these middle-class values. When not threatening adult sensibilities, SRU activism was understood by some parents and SRU activists alike as a useful, meaningful, and organized activity that cultivated their intellect, critical-thinking skills, and capacity for civic engagement.

Meanwhile, YP politics was more ubiquitous in Oakland students' lives. Every aspect of their lives became politicized: their academic achievement in school, their health, their relationships with family and friends, even the way they viewed themselves.[2] Through the political framework of YP, students began to understand their academic disengagement as a kind of acquiescence to an ongoing Euro/white supremacist campaign that stretches back five hundred years, one that would like to see people of color "end up in prison, low-wage work, or dead," as YP workshops on Five Hundred Years of Miseducation and The Cycle of Violence emphasized. Therefore, academic achievement was reframed as collective resistance to white supremacy.

In this sense, the politicized terrain of youth activism in Oakland included community spaces, school spaces, and even the inner spaces of the self. When I asked Jazmin, a seventeen-year-old YP organizer, what her life would be like without YP, she talked about her life in terms of personal and political transformation and specifically addressed the role of academic achievement in this transformation:

JAZMIN: I don't know exactly what has brought me into having this passion to want to change things, but I think it is so strong it would have come out whether YP was there or not. I just wouldn't have been able to do what I am doing now. I wouldn't have known how to organize, how to talk to people if it hadn't been for YP. It would have just been undirected anger.

HAVA: And where would you have put it, do you think?

JAZMIN: I know when I was in junior high I was cutting school, I was drinking, I was doing drugs, I was just totally unfocused . . . and I got into YP
and I ended up going to class all the time. The only time I miss class
now is when I am at a YP special activity or something. Like, it's not
just about organizing to make a change in your community. But like,
changing yourself, having a healthy life, it's about so much. Like, alco-
hol and drugs come into a community to oppress it, so you have to stay
away from it. It's just so much [about YP] that changes you.

YP as an organization required that high school organizers keep up their
grades: a requirement that took on political and strategic significance
within the organization. YP reframed dominant school drop-out discourses
into a critical "push-out" discourse. A significant YP worldview emphasized that students of color are in fact pushed out by the public school system to channel them into the prison industrial complex, low-wage labor,
or the violence of the underground economy.[3] This push out political critique of schooling was not an abstract notion: YP students experienced
firsthand, with all of their senses, this feeling of being pushed out by their
schooling.

   During one hot July day, Shandra, Salvador, Pilar, Guillermo, Alisha,
Bert, and I all met in a far classroom in Patterson High School, way out in
East Oakland. This daily meeting was supposed to have lasted about five
hours, so that the Patterson High YP lead organizers could have enough
time to perfect the political workshops that they would be teaching the
next day in this same classroom to incoming Patterson High freshmen.
With reassurance that a YP adult ally would be there to supervise the students, Mr. Nelson, a supportive teacher, had granted YP the use of his
classroom over the entire summer so that the Patterson team would be
sure to have a stable space to meet for the duration of their summer program. While the classroom was somewhat of a haven for YP students, especially because it was the only classroom in the entire school that had three
working computers with Internet access, it was still a classroom at
Patterson High: barren, bars outside of the windows, and broken window
blinds inside. No pens, pencils, paper, or chalk could be found. All the
desk drawers were locked, as was an old file cabinet standing in the corner.
Next door to the classroom was a locked girls' bathroom. During days like

this, if I was lucky enough to track down the exasperated janitor, I would ask him if he could unlock the bathroom for us girls. Each day I had to promise him that the YP students would not destroy or tag the bathroom and that only a few of us would use it quickly before he returned to lock it again.

Shandra, Alisha, and Pilar had just dragged themselves into the classroom after finishing summer-school classes for the day. They carried Styrofoam boxes heaped with gooey chili-cheese fries from the cafeteria and began to eat them and discuss their morning. Pilar's science teacher could not remember her name. He kept calling her "Margarita" instead of Pilar. This struck Salvador as hilarious, and he laughed, teasing her and calling her Margarita. Pilar became instantly annoyed with Salvador, and he stopped teasing only when she explained how many times she has corrected her teacher and how frustrated she was about this. Salvador apologized for his teasing. Alisha was taking an English class she had already taken and passed the year before. She really needed to enroll in biology, but the class had been full for months. The school counselor enrolled her in English instead, despite her objections. The students swapped chili-cheese fries and their stories of frustration with summer school, as they gazed through the barred windows at the portable classrooms outside.

Later, I would witness a YP adult mentor show them pictures of Patterson High taken decades before they were born and point out the portables in the photos. "See," she said, pointing, "The portables were there, even then. And they're *still* here. Portables are temporary buildings, for temporary educations. You would think that schools should at least have real buildings! But these portables have always been here. We weren't ever *meant* to receive a real education. You understand? *You* weren't ever meant to receive an education. This system is not set up for you." Her words were harsh. They stung. As a white, middle-class person, I had never once been told that my education was not designed for me. But her point fully resonated with YP youth, who experienced schooling through these everyday fragments: barred windows, locked and dirty bathrooms, suspicious security guards, redundant classes, a shortage of textbooks, empty and bleak hallway walls, a shredded auditorium projector screen, and an endless string of substitute teachers who did not know students' names. For YP students, these fragments first crystallized into a suspicion that their schools were actually *blocking* their educational opportunities and facilitating their disengagement.[4] After participating in YP, students transformed this suspicion into a powerful political critique of schooling, in which they began to recognize their own academic disengagement as a kind of self-defeating collusion with the school systems that worked to push them out. Academic engagement and getting good grades were then reframed as an essential form of political resistance. If their systems of schooling were not designed to ensure their education, then the students would have to fight to claim it.

This politicized academic resistance differs from the well-documented strategies that many working-class whites and students of color employ to resist domination in schooling (Valenzuela 1999; Fordham 1996; Ogbu 1991; MacLeod 1995; Willis 1977), strategies that create oppositional identities in school but ultimately exacerbate students' academic disengagement and compound young people's downward mobility.[5] YP is not the only youth-oriented organization to recast academic achievement in this political light. Many other social justice youth organizations that fight for changes to their school systems also view high school academic achievement as a means toward higher education, and thus toward social and political advancement for people of color. As described in chapter 2, YP's framing of academic engagement as political resistance even expanded to reclaim other school spaces, such as school bathrooms. Alongside campaigns for comprehensive ethnic studies programs, bathroom campaigns went hand in hand with politicized and radical claims to students' right to an education.

Academic Achievement as a Social Movement Strategy

I have never heard any school get as much bad press as Patterson. Patterson is always in the papers. I could go anywhere and tell people I go to Patterson, and it's always three things: "You got a baby?" "Who you be fightin'?" "Did you get kicked out?" They look at Patterson as a continuation school, as though it's not a public high school. There's this kind of thing like, "This is the school where all the bad kids go." That is how ignorant people are about it. And that is basically how the media makes it look. That's how the students are grown to feel. (Gayle, eighteen-year-old YP organizer)

As Gayle illustrates, low-income students of color encounter a wide array of negative stereotypes about them that are held by adults, mainstream media, and other youth. In the process of becoming political organizers and agitators, these students must find ways of disrupting these stereotypes to gain some political leverage and legitimacy in the eyes of powerful adults. Students found that academic achievement not only was a way to resist the forces that conspired to push them out of school, it also became a central organizing strategy that made adults' ability to dismiss their concerns and demands much more difficult.

The political framework of both YP and SRU encouraged student organizers to find a voice and confront (adult) power (whether in the school, the streets, or the government). Many students noted that as their movements picked up steam and they emerged as leaders among their peers, they became increasingly seen as threats by their administrations. Gayle pinpointed the love-hate relationship Patterson's administrators had with her as both a prominent student and a prominent student organizer: "I am the student that the administration loves to hate. And hates to love. *Because I'm a good student*, I'm a good person, I am kind, but my views I always let control everything. If I don't agree with something I am going to speak on it. I am not going to be a silent witness." Importantly, when YP students achieved academically, their good grades gave them leverage for negotiating student needs and visions with adult administrators.

Although SRU students in Portland were critical of their "irrelevant" education, they did not perceive themselves to be pushed out by their schooling in the same way that students of color perceived themselves to be pushed out of their urban school systems. SRU students ran the gamut from high achievers like Curt and Shae, who excelled in their AP classes and ended up graduating from high school with honors, to students like Hayden or Troy who were on the verge of dropping out and sought to attend an alternative high school or early community college instead of compulsory public school. Despite this range among SRU students, academic achievement never took on a political or strategic reframing in SRU. Instead, academic achievement emerged as a divisive issue in SRU: students who prized academic achievement and their links to supportive teachers sometimes clashed with the more radical or hard-core SRU students who were on the fringes of their schools and their teachers' good graces. I witnessed this when SRU founder Vlad, angry and fed up with the downturn in SRU's level of activism at the end of the 2003 school year, expressed disappointment to the group about their lack of preparation for a unified showing at the annual May Day march in Portland. Shae snapped, "You know, Vlad, some of us actually care about doing good in school. We have a lot of stuff going on and we can't be devoting every minute of our time to activism." In Shae's view, doing well in school on one hand, and her activism on the other, represented two mutually exclusive activities that competed for the same block of precious time.[6]

Thus, in SRU, academic achievement remained a private, quiet, and depoliticized issue—and sometimes even an embarrassing issue, lest some students appear too cooperative with school adults and not committed enough to radical activism. Although Shae publicly challenged Vlad in the SRU meeting about the competing demands on her free time and the importance of keeping up with her homework, she told me privately how difficult it was for her to reveal herself as a SRU activist to her teachers. Rather than risk disapproval from her teachers, Shae tried to hide her association with SRU at her school to preserve her good student image. Shae wrestled privately with the seeming incongruence of doing well in school and pleasing her teachers on one hand and emerging as a visible student organizer on the other. Girls like Shae never brought this to SRU meetings as a public issue, because they might have been perceived by boys as less radical or less committed. Academic achievement—although not a politicized issue in SRU—certainly became a hidden gendered issue within the organization.

While Shae worried about disappointing her teachers and viewed overt SRU activism as a possible threat to her legitimacy in school, white, middle-class boys in SRU did not express this same tension. It was striking that these boys could be medium or low academic achievers, or could be punished, disciplined, and reprimanded by their school administrations for their political organizing, but could bounce back and reestablish communication with powerful school adults without having lost their legitimacy to negotiate. For example, SRU activist Pete was suspended from his relatively wealthy Shoreline High School for helping to organize an unapproved walkout against the war. Within three weeks he was back in school, leading negotiations between student activists and the principal around the creation of a SRU satellite activist club at Shoreline High. When his administration automatically listed the new SRU group as an official school club, Pete's brand of negotiating moved from assertive to almost confrontational. The listing of the SRU satellite as an official school club became problematic for SRU students, because all school clubs required an adult sponsor to oversee and approve club activities. Under Pete's leadership, SRU students decided to circumvent this adult power by presenting to the administration their own perimeters for the satellite SRU club. As Pete recalled,

> Basically we wrote an ultimatum to the administration that we recognize that there needs to be an adult at our meetings, but we also reserve our power to have meetings at any other point during our time at school, like, without a sponsor, in order to organize. And that's basically just what we said. Like, we realize that we need to work within this club thing, but if we feel the need, we are going to say, "Hey, Mr. So-and-so, we want you to leave. We want to talk about some things now that we don't want you around for." But, they really didn't respond to us; they just kind of said, "Okay, okay."

Their ultimatum was not a clear and unqualified success, as evidenced in the dismissive response, "Okay, okay." Yet Pete interpreted the administration's weak response to the students' ultimatum as a clear victory. Later, as SRU antiwar activism became more controversial and began to lose teacher and parent support, the Shoreline administration would return to the SRU quasi-club and insist that they abide by school club charter rules completely, or not exist at all. Although the innovative design of their satellite SRU chapter as a quasi–school club meant that it would be vulnerable to administrative betrayal and control later on, it was significant that SRU's ultimatum initially met with little resistance from the administration at Shoreline High. Under Pete's leadership, himself a student who had been suspended, Shoreline's SRU chapter was still able to retain the legitimacy, visibility, and, most importantly, the staying-power of a school club, while maintaining the flexibility to operate outside of the school's adult power structure. White, middle-class students, unlike YP students, possess a white and middle-class privilege that somewhat affords them the assumptions of "competence" and "innocence" (Cullinan 1999). As Cheryl

Harris explains, white privilege by itself, regardless of class, is valuable as property and political leverage: "Whiteness, the characteristic that distinguishes them from blacks, serves as compensation even to those who lack material wealth. It is the relative political advantages extended to whites, rather than economic gains, that are crucial to white workers" (1995, 286). Although this white privilege, along with class privilege, was mediated by their delegitimization as youth, SRU students' white and class privilege eliminated their need to make school achievement into a central organizing strategy as they wrestled with school administrations over the establishment of new political clubs, student unions, and other infrastructure that would connect their schools to the larger political movements in their city.

The presumption of innocence and competence that SRU students' whiteness and relative class privilege afforded—although mediated by age inequality—may have played into the initial success of the Shoreline SRU satellite in securing a semiautonomous space on school grounds (however shaky this autonomy turned out to be). Of course, this race and class privilege is not simply the property of students; it also knitted into the school culture itself at public institutions such as Shoreline. At relatively wealthier public schools, even the built environment is constructed to "encourage the freedom of mobility and thought to discover, problem-solve, and create. . . . Relaxed, but rigorous learning environments seem to be the natural outgrowth of their [students'] self-directed, responsible, inquisitive, and creative spirits" (Enora Brown 2003, 127–128).

In contrast, YP youth who attended severely impoverished East Bay schools were often denied the autonomy to even go to the bathroom without suspicion that they would destroy it. A security guard was posted at the end of each hallway. Security cameras were planted in several strategic corners of the building, constantly monitoring students as they moved through hallways, across the cracked cement of the school courtyards, and even just beyond the iron gates of the school. In a climate where unsupervised student activity was especially criminalized, YP students stood less of a chance in demanding a school-club structure on school grounds that allowed for the absence of adult surveillance.[7] To even attempt such a negotiation, YP students had to be vigilant that their academic credentials would not work against them. On the other hand, in Pete's negotiations with the Shoreline administration, school authority figures never once used his recent suspension, or his grades, as an illustration of why SRU students at Shoreline were not capable, responsible, or deserving of having their own semiautonomous space on campus.

Class and cultural capital are central to how student organizers are able to negotiate with their administrations over student visions for better schooling.[8] SRU activists prided themselves on being part of a youth-only movement, deftly avoiding the need for adults to speak for them. They recognized that to be able to speak directly with adult power, they had to employ adults' language. Alana had a series of several meetings with her principal, plotting and planning an administration-approved sleep-in at her school. She reflected on her experience: "Yeah, I had to really argue why the sleep-ins would be so important to saving our schools. But carefully argue, you know what I mean? Not just marching into her office all angry. I was careful to say which parts of the event that the students would take care of, and which parts we needed from her. I made it seem totally nonthreatening and in her best interests too—since she was also upset about the [school budget] cuts. In the end, she was totally on board and even gave us a PA system!" SRU activist Curt reflected on what he had learned about the delicate art of negotiating with school administrators—an art that Alana had also learned—that relies on using "linguistic trades" made available only through relatively resource-rich schooling and middle-class family structures:

> I mean, it seems like we have to do a lot of talk with the administration, and it's just like reformatting everything we have said to them in a way they would say it to themselves. And then we're like, "Okay, now we're going to do this, so can we just do what we said in the beginning?" and they are like, "Oh yes, now that you have put it in some kind of linguistic way that we can understand."
>
> It's just about different linguistic trades between ages. Like, my principal needs to understand things in a way she can understand. . . . I don't think the U.S. government will understand something unless we put it in the terms that maybe they will get. And I would say it's been pretty successful at my school, and it works in SRU.

Curt lauded his ability to span "linguistic trades between the ages," bridging an age gap and a power differential between himself and adult administrators. However, what he did not recognize is that his class status and educational advantage enabled him to bridge this gap. Instead of relying on their grades as leveraging tools to negotiate with school administrators, SRU activists relied on their abilities to speak the "administration's language," a tactic that many YP student organizers felt they could not use. At one YP strategizing meeting, student organizers role-played voicing their concerns about their curriculums to their administrations. Several were scheduled to do the real thing the following day. During the role play, students would snicker as some pretended to be hard-headed principals: cold, stoic, and deep-voiced. Afterward, we all gathered in the kitchen for some baloney sandwiches. Although the role play was supposed to prepare students for negotiation, I caught Tevin shaking his head and sighing as he slapped baloney onto a piece of white bread: "Man, I don't know if I can do this tomorrow. I get so nervous with this. I don't know how I'll remember to say all that stuff. And what if they don't listen?" Middle-class, white SRU youth in Portland did not express this same frustration. Students like Curt or Pete, who came from a middle-class background, held a marked confidence in their abilities to confront the administration head-on, using their language. Likely an outcome of concerted cultivation, they had developed a deep sense of entitlement that further facilitated their ability to question adults and address them as equals (Lareau 2003). SRU activists negotiated directly with their administrations over approved school sit-ins. They argued with their administrations that failed to see the importance of school-based youth activist clubs. They challenged them when administrators threatened to suspend student activists for participating in walkouts against the war. Although YP youth organizers also engaged and confronted their administrations, they did so with adult allies ready to back them up. They also had to consciously work to build their confidence, skills, and desire to confront their administrations before they even attempted these challenges to adult power.

Compared to the ever-present political importance of academic achievement in YP, the same issue rarely emerged in SRU, even in individual interviews. After speaking with Alana for nearly three hours, she revealed to me only toward the end of her interview that she was receiving dismal grades in school. She discussed her academic disengagement in the context of her conflicts with her parents over her activism. She shared her perception of schooling as irrelevant, and how her parents complained that she was spending too much time on political organizing and not enough time on her homework. Although her grades were a huge issue with her parents, they did not interfere with her legitimacy—among administrators, teachers, and other students—as a prominent student organizer in her school.[9]

Academic achievement among YP students, in contrast, was a ubiquitous issue in interviews, YP workshops, retreats, and everyday interaction. At every YP weekend retreat or weekly meeting, there was always time set aside for students to work on their homework. YP and SRU students, who were passionate about education and were fighting to save their schools as a public good and a democratic right, simultaneously advanced a political framework that was highly critical of their current school systems. This double-sided battle was even more pronounced among YP students, with their critical emphasis on academic achievement as political resistance. How does a student simultaneously criticize her schooling, fight for her education, and strive to achieve academically in what she perceives to be an educational system based on Eurocentric forms of knowledge and values? Seventeen-year-old YP organizer Naomi explained how she made sense of these tensions between schooling, achievement, and social justice in her own life:

> It wasn't until I got into YP, that I was like, I need my grade because I am talking to all these people, the vice principal, these teachers, these community people, and how is it going to be when they are like, "How you doing in school?" and I am like, "Oh, I am getting F's." You know what I am saying? Or they would talk to a teacher, and the teacher would tell them, "Oh, she never comes to class."
>
> And I have a focus. I don't want to be mediocre. I want to do my best so I can get a scholarship and go to college and get educated in something that I want to get educated in. Take women's studies, ethnic studies, you know? I have a goal now. Why I want to do good in school. So even though what we learn in the classroom is so irrelevant to me, this is something I have to learn in order to get to my goal.

Thus, YP adult mentors became YP student tutors and champions of students' academic achievement, even when both YP students and adult allies openly recognized and criticized assignments and teaching styles that they perceived to be alienating or colonizing. Ultimately, students' success in the classroom affords them more legitimacy in the eyes of administrators, teachers, parents, and even other adults in the community who view student worth and intelligence in terms of grades. When students gain this legitimacy, it lends them power to further openly critique colonizing classroom lessons and assignments and to negotiate with the administration to achieve student visions for school change. Gayle, a good student and a prominent school organizer, described her complex relationship with her administration: "You know, I have my problems with them and they have their problems with me. But it's like, 'What are we going to do? *She is a good student*, a good girl. She's not horrible. We can't kick her out because she is not doing anything. She is just speaking her mind; she is being resistant.' And, you know, you can't knock a person for doing that." Gayle's analysis reveals how her academic achievement (here also linked to a gendered "good girl" image) gave her leverage as a student organizer and complicated her administration's efforts to simply write her off as a poor, urban, black teenager.

Conclusion

What does the politicization of academic achievement in Oakland tell us about schooling, student resistance, and the intersecting forces of racism and poverty? First, much of the literature on race, resistance, and schooling focuses on academic disengagement as resistance. The processes of student political organizing and politicization introduce a different mode in which students resist schooling. In Oakland, student organizers developed a complex political framework that reconciled a seemingly paradoxical relationship: that of schooling as white supremacy on one hand, and academic engagement and achievement as an ideology of political resistance on the other.

Secondly, this political reframing of academic achievement is born from a particular intersection of racism and poverty. White, middle-class teen activists who fought for the survival of their schools did not politicize academic achievement, largely because they did not articulate a perception that they were being pushed out of their education. Although they decried school budget crises and rallied for the continuation of public school education, they never doubted that their education was for them, nor did they ever doubt that they deserved their education, nor did anyone ever communicate explicitly or implicitly to them that they did not belong there or insinuate that they would not make it to graduation anyway. In contrast, the political transformation of students in Oakland required that they recognize their right to an education and that they actively claim that right. Bars on the windows, overcrowded classrooms, school violence, punitive standardized testing schemes like the California High School Exit Exam, and widespread negative stereotypes of youth of color as degenerate and dangerous all converged into a strong and consistent message that low-income black and brown youth do not deserve a quality education. YP's politicization of academic achievement became central to students' ability to counter this consistent message.

The use of academic achievement as a political tool in Oakland also reflects how low-income students of color are subject to adultist stereotypes that are at the same time racist and classist. Academic achievement in YP became a tool to challenge adult administrative power, as much as it was a tool to disrupt broader racist and classist stereotypes. In contrast, although SRU students in Portland also had to learn to negotiate with adult power in their schools, and at times they believed that school administrators would dismiss their concerns and status as serious political negotiators based on their age, they were secure in the fact that the administration would not delegitimize their demands or concerns *based on their academic record*. Their ability to negotiate with the administration using adult vocabularies, and their whiteness and middle-class status more generally, were used as tools to interrupt adult power and gain political leverage on school grounds.

This provides us with a moment to theorize how the age-stratified power differentials within school systems—namely those between adult administrators and teen students—are structured along lines of racial and class (and, less developed here, gender) systems of power and privilege. The adult gaze is powerfully constituted by racial and class imagery and discourses. Students intuitively know this and develop appropriate strategies to challenge the many stereotypes and images that work to keep them marginalized from adult decision-making processes on school grounds. In the case of YP in Oakland, students' use of academic achievement as both a political ideology and a key strategy toward actualized political power reflects the intersecting racial and class subordination that shapes their intertwined experiences of schooling and political powerlessness. In contrast, the absence of this ideology or strategy among SRU activists in Portland, as well as their use of adult languages to gain legitimacy as negotiators with their adult administrations, reveal the ways in which white, middle-class youth depend upon racial and class privilege (even unwittingly) as they work toward building student movements on school territory and confront the adult gaze.

5

Toward Youth Political
Power in Portland

The Adult Gaze, Mainstream Media, and the
Problems of Social Visibility

SCOTT: I definitely feel freedom being under the age of eighteen. Like, being under the age of eighteen you're exempt from a lot of things. You know what I mean? Like, in two months I could get in big trouble for something that I'd be just, like, fined for now, you know what I mean? I know it sounds bad but it's totally true. Like there's another article about impressionable teenagers, or whatever, like it's . . .

STEPHEN: Not necessarily impressionable teenagers, but teenagers that are willing to do something. Because nothing will happen to them!

SCOTT: Teenagers do have special abilities, they have this security . . .

STEPHEN: Superheroes!

SCOTT: Yeah, superheroes! [laughing]

STEPHEN: Yeah, they definitely have an advantage.

SCOTT: I think that they're not necessarily listened to as much, but I feel like they definitely have the opportunity to *do* more.

Police Power and the Adult Gaze in Portland

It was not lost on SRU youth that there were moments of irony about the adult gaze, which filtered through adult-dominated media, schools, police, and even social movement networks. Although these activists often criticized this gaze for infantilizing them as serious organizers and dismissing their political aims and capabilities, they also noticed that this infantilization, the childlike innocence or rambunctiousness attributed to their motivations and actions, could sometimes be a crucial asset. In Portland, there was a perception among some adult radical activists that SRU youth held a special advantage over adult radicals: in the eyes of these young adults, SRU activists, by virtue of their age, could afford to take the leading edge in direct actions. They could take the most risk to block city streets, commit the most courageous acts of civil disobedience, and could even physically block a whole line of riot cops using nothing but their bodies, protecting the many adult radicals standing behind them. Although these adult radicals did not necessarily look to these youth as movement leaders in terms of their organizing skills or political visions, they recognized that youth had an advantage when it came to the basic physicality of participating in direct action protests. Why? Because these adult radicals, and even SRU boys like Scott and Stephen, believed that police response and state punishment would be less harsh for people under eighteen years of age. Therefore, youth could be utilized for their special legal status as juveniles, able to take risks for the entire movement in ways that adult radicals could not.

Some SRU activists were intensely proud of this special status their age had earned in antiauthoritarian movement networks. It is no coincidence that this pride came more from SRU boys, who, like Scott and Stephen, viewed themselves as radical teen "superheroes." Although SRU girls often felt empowered by their participation in direct action protests, they did not necessarily view themselves as activist superheroes. Unlike boys, many SRU girls worried about their parents' ability to punish them as much as they worried about state punishment. [1] SRU activists Myra and Suzanne explained this predicament:

MYRA: The arrests are more severe above eighteen years old. Like, other activists try to get us to be more radical because we can't get punished harshly. That will change when we are eighteen.

SUZANNE: Well, we can't get punished as harshly by the law, but we can by our parents!

In fact, girls' orientation to parental authority was at times a point of disjuncture between themselves and radical young adult activists in street protests in Portland. Young adult activists once tried to persuade Myra and Suzanne's affinity group to put their bodies between the riot police and other adult activists. This was the very first street protest that the girls had ever attended. When Myra and Suzanne tried to explain to these older activists that they couldn't take this radical step forward because they'd face the wrath of their parents, older activists replied, incredulously, "So what? Do it anyway!" Although parental power seems insignificant and manageable to adult activists, especially compared to the formidable specter of police in riot gear, for Myra and Suzanne parental authority was very real and powerful.

Even with this gender difference in attitude toward direct action risk taking, however, SRU boys, SRU girls, and radical adult activists in Portland all seemed to agree on one thing: that there was a clear legal advantage to being under eighteen when it came to protest politics and state punishment. This did not mean that SRU youth were not critical of police or did not experience police punishment, repression, or even violence as a result of their activism. SRU youth, both boys and girls, became explicitly anticop as they became politicized. The group's emphasis on "action" and "doing something" often took student movements out into the streets and in direct confrontation with police. When SRU students found political power and agency in direct action, even for the girls who were less comfortable taking this action, they also encountered police repression. In this way, SRU teens' politicization in street protests was interwoven with new experiences of police violence, and their political identity became explicitly anticop.

Police infiltration (real and perceived) of radical communities in Portland and the general tightening of security infused Portland student organizing with a heightened awareness of police danger and destructiveness. The centrality of antipolice identity among SRU students was clearly evidenced in Zoe's answer to my question: "How do you feel like you've personally changed since becoming a member of SRU?"

> Well, I've lost my respect for cops. I used to have a lot of respect for those people. I used to categorize them as individual people, but since then I have kind of like . . . they all seem the same. I have been more conscientious of who I talk to on the street and how I give out my personal information. Sometimes I won't give people my real name. Security culture is much tighter for me.

Her relative lack of previous contact with police, and her prior ability to see police as individuals and not as instruments of oppression, was a reflection of her white and middle-class privilege. Zoe's observation about this change in her understanding of police was echoed in several other SRU students' narratives about their own political transformations since joining SRU. Several SRU students mentioned how they had seen their peers change as a result of engaging in direct action. Many observed that once "liberal" youth got out into the streets and faced police repression, they transformed from believing in the workings of the United States as a democracy to understanding that their dissent would bring down the wrath of the state. That is when they became "radical." SRU students' experiences with police represented defining moments when white, middle-class students became politically conscious of how state power can limit speech and protest.

In contrast, YP students, who encountered police power, harassment, and even violence in their schools and communities on a daily basis, did not necessarily need a political framework to adopt a critical analysis of police power. During YP workshops on oppression, I witnessed even new YP initiates criticize police based on their own interactions with officers or on interactions that their friends or older siblings had with police. In impoverished schools that can no longer afford counseling services, students who fight or engage in other troublesome behavior are immediately taken into police custody. Every time I visited Patterson and Kendall high schools, I noticed that it was the police who always had the best parking spots. In YP student narratives, meetings, and workshops, there was little evidence of students undergoing this same radical transformation in the way they viewed police. Police power was already stitched into multiple spheres of their lives.

An important distinction here is that SRU activists experienced police control, harassment, and violence as teenage activists in ways they usually did not as nonpoliticized white, middle-class youth. SRU activist Michelle explained, "We're students and we're supposed to be unruly and rebellious. We have these titles on our heads, so we get poked at more [by police] when we're at protests, and it's frustrating." At one antiwar march, Stephen told me that the police had harassed him just the night before. Police had stopped Stephen and his friends as they were walking downtown at night and asked them if they planned to cause trouble at the march the following day. Police harassment of Stephen and his friends was framed in terms of activism and the protest the next day. In contrast, YP youth in Oakland experienced to varying degrees police control, harassment, and violence as youth of color and as people of color, regardless of whether or not they were engaged in political movement.[2]

Despite SRU students' criticisms of police, and despite their belief that police would target them for discipline and punishment as teenage activists, SRU students still viewed their youth status as protecting them from the harsher state reprisal that awaited adult radicals. To a certain extent, SRU youth still banked on the innocence that their youth afforded them. Even though they recognized that police would target them at protests because they believed police viewed them as "unruly and rebellious" teens, these youth intuitively anticipated that their protest tactics would ultimately be written off as teenage rebellion.

In contrast, YP youth of color were neither routinely disciplined by police as rebellious youth in street actions, nor did they enjoy the protection of being under eighteen vis-à-vis the state penal system. Police and state approaches to youth of color read black and brown, as well as young, through a racist matrix of cultural signification that spells crime instead of rebellion, and menace and "superpredator" instead of a more disciplinable, reformable, and containable unruly and rebellious.[3] As Mike Males explains, "Today, national leaders skillfully meld racism and fear of the young into a potent political crusade that menaces the fabric of American society in new and complex ways" (1999, 3).

Acutely aware that adults such as principals, police, parents, and even older activists would consistently dismiss them because of their age and their assumed immaturity, SRU youth sometimes relied on their status as child innocents to further their social movement goals. Much of the time they perceived their status as youth to be a kind of weapon that adults used against them to delegitimize their efforts in making political change. But at other times, SRU youth understood their presumed childhood innocence could work to protect them and even manipulate adult sensibilities. SRU youth never recognized that this youth innocence, commonly attributed to them by the adult gaze, was also projected onto them by virtue of their whiteness and middle-class status. They simply recognized it as one potential tool, albeit a problematic tool, that they could employ to achieve some of their social movement goals. If some SRU activists viewed themselves as superheroes, the superhero's special power was invisibility: the ability as middle-class, white youth to slip under the radar and not be held fully accountable for their political activity. The same facet of the adult gaze that dismissed their efforts to make political change, the same social view that objectified them as children affected by public policy rather than recognizing their capacity to influence public policy, also worked to their benefit in limited ways. This was as true for their portrayal in the mainstream media as it was in the street protests of Portland.

The Corporate Media and the Adult Gaze

Proeducation Activism: "Happy," "Sad," Infantilized Youth

At almost every SRU meeting, activists talked at length about how to frame their actions to the media, and, by extension, to the general adult public. Media coverage was central to their movement. Unlike YP students who had strong connections to stable young adult allies who served as interfaces to a larger adult public, SRU's biggest adult interface with the adult public was the mainstream media. When I asked Megan why media coverage was so important to SRU, she explained, "It's so important because we want the public to know that we have the power. That there are so many things we can do for this world. That we are the ones that have to live with grown-ups' decisions, so we have the ability to prevent mistakes now." When I posed the same question to Hayden, she responded, "Because otherwise we're totally invisible." To illustrate her point, she frantically waved her arms as if she was drowning. "It's like we're saying, 'Hey, we're over here! See us? We're over here!'" Kristin put this another way:

> We're trying to reach the public. Sometimes the general public watches channel 6, 8, 2, 4, you know, 12. And it's really hard for us to get noticed and to get recognition. It's not like our goal is to get recognition, but we want to change the public's opinion on things. That's what most demonstrations are for. And we're such a small group of kids. To reach the mainstream people we have to get media. You know, that's the goal of most acts.

Megan and Kristin pointed to the mainstream media as a crucial means of publicly reconstructing the image of apathetic, objectified youth into political actors who hold the promise and ability to fix older generations' mistakes and to prevent new ones. In addition, SRU activists recognized that the mainstream media was a way of making visible young people's efforts at making social change, as well as their dissent. In fact, SRU activists relied so much on media coverage that they often equated this coverage with their voice. Getting media coverage was often taken to be their barometer of success. Because young people have no sanctioned channels for political participation, media becomes particularly important in changing public opinion and influencing an adult public that does have access to political decision making, such as voting. As Jacob explained, "I mean, we kind of have to suck up to corporate media because they are the ones who can get the message out there." And at times, corporate media even praised youth for their deference. One news story mused, "They've grown up in a networked world, using e-mail and cell phones. But there is no replacement for the traditional political skills: talking to people in the halls, handing out fliers, being nice to the media and putting aside school rivalries to pool ideas." SRU identified corporate media as one tool that young people could use to influence local voters to support tax increases that would keep their schools open. SRU orchestrated multiple school sleep-ins, in conjunction with citywide student walkouts against school defunding.[4] The sleep-ins garnered media coverage on several local TV stations. Student occupations of their schools sent out a powerful message to the local voting public that students cared about their education so much that they chose to stay there in their free time and to even spend the night.

As much as SRU students depended on mainstream, corporate media as a tool to carry their messages to a broader adult voting public, in their meetings they were openly critical of corporate media. With the jaded sigh of a veteran activist, Troy shrugged his shoulders and explained, "Media is a gamble. I mean, the media is and always will be. Corporate media is always political cooperation with capitalists." SRU's true allegiance was to the relatively recent independent media movement that sprung up in Portland following the WTO protests in Seattle. The independent media movement arose explicitly as a critique of, and an alternative to, corporate media. However, SRU students recognized that the corporate media, rather than independent media, had the ability reach a wider array of adult voters who might vote in students' interests on local tax measures that would save education.

SRU youth's reliance on corporate media as the major interface to an adult public meant that they had to endure corporate media's distortions of SRU actions and political messages. Although student actions that communicated a proeducation message were highly politicized issues for SRU activists themselves, the media quickly depoliticized their messages and effaced their radical potential. SRU activists recognized that their youth-only organizational structure was a huge draw for the media. Proud of the media attention, but critical of the adult gaze it represented, Tory recalled, "At first, everyone was paying attention to us. It was like, 'Wow! We're on the news every night! Look, we walked out! Look, we sat in! Look, we jumped!' and they wanted to film it all, to put it on TV because we're all kids [laughter]." On one hand, this media attention was gratifying for youth activists as it publicized their organizing work and helped to dispel stereotypes about youth as inherently apathetic, passive, and uncaring about their own education. On the other hand, student organizers were dismayed at the ways the media infantilized them, alternatively describing student protests as either "happy" or "sad" rather than angry and political. One local news reporter, standing in front of a lit-up Portland high school at night during the sleep-ins, looked into the camera and remarked,

> You would think this is the last place that teenagers would want to be in their free time. But students here are refusing to leave, and are showing just how much they care about education. And let me tell you, they are making the most of this sit-in. There are bands playing in the auditorium. Students are working on projects together in the hallways. They're sitting on the floor eating dinner together. I mean, this is amazing. As you can see behind me, these kids are just full of excitement and hope that they might be able to do something to keep their schools open. And with all this activity, I'm not sure how much actual sleep these kids are going to get tonight.

Sara analyzed this kind of corporate media coverage of SRU proeducation activism: "I think a lot of liberal student actions get so much good media coverage, because it's like, 'Oh, look at these happy little kids, holding candles and making flags,' you know? I mean, everybody was about to wet their pants; they were like, 'Oh my god! Kids want to go to school!'" SRU activists knew that although their radical, political critique of school defunding was lost in the media coverage they received, their proeducation message ultimately pleased adults. In these messages, students were not criticizing their education, their teachers, their nation, or adults in general. They simply wanted to preserve their institutions, their schooling, and essentially the educational status quo. Through their proeducation message—filtered by the mainstream media—SRU activists even disproved adults' suspicion that Portland youth would be thrilled with early school closures, because it would mean a longer summer vacation. In an infantilizing twist, Sara pointed out that adults watching SRU education activism unfold were so impressed that they were "about to wet their pants" when they discovered that kids actually cared about school.

In contrast, SRU activist Amanda's analysis of corporate media coverage stressed the image of sad students, reflecting an innocence and youth vulnerability that appealed to the media and the adult gaze it represented: "The media coverage was like, 'We really need to get money for our poor children; they're sad,' you know. What got the most attention from the corporate media was showing what would be cut, how many things would be cut, and how sad it would be for the kids." Indeed, local media coverage of the student sleep-ins and the student walkouts alternately used infantilizing images of "happy," "sad," and even "worried" children rallying for their education. Commenting on why students decided to protest the school budget cuts, one local journalist summed it up this way: "Students are worried that out-of-state colleges won't want Oregonians . . . and that the lack of extracurricular activities will degrade the quality of life for many kids." One local article about the Portland citywide student sleep-ins quoted a parent's perspective, which praised students for restraining any possible rage or radicalism: "They could have thrown up a fist. . . . But instead they took the time to make this building wholly in their own terms."

While this media coverage acknowledged that students were claiming their schools and therefore possessed agency, what was missing was a report of exactly the kind of fist in the air that the parent mentioned. Invisible here was the anger and politicized outrage that fueled students, and their connections to larger political ideologies. These elements were overtly symbolized in SRU's insignia: ironically, a fist in the air. SRU organizers mobilized other youth in their high schools by handing out patches with this insignia, or spray-painting it on T-shirts. Sometimes this insignia accompanied the phrase "ACTYOURAGE!" This symbol of student rage proved to be a successful organizing tool within the high schools among students and also aligned the adolescent movement with radical direct action movements in Portland.

The imagery of a fist was also ubiquitous in YP organizing. When YP students led workshops, their mentees learned to raise their fists instead of raising their hands when they had something to say. Integrating this symbolic gesture into YP's organizing practices resonated with their vision of education-as-liberation. For YP, the fist symbolized collective resistance and the power that comes from multiracial unity. However, adultist mainstream media coverage of Portland student activism rarely spoke of student organizing in political terms, or even in terms of collective student anger as resistance. To recognize student anger, dissent, or political frameworks would have required the media to reconceptualize teens as highly cognitive, critical, reflective, and legitimate political beings—conceptions not in line with dominant images of youth.

Instead, mainstream media coverage of proeducation actions often infantilized and depoliticized SRU student organizing. Implicitly attributing SRU actions to more childish emotional responses to school budget crises rather than to social outrage and/or political critique, the mainstream media constructed white, middle-class youth in terms that reproduced the image of them as innocents for the adult public.[5]

SRU students spoke openly in meetings about their distorted images in the mainstream media but ultimately agreed on the dictum that "any media coverage is good media coverage" in that it meant public visibility, even if distorted. Aware of mainstream media distortion, SRU organizers purposefully kept symbols of student anger and radicalism, symbolized by the SRU insignia, out of the view of mainstream media, particularly during proeducation rallies and actions. In this sense, they depended on media images of infantilized, youthful innocence to influence adult voters. There were key moments, however, when SRU youth projected more complicated messages to persuade adults to vote on tax increases for education. These messages both played upon adults' sympathies for childhood innocence and their fears of adolescents "taking over" public spaces.

Proeducation Activism: SRU's "Threat" of Youth Takeover

> Because all these kids come together and do it, and just, like, take over city hall and take over the Capitol building in Salem, just proves that something is really messed up in the way the country is moving. It just says the country is so messed up that even the kids are walking out of school. Like, that is really messed up; like, that really sends a message to someone. Like these kids are so angry that they are taking over a building, and they are taking over the city at night; they are *taking over.*

In this quote, SRU activist Pete cast youth occupation of adult public and civic spaces as a simultaneously empowering and pathological action. Even as young people's occupation of public spaces empowers youth activists, Pete inferred that the adult public might (and should) interpret this occupation as an undeniable expression of youth dissatisfaction and a symptom that the world is terribly out of balance. Although SRU students believed that their childhood innocence could be an effective tool in persuading adults to vote on their behalf, they found it even more powerful to combine these projections of innocence with the simultaneous threat of teen takeover. As Spencer Cahill argues, "the very presence of groups of preadolescents or adolescents in a public place is apparently considered a potential threat to public order" (1990, 398). Gill Valentine (1996) asserts that two contradictory concerns about youth work together to produce public space as adult space: that children are susceptible to stranger danger in public spaces and should therefore be kept safely in the home and that teenagers are threats to public order and should therefore be kept out of public spaces. SRU activists were well aware of this double perception of youth and conceptualized public spaces to be adult spheres rather than their own. Their occupations of these spaces were deliberate attempts to tap into adults' panic about youth taking over. Their aim, especially with the proeducation activism that took place in the streets or at the State Capitol, was to alarm adult publics into taking political action on their behalf. This conscious attempt to tap into adults' fear of youth was evidenced in the SRU student walkouts against education cuts. During their unpermitted march through Portland's downtown streets, SRU organizers shouted for more monies for school funding, while holding a huge banner meant specifically for an adult public: "Keep Kids Like Us Off the Streets!" In this sense, their physical occupation was the political message, carrying the implicit threat that if adults did not take action to fund schools, they would bear the brunt of their worst fears about youth.

Some proeducation SRU actions skillfully threaded childhood images of playfulness into these threatening takeovers. On a cold, wintry day, nearly a hundred SRU students from all over Portland gathered on the Capitol steps and played guitars, recited poems, and gave speeches to a crowd of parents, teachers, and local media reporters about the injustice of their school crises and the importance of education. Joni, a Rose Valley High senior and a powerful SRU speaker, got on a bullhorn and announced to the crowd that they would be moving the rally inside the Capitol to demand that legislators hear the students. The protesting students and a handful of adult supporters filed into the Capitol building, and police immediately ordered the crowd to leave all our signs outside. We stacked our signs on the Capitol steps, and then inside students linked arms in a huge circle, chanting, "What do we want? An education! When do we want it? Now!" They danced and skipped. Someone brought a soccer ball and the youth kicked the ball back and forth, still spinning and chanting, until students made enough noise to disrupt meetings and draw a crowd of legislators to safely watch the spectacle from the balcony above. After a half-hour, the police ordered us out of the Capitol. Students lingered until they were warned a second and third time, and then they finally finished their rally outside on the steps.

SRU activist Michelle identified the rally at the State Capitol as her most empowering moment as a youth organizer:

> I thought it was awesome; I really loved the energy. Because it was kind of mellow outside, but when we got inside [the Capitol build-ing], everything just exploded. Because we were invading someone else's space, and our sounds were echoing off the walls. We were playing and stamping and clapping and running in a big circle, and we were linking arms. And they couldn't really do much about it, which was great! Because people don't realize, we have the power; people are trying to take it away from us everyday. And just for kids to unite and do something like that together, it was just awesome!

High school students brought a youthful sense of play and fun into the State Capitol: a space that Michelle identified as "someone else's" space. For these activists, the combination of childlike playfulness and youth takeover merged into an empowering SRU-style disruption of the public order. Yet from the perspective of the adult gaze, the threat of this takeover was neutralized by two interrelated messages that reinforced childhood innocence: SRU students' focus on saving their schools—a message easily depoliticized for an adult public—and their projected images of childhood play: skipping, dancing, and kickball. Although transgressive, an action like this did not garner the same kind of negative media attention that SRU antiwar activism garnered. As SRU activists took their social justice activism into the larger antiwar movement brewing in the streets of Portland, media coverage and adult reception of their political messages began to turn.

Antiwar Activism: "Violent" and "Corrupted" Youth

SRU activists saw no discontinuity between their antiwar/anti-imperialist critiques and their proeducation values. However, they found that they had to sever their antiwar critiques from their proeducation messages to attract mainstream media and influence adult voters. Sara lamented, "I feel like sometimes we have to manipulate what our groups do to get the media coverage that we want. Like, we would rather be doing a different, separate action, but we need good media coverage. So we go to a lesser extent than we would. You know, we just can't support everything that we believe in, because we need the support of our schools and parents, and things like that." However, when aligning with the antiwar movement and a community of young adult radical activists, SRU was more overt in making the connection between schooling and war. Managing these multiple images— and especially the image of innocent, depoliticized, happy kids feeling sad about education cuts—became problematic as SRU students tried to make a visible student showing at antiwar protests.

The centrality of mainstream media to student visibility and the crisis this posed for SRU activists came to a head on the day of bombing in March 2003: during an event that SRU activists would later refer to as "the incident on the bridge." Students in Portland led unpermitted school walkouts (as did YP organizers in the East Bay) and gathered with other protesters downtown. At first, students gathered with SRU banners and marched in the streets with thousands of other people. Then, some students with SRU banners joined activists who were occupying one of Portland's bridges, trying to use civil disobedience to block traffic and shut the city down, as activists were doing in the streets of San Francisco and elsewhere in the United States. SRU students soon found themselves holding their "Students Rise Up" banner while standing face to face with a line of police in riot gear on the bridge. As protestors refused to leave the bridge, the police began to push protesters back, using police batons and pepper-spray on protesters to clear the crowd and restore the flow of traffic. After this face-off with police, SRU students, their faces swollen red and eyes tearing from the pepper-spray, ran from the bridge and rejoined the larger antiwar march downtown.

This confrontation between activists and police on the bridge, with SRU students at the forefront, became a focus of debates on protest tactics and police misconduct in mainstream media coverage of antiwar protests. Mainstream media outlets were quick to label the protestors on the bridge as "violent."[6] Central to these images of protestor violence were images of SRU students using their banner to push against the police and to shield themselves from police with batons and pepper-spray. This helped to fuel the image of SRU antiwar student activism as confrontational and even destructive, and parents, teachers, administrations, and even other students began to denounce SRU for its antiwar activism. It should be noted that while negative media coverage of antiwar activism gave rise to a new image of high school antiwar activism as confrontational and destructive, some media coverage still managed to preserve the image of youth as innocent. One media piece reported, "While the vast majority of protesters remain peaceful and nonviolent, a rumor circulating among Portland lefties has it that a small group of extremists has been recruiting impressionable teenagers to fight the police." Some SRU activists were outraged by this piece and identified this coverage to be especially ageist, as it effaced them as political agents. However, this coverage preserved the dominant image of white youth as innocent, as it implied that teenagers were simply objects of corruption and victims of older activists' influence. In this sense, it was in-line with the media coverage of SRU proeducation activism, as this coverage too relied on assumptions of youth innocence.

The turn of adult support for SRU activism, spurred by negative media coverage of antiwar activism in general, produced a crisis within SRU itself. At a pivotal meeting following a series of antiwar protests in Portland, SRU students engaged in intense debate over whether or not to keep antiwar activism and proeducation activism separate. For Vista High students who were facing the loss of support from Mr. Mesner and their formerly cooperative principal (both key to facilitating successful student organizing within Vista High), radical antiwar activism proved to be risky to student organizing efforts to promote funding for education. Vista High girls in particular argued that SRU should separate its antiwar and education activism. Amanda suggested formally severing SRU from antiwar direct action:

> I don't know if SRU should be officially involved in direct action. I think it would be safer for a lot of people if they weren't connected to a specific group. So that way it wouldn't be able to carry any consequences back to the larger group. And so SRU members could form affinity groups and individually go out and take direct action. They could do that, and have their presence made in their affinity groups.
>
> It would help the image of SRU better, and it would still be the kids from SRU, but it wouldn't be that media subtitle "SRU kids." It would just be as students, as people. That way we can have something that is media-presentable, you know, nonviolent, not scary. Something people would be willing to support.

Troy and other SRU organizers with ties to older, radical activists vehemently disagreed with this proposal. Troy argued,

> I think that as a social justice group and fighting for those issues, means fighting against war. That's just how it goes. Killing people, for the sake of killing people, for whatever reason, is just plain wrong. So as a social justice group I think we should be able to oppose war pretty actively.
>
> So we went to a protest that turned violent. Well, how do you know from the start that a protest is ever going to be violent? How do you know when the police are going to riot? You just don't. And I'm all for protecting yourself. You know, if police actively hit my

friend in the head with a baton, I'm going to shield the baton. That's just a common sense kind of thing to do. How could we regulate any of that?

This kind of debate went on for another hour and branched into conflicts over direct action tactics and the differential access to adult radical activist affinity groups among SRU boys versus SRU girls. This debate also revealed SRU students' struggle to manage their image to multiple adult publics (i.e., young adult radical activists on one hand and parents/teachers/mainstream voters on the other). Alana and Amanda, both exasperated, argued that SRU boys were being "elitist" because of their insistence on aligning SRU with adult radical activist groups at the cost of alienating a broader base of high school students (many of whom had few to no connections to young adult radical movements) and a broader base of adult support. This issue was left unresolved, and this would be the last SRU meeting that Alana, Amanda, and several other girls would attend.

Within the larger context of negative media coverage of antiwar protest in general, SRU's double nature as a proeducation and antiwar movement became difficult for student activists to reconcile. This difficulty was exacerbated by SRU's dependence on mainstream media and on more general images of youthful innocence to elicit an adult response to education budget crises. SRU's antiwar activism threatened this image of youth innocence and thus delegitimized student organizing. The price paid by SRU members for their visibility through mainstream media proved to be costly, because this visibility hinged on an infantilized vision of youth innocence. Ultimately, SRU students' dependence on mainstream media as an interface to a larger adult voting public limited their abilities to combine their education values and their anti-imperialist values into a public, cohesive social justice movement.

SRU Invisibility and YP Hypervisibility

While white, middle-class activist youth traded their usual social invisibility for distorted visibility, urban youth of color in the East Bay did not speak of the same social invisibility. In fact, they perceived themselves to be hypervisible in images put forward by the mainstream media. YP student organizer Tevin remarked, "The images in movies and news and stuff is that youth of color are all drug dealers, lowlifes, not wanting a good future, not having an outlook." After my interview with student organizer Jazmin, she told me proudly that she was off to go make a statement for a local news channel about the campaigns that YP was working on. She was looking forward to this opportunity. "We're bombarded with so much negative news, and they hide so much of the good stuff. They especially portray the youth of color as negative people. And you never find out what are the good things that they are doing. So, by going out to this station and giving them a story to pitch where youth are doing something positive, doing something good, then people can see that, you know? Then we can get more support from the people." After our interview, Javier, a YP adult ally, drove up and Jazmin and I piled into the back of his car. In the front seat was another YP student organizer, Anita, who would also make a statement on the news with Jazmin. Javier braced himself and explained to Jazmin that he was just coached by a woman from the station on how to frame YP's message. The station representative told Javier that the students should communicate something to the effect of "no one will help the youth of color, so we are going to help ourselves." This "pull ourselves up by our bootstraps" message was not the message that Jazmin and Anita wanted to communicate to the public. They wanted to use this media moment as an opportunity to talk about interracial conflict, poverty, school budget cuts, and how YP was trying to unite and empower students of color under these conditions. Jazmin grew quiet and upset. Javier, looking at her through the rearview mirror, tried to turn this into a lesson about the media: "I know this isn't the way you would choose to frame it. But this is a good opportunity to look at how the media works, and how you have to frame your message in certain ways in order to get it out there."

According to YP participants, mainstream media coverage of YP activity has been, for the most part, favorable—although sparse. In Oakland, corporate media was not looked on by YP as a voice for youth. In fact, YP as an organization took pains to deliberately keep mainstream media out of YP activities that specifically addressed issues of violence on school grounds. As one YP adult ally explained, this is when the mainstream media has tended to reinforce stereotypes of urban youth of color as criminal and violent. In one 2004 news story about a shooting at an Oakland high school, a city council member was quoted as saying, "It's just depressing. I don't know what we can do to get through to these kids. I'm tired of seeing African Americans and Latinos dying in the streets. They have no sense of value for human life." In this context then, youth of color neither relied on presumptions of their childlike innocence, nor did they experiment with scaring adult publics—because their threat of takeover would have been futile. These youth were already perceived as a danger to the public order, so there was not much hope that adult political action on young people's behalf could be prompted by the desire to prevent the threat from actually materializing.

Because YP youth depended on YP adult allies as the main interface to an adult public, they depended much less on mainstream media to communicate their messages. In fact, as a geographical center of youth organizing, Oakland has an unusual and impressive array of alternative youth media outlets specifically designed by and for youth of color, so YP youth had access to these outlets as well. Importantly, YP youth of color did not see the mainstream media as a way to become visible to the adult public because the problem, at its core, was not their invisibility. On a hot summer day in July, I witnessed a YP moment that exemplified the politics of YP youth hypervisibility. YP student organizers and new YP freshmen initiates converged from across the East Bay at the University of California at Berkeley. After a week-long intensive training on organizing tactics, social movements, and ethnic studies, YP student organizers decided to introduce one hundred new YP initiates to the power of protest. We all filed out of our meeting room on campus into a spontaneous march through the UC Berkeley campus. YP student organizers led younger students in chants such as "We are the students! The mighty, mighty students! Fighting for our rights! And equal education!"

Just two minutes into the march appeared two police officers on bicycles cautiously eyeing the mass of high school students and murmuring into their walkie-talkies. We found a grassy place on campus to sit down, right near where Mario Savio, the student leader of the free speech movement, made his fiery speeches in the 1960s. Our tension was palpable, as several of us looked at the police staring at us and wondered if they would order the group to leave. Even with that tension, new YP freshmen took turns getting up in front of the crowd and spoke to us, reciting love poetry, angry speeches, and wishes for their futures. Two middle-aged, white men walked by and stopped to gaze at the students. One took out his camera and began clicking away. YP youth organizer Mashid stood up and shouted at him: "Hey! What are you doing? We're not animals in a zoo, you know!" Embarrassed, the man put down his camera and walked away.

Unlike white, middle-class students like Hayden, youth of color are not frantically waving their arms shouting, "Hey! We're over here!" They are already hypervisible in prevailing images in the mainstream media, which depict them as criminal, degenerate, predatory, and violent. Thus, securing mainstream media attention did not become a central YP strategy in advancing the goals of student movements. Students of color must navigate a mainstream adult gaze in ways that challenge their hypervisibility as objectified and caricatured images of violence, degeneracy, and danger. Sometimes this means keeping student organizing away from the media's glare.

Conclusion

Mainstream media coverage of youth movements (or the lack thereof) reveals the ways in which the politics of invisibility and hypervisibility limit youth agency and the legitimacy of political personhood. Media emerges as a major institution that constructs youth—along racial and class lines—as citizens-in-the-making, rather than as actualized agents of social change. It is an institution that portrays youth alternately as innocent, infantilized children or as menaces to public order.

In the case of SRU activism, corporate media visibility was voice. Without rights to electoral political participation, SRU youth aimed to manipulate adult spectators into exercising adult political agency on the behalf of young people. More than this, however, was the collective empowerment that SRU youth experienced when they saw themselves reflected in the media. As SRU organizer Tory explained, "When the media pays attention to us, we feel all mighty and strong." Like many new social movements rooted in middle-class constituencies, social movement actions are often theatrical and transgressive. They are geared toward changing or disrupting diffuse social perceptions, processes of normalization, and cultural power rather than aimed specifically at state power. The media-as-audience is central to this process (see Gamson 1989). However, young people's use of the media was only as beneficial as the extent to which they could sync their messages with, and actually reinforce, widespread adult beliefs about white, middle-class youth. To resonate with adult sensibilities surrounding youth and childhood innocence, they deliberately kept images of youth radicalism and student outrage out of their proeducation public actions. They also tapped into adults' fear of youth and played on their suspicions that, if not properly socialized and guided, teens might take over adult public spaces. At times, SRU youth subtly threatened adult audiences if they failed to take swift action to ensure young people's proper place: in the schools and *not* in the streets.

Trapped by the limitations of the adult gaze, SRU youth found that the distorted, depoliticized media coverage of their proeducation activism was incompatible with their angry antiwar and anti-imperialist message. Even though SRU activists considered a proeducation and antiwar agenda as two intertwined threads of the same vision for social justice, the adult public viewed student activism as much more threatening when it became explicitly antiwar. Josh explained it like this:

> Our message, it's so sad to say, but people viewed it as this liberal kind of message: school and education and stuff like that. But a lot of us consider it really radical thinking to educate people. . . . But it's the *image* of kids fighting for their education; it's a good thing. People can feel warm about that inside. But media coverage started to turn. It turned the public eye from kids fighting for their education to kids fighting against imperialism. Which means fighting against patriotism, you know? I guess that doesn't make people feel so warm inside.

Mainstream media was largely unable to portray SRU youth activists outside of dominant conceptions typical of white, middle-class youth. Comfortable with reducing youth political critique to happy and sad childish emotions but uncomfortable with youth outrage, the corporate media ultimately demonized and pathologized youth political critique when it became explicit, unpatriotic, and confrontational. With the stakes too high, some SRU activists felt they could not sacrifice the favorable media coverage they had previously received. As the corporate media and many parents and teachers began to withdraw their support, some SRU activists felt compelled to separate their proeducation and antiwar activism. It was their overreliance on mainstream media coverage, and the larger problematics of distorted social visibility for white, middle-class youth, which began to fracture the SRU youth network.

Meanwhile, the dominant conceptions typical of working-class and poor black and brown youth made the prospect of relying on the corporate media, for YP, unrealistic and unhelpful. Always seeing grossly distorted and frustrating reflections of themselves in the media and in the adult gaze more generally, YP activists ultimately found little redeeming value in mainstream media coverage. While SRU students strived for media visibility, even if distorted, YP students, at times, worked to keep corporate media away from their politics to lessen the harm done by the media's constant hypervisibility of youth of color. Both strategies, although at times problematic and limited, have been essential in building student movements and transforming young people from citizens-in-the-making into agents of social and political change.

6

Gendering Political Power

Gender Politics in Youth Activist Networks

By the early summer of 2003, the SRU network had begun to fracture because of internal struggles over how to project the groups' aims, identity, and political visions to multiple adult publics. This struggle was due in large part to these young activists' overreliance on mainstream media, whose contours refused to recognize their political outrage or their critique of U.S. foreign policy as anything but pathological and corrupted. After the early street protests in Portland and the "incident on the bridge" during the tumultuous Day of Bombing, SRU activists found themselves split between two sides of a seemingly irreconcilable dilemma: do they proceed to openly engage in antiwar activism and risk losing the adult support of parents and teachers? Or do they sever their antiwar activism from their proeducation activism and compromise their vision for social justice and their collective identity as radical youth?

SRU activists were split on either side of this dilemma, and it was not accidental that the dividing line was a gendered one. Boys were overwhelmingly in favor of openly engaging in antiwar activism as the same SRU network that had previously rallied for education funding at the State Capitol. Girls proposed that SRU students salvage whatever parental and teacher support that they could, hiding their more radical orientation from this adult public and establishing their antiwar activism as both covert and secondary to the network's overt educational activism. This fracture in SRU revealed more than just the problems of distorted social visibility and the adult gaze. The split also signified the culmination of deeper gender politics that slowly manifested within the organization: politics that were not discussed openly between boy and girl SRU activists, politics that quietly and privately stemmed from their different positions in family life, politics that were not even interpreted as *gendered* but nevertheless were powerful enough to tear the group apart.

Boys and girls are situated differently within institutions such as schools (Orenstein 1994; Thorne 1993) and families (Taylor et al. 1995; Weitzman et al. 1985). The gender split in SRU stands as evidence that young people's orientation to civic and political organizations in their communities, and their participation within civil society more generally, are also profoundly affected by gender. Without a consideration of how gender affects teenage political participation, gender-neutral strategies to engage youth in social justice campaigns will fail by overlooking the particular ways in which girls' and boys' possibilities to emerge as public, political actors are strongly tied to their different positions in their families, schools, and other institutions.

The revelation that gender shapes social movement participation is by no means a new one. Gender inequality can channel women away from leadership roles and into more informal positions within social movements. Gender can shape the informal and formal social networks that serve as bases for movement mobilization. Women's roles as caretakers, mothers, and community members profoundly shape their activist commitments in ways that are both empowering and problematic.[1] Although many studies have revealed the ways in which gender structures social movements—especially women's participation—almost all of these studies focus exclusively on adult women's activism. The question remains: do the same gendered forces that shape women's political participation also explain the struggles that teenage girls face as they try to transform from citizens-in-the-making into actual political forces?

What is missing from many of these gendered analyses of women's activism is the key issue of spatial and civic mobility: the basic but essential ability of an activist to access public spaces, insurgencies, and conversations about political issues. Being a social movement participant requires that one attends community meetings, participates in protests and demonstrations, and forms alliances with allied activists, among many other activities. There is a fundamentally *public* character to these social movement activities and a requisite mobility needed to engage in them.[2] It is worth considering that young people, as a demographic, are spatially constrained in ways that differ from adults, and thus face age-related obstacles to participating in political and public life.[3] It is this key issue of spatial and civic mobility, and the barriers to this mobility faced by young people, that render teenage girls' struggles with activism qualitatively different from women's struggles.[4] While youth movements help to facilitate girls' participation in a mostly adult-dominated sphere of community politics, youth protest groups, like all protest groups, are also structured by gender politics (Taylor 1999). YP and SRU boys' and girls' experiences demonstrate that the gender politics of youth protest groups can both stem from and become exacerbated by teens' gendered relationships to parental power.

Gender, Parental Power, and Youth Civic Mobility

In the wake of the student movements of the 1950s and 1960s, scholars have tried to understand the impetus behind youth activism by focusing on the relationships between young activists and their parents. These scholars have debated whether or not youth activism can be read as "youth rebellion" against parents and previous generations. Although Erik Erikson (1968) and Lewis Feuer (1969) make this argument, other scholars, such as Richard Flacks (1971) and Kenneth Keniston (1968, 1971), argue that young people's political participation is actually an expression and continuation of their parents' political sensibilities. Indeed, more recent literature also supports this assessment (Watts and Guessous 2006) and argues that parents play a central role in encouraging their kids to become civic-minded and even politically active.

When examined through a gender lens, however, this key relationship between parents and youth activists proves to be a much more complex phenomenon than either the older or newer literature would suggest. Because many of these studies generalize from boys' or young men's experiences, or neglect to consider gender as a significant variable in parent-child relationships, the salient issue of spatial mobility, as it is negotiated between parents and youth, is often left out of the analysis. Some key questions remain: Which youth activists have the requisite mobility to engage in public demonstrations, public debates, and social movement networks? What kind of mobility is necessary for teens to become community organizers and social movement leaders? What role do parents play in determining this mobility? And also of importance, how do racial, class, and ethnic contexts combine with gender in ways that structure parent-child relationships and young activists' mobility? Of course, parents can be, and often are, key supporters of both boys' and girls' political development. SRU and YP activists shared with me story after story about how central their parents were in shaping their political outlook on the world. Take for example YP organizer Gayle, who viewed her political roots as an almost biological given:

> Organizing is actually something that runs in my family. My father, he is a public defender. . . . He has always been the type of person to help out the smaller people and try to group up. And he always taught me that power is in the masses. That is something I have always known.

A gender lens complicates this picture, however, by allowing us to recognize why both YP and SRU girls in particular, even those like Gayle, could share stories like these while still perceiving their parents to be significant barriers to their activism in the public sphere.

One factor that can help to explain this is the gendered expectations that parents hold of their kids. Parents often expect a measure of independence and even defiance from their sons that they do not expect from their daughters. Indeed, parenting patterns can promote boys' independence and autonomy and girls' interdependence, dependence, and/or passivity.[5] However, gendered parenting patterns are also profoundly shaped by socioeconomic and racial ethnic contexts (Hill and Sprague 1999) and cannot always be characterized as clear-cut forces that disempower girls. In communities of color, parents have been essential transmitters of ethnic and cultural identity, enabling children to develop ideologies that resist oppression. In black communities, black women in particular have been central to this transmission and have long provided a "private sphere in which cultures of resistance and everyday forms of resistance are learned" (Collins 1990, 51). Furthermore, girls are not always the main objects of parental worry: given the high incidence of racial profiling and police harassment of young black men, single black mothers express a particular concern for their sons' safety (Ward 2000).

Race, gender, and class together shape parental worry and strategies of caretaking and control (Kurz 2002) in various ways that inevitably affect young people's mobility and participation in civic life. Annette Lareau (2002), for example, notes that social class in particular creates distinctive parenting styles, as evidenced in her example of middle-class families who practice concerted cultivation by restricting their children's activity to participation in highly structured, adult-supervised, age-specific organizations. Intersecting dimensions of power such as race, class, and gender are also crosscut by ethnic cultural contexts and family type, producing a variety of parent-child interactions that have the power to shape young people's mobility as activists in very different ways.

Despite these many variations in parent-child interactions and in young people's mobility, Amy Best finds a marked difference—across socioeconomic and racial ethnic groups—in the parental restrictions placed on boys' and girls' spatial mobility: "Boys across cultural groups seemed to enjoy greater freedom and fewer restrictions when it came to driving and having cars. . . . This has significant consequences for how girls then move around public settings such as school, social events, shopping malls, and public streets as adolescents" (2006b, 73). The struggles that girls in this study encountered as they tried to become community organizers, especially in relation to their parents' opposition, worry, and control, stand as testaments to the consequences that Best describes. However, these consequences go beyond girls and boys moving about differently in public settings. Girls' constrained civic mobility, in the context of youth political development, also restricts their ability to break from the model of citizenship-in-the-making and become social movement participants, organizers, and leaders in the public sphere. Although parental boundary-setting around young people's mobility is not in and of itself an unfair exercise of power, and in many cases this boundary-setting undoubtedly constitutes good parenting and significant care work (Kurz 2002), these boundaries can nevertheless emerge as barriers to youth political action.

Parental constraint, however, is not a one-way street. As Best (2006b) and Demie Kurz (2002) argue, it is not simply parents' will that results in girls' limited mobility relative to boys: it is also girls' and boys' perceptions of and active struggles with parental constraints that determine their mobility as activists in the public sphere. While recognizing that parents' boundaries around young people's mobility can be gendered in themselves, and thus hold their own power to shape teenagers' forays into community activism, this chapter emphasizes YP and SRU teens' own negotiations with these boundaries as gendered forces that ultimately shape their relationships to each other, as well as determine the form and the extent of their political participation in larger community movements. This partially explains why struggles in SRU, such as the struggle over how to project their image to adult publics, became gendered struggles.

Gendered Strategies to Navigate Parental Opposition

Although many SRU and YP students cited parents as their original inspiration or influence on the development of their political leanings, parents were not always supportive of their children's activism. Student activists' narratives reveal that parental opposition to youth activism stemmed from a variety of concerns. However it became clear that parents' concerns over their children's activism, as well as student strategies to navigate these concerns, were deeply embedded in overlapping gender, race, ethnic, and class contexts. Students in both Oakland and Portland perceived that parental opposition stemmed mainly from three major concerns: children's physical safety, children's developing political ideologies, and the potential threat that student activism posed to children's roles and responsibilities in family life. Despite these various reasons for parental opposition to youth activism, the overall theme of parental opposition was much more pronounced in girls' narratives in both sites, as girls expressed more vexation over parents' opposition to their activism than did boys.

Parental Concerns over Physical Safety

When YP student organizer Shandra discussed barriers to activism, she identified her mother, a black, single parent, as the ultimate barrier: "You know, as long as I don't have no problems with my mom, everything is fine." Her mother's worries over what Shandra referred to as "little issues" included Shandra being out late in Oakland, not being able to reach Shandra by phone, and not having a car to pick up Shandra from organizing meetings. Shandra's mother's concern over these issues was particular to the conditions of single-parenting in a deindustrialized, racially segregated, and impoverished urban area. Parental worry generated within conditions of poverty and racial violence was certainly different from parental worry among middle-class whites in what is widely perceived as "livable" Portland. Issues such as not having a car to pick up one's child (as affordable public transportation is becoming more scarce) and worrying about children navigating especially dangerous and violent neighborhoods at night are windows into the racialized and classed, as well as gendered, components of parental worry over youth political organizing.

There was the occasional student in Oakland who joined YP but was then pulled out by concerned parents or grandparents who objected to their youth being involved in anything political at all. YP adult ally Yesenia discussed the context of political uprising in countries such as Nicaragua, El Salvador, and Guatemala, and how the experiences of older generations who emigrated from other nations can shape their perceptions of political organizing in the United States: "It's interesting in the Latino community because people come from very, like their countries of origin—the political turmoil, you know—like my friends, they feared for their lives. But over here, you can engage politically and not, thankfully at least up till now, you don't have to really fear for that." Nevertheless, for some parents political activism means risking violent reprisal from the state. For older adults who lived in Oakland during the turbulent 1960s and 1970s and witnessed violent police action against young activists of color, activism means facing off with police, which can spell trouble. For older generations of caretakers (such as grandparents) who help to raise the new generation of teens in Oakland, Oakland's activist past portends danger for politically active youth of color. This worry, coupled with the widespread perception among residents of Oakland that the city is already a dangerous place, means that in this particular deindustrialized and impoverished urban context, parents worry about their sons' physical safety as much as they worry about their daughters'.

Because white, middle-class SRU activists and many of their parents perceived Portland as largely safe and livable, parental concern over teen activists' safety was most pronounced around the unpredictability of direct action street protests. Thus, while Portland parents did not express a great degree of worry over the day-to-day demands of student activism, such as attending regular activist meetings, white, middle-class parental support for student activism waned as student protest became enmeshed in direct action antiwar protests in city streets.[6]

In the context of parental concerns over physical safety, YP adult allies were crucial facilitators of both boys' and girls' activism in Oakland, as they often provided safe transport of young activists to various organizing activities and events when YP teens needed it. Thus, the presence of adult allies mollified parents' worries over their children's whereabouts in particularly violent and impoverished neighborhoods.

Since their organizational structure was youth-only, SRU activists did not have these same adult allies to mediate their relationships to parents. Because of this, SRU girls in particular developed complex ways of negotiating and navigating parental worry, opposition, and constraint in order to become engaged activists and organizers in Portland politics. Portland girls often simply withheld information as a way of navigating their parents' worry over their physical safety during direct action protests. SRU boys, YP girls, and YP boys did not employ this same strategy.

A telling example was Zoe, a vivacious SRU activist who had described her parents as "very supportive" of her activism. In her interview with me, Zoe explained the importance of knowing one's own limits in street protests. She expressed an unusual kind of confidence in managing her relationship to her parents, one that was not echoed by other girls in this study. Her confidence was more akin to that expressed by many SRU and YP boys:

> If I get hurt, like bruises, and I feel like I don't want to run around, I will go home. I know what my limit is and I think everybody should. Because your parents generally have to put limits on you. But if you are adult enough to do it yourself, that really shows something to your family. And they'll start letting you grow up a little bit more, which is good. And if you don't tell them everything, that makes it more difficult 'cause then you have no trust from your parents and your parents might tighten the noose a little bit more.

However, Zoe qualified this sage advice by admitting how she herself with-held information from her parents to circumvent their worry and control:

> I've had to keep stuff secret from my parents though, actually.
> Like . . . I told them I was going to a protest; I don't tell them when
> I am going to be home. I don't tell them I am going to block free-
> ways. I don't tell them that I am going to sit down in the streets. I
> don't tell them I might get pepper-sprayed. . . . If I do get hurt I usu-
> ally don't tell them right there. . . . I usually tell them when I get
> home and after it's all over with, so that they won't tell me to come
> home right now.

Importantly, girls' strategies vis-à-vis their parents are not only reflections of their constraint. They are also ways of caring for their parents and main-taining familial harmony. As Best notes, "teenagers engage in significant family care work and, in doing so, support family well-being" (2006b, 79). While SRU girls spoke at length about their strategies to circumvent their parents' worry, control, and opposition to their activism, they also recog-nized their parents' opposition as legitimate—especially when it came to parental worry over their physical safety. As SRU activist Hayden explained, "Even adult activists don't have to deal with what we have to deal with: going back to their parents and talking about all this, 'cause a lot of parents may not be supportive with being involved in activism. And I think a big thing in SRU, like with the protests and stuff, parents are really concerned about the students and their safety. Which is totally justified."

Parental Concerns over Children's Political Ideologies

Some SRU teens discussed their parents' concern over their growing radi-calism. In the case of SRU Portland activism, parental concerns over their children's growing radicalism did not stem only from worries about physi-cal safety in radical street protests. These concerns also reflected worries over children's actual political ideologies and what these represented about the corruption of childhood innocence. While many parents expressed pleasure that their children longed to be more active in their communities and even wanted to save their own schools, they were not necessarily pleased when the motivation for young people's community action clearly stemmed from political outrage, sharp critique of U.S. foreign policy, or the kind of antiauthoritarian philosophy that has made Portland famous for being a hub for anarchism.

Parental support of SRU student activism was highest during rallies and student sit-ins for increased school funding. This parental support dovetailed with the local mainstream media coverage that depoliticized SRU students' educational activism by effacing their political critique of school budget cuts: portraying youth activists as sad about budget cuts rather than highlighting their political outrage. Later, local media coverage of antiwar protests portrayed SRU students as rogue troublemakers, corrupted by the influence of older radical activists. Some Portland parents expressed concern over their children being corrupted by angry, antiauthoritarian activists, a concern that carried assumptions of childhood innocence often accorded to white, middle-class youth but rarely to youth of color (see Ferguson 2001; Roberts 1997). In the following exchange, Suzanne and Myra, two SRU activists, discussed this parental concern over corruption, and the ways they navigated parental worry and opposition to their radicalism:

SUZANNE: I have to respect that they don't want me to go to a protest. It doesn't change my mind. My opinions are the same. It just means that I can't be there sometimes.

MYRA: For a while I didn't want other parents to think I was a radical kid trying to corrupt their kids. You just want to be sensitive to those issues.

SUZANNE: So it's hard to talk to parents. You have to hold it in. Negotiate. Keep calm.

Suzanne and Myra pointed to several strategies here: succumbing to parental opposition by withdrawing from protests, maintaining sensitivity to parents' worries over ideological corruption, and the strategy of "Hold it in. Negotiate. Keep calm." Suzanne emphasized that although parental worry had not changed her mind about important social issues, it meant that she could not always act on her beliefs. While drawing attention to the autonomy of her beliefs, the fact that Suzanne's actions were limited by her parents' dictates meant that her political and public voice and presence were compromised. This is striking, because Roderick Watts and Omar Guessous (2006) find that girls' political commitment (as distinct from behavior) is on average higher than boys' commitment. Succumbing to parental constraint means that although a teenage girl might have a political consciousness and commitment to a cause, she may be unable to engage with others in public dialogue, dissent, and action. In this example, the strategies of SRU girls to succumb to their parents' dictates and withdraw from street protests, as well as to maintain a sensitivity to issues of corruption, are shaped in a specific racial and class context where white, middle-class parental concerns around street protests read youth radicalism as a threat to both children's physical safety and children's innocence.

Of course, many girl organizers develop strategies to work around adult worry and authority, even if parental power seems absolute. Often, girl organizers who are constrained by their parents not only withhold information (as in the case of SRU activist Zoe); they also lie to their parents to get out into public arenas and act on their political and social beliefs. In the following exchange, SRU activists Sara and Kristin discussed how they both withheld information and lied to their parents about their political ideologies and the extent to which they were active in street protests:

SARA: I think the worst thing is my parents. 'Cause they always want me home at a specific time. And like, I got pepper-sprayed twice: once on Saturday and then the next Thursday. I got pepper-sprayed both times. And I had to look presentable in front of my parents when I came home.

KRISTIN: Did you not tell your parents?

SARA: No, I couldn't tell them. Because I told them I was at a candle vigil. So they have no idea of my true political views, because if they did, I wouldn't be allowed to go to the more radical things.

Although secrecy and lies allowed Sara and Kristin to protect their political ideologies and attend political meetings, protests, and rallies, maintaining secrets and lies came with a cost to their relationships with their parents. As SRU girl activists described strategies of withholding information and lying to parents, these girls also expressed dismay and worry about having to do this. Sara spoke at length about her parents' disapproval of her political views and lamented: "I wish I could tell my parents everything. If they would support me. But I really don't feel like listening to them lecture me. Because then it would be ongoing. But it would be nice if they would just be like, 'Oh, that's cool.' You know, I could tell them what I've been up to. I don't like lying to them." Although it buys them precious mobility, lying to parents presents a deep tension for youth organizers. It creates a wedge between youth and their parents, and stands as a lost opportunity to be taken seriously by parents as legitimate political beings. It also reminds them that despite their own conviction that they are fully capable of participating in community politics on par with adults, they are still considered children within their families.

When both YP and SRU boys talked about parental worry and control, they did not speak of such nuanced strategies, nor did they speak overtly about the angst they had in navigating their parents' opposition to their activism. Boys expressed much more confidence in dealing with parental power than did girls and also tended to see parental power as less absolute and more manageable. For example, YP organizer Salvador echoed a determination consistent throughout boys' narratives in both sites and discussed how his parents had to come to terms with his political ideology and his political action (rather than the other way around). With a brother in the military and stationed in Iraq, Salvador's parents gave him a lecture about the importance of supporting the troops instead of protesting the war in Iraq. Even though Salvador had heard his father express criticism of the Bush administration when his older brother went off to Iraq, his parents still opposed Salvador's antiwar activism. This opposition to Salvador's antiwar ideology may have come from a specific racial, ethnic, and class context that differed from that of white, middle-class families in Portland, who were not as likely to see their children recruited into the military and serve in Iraq. In fact, while virtually no SRU activists had siblings stationed in Iraq, nor did they have permanent military recruitment programs instituted in their schools, YP activists had family members and friends who viewed military service as a much more realistic post–high school track than college. They had thriving ROTC programs in their crumbling schools. Salvador's antiwar ideology could have threatened to delegitimize his parents' patriotism: in a larger context of heightened anti-immigrant sentiment, their patriotism—and social inclusion more generally— might have already been suspect simply because of their immigrant status. Despite the gravity of these concerns, Salvador perceived them to be of minimal consequence: "My mom and my family, they don't really support my activism, but they let me do it. It's like, 'We don't support it, but we really can't stop you. You're still gonna end up going and doing it.'" In Salvador's experience, parental opposition neither resulted in family disharmony nor the curtailing of his political activity.

Parental Concerns over Children's Roles in Family Life

While Salvador perceived his parents' opposition to his activism to be a minor issue, YP student organizer Pilar, a teenage girl from a Mexican immigrant family, told me "family is really one of the hardest things about being a youth organizer." Pilar explained her difficulties in balancing her organizing work and time with her family. For her, parental control and worry arose from an overlapping matrix of gender and ethnicity, and she perceived her father's authority in the specific context of Latino family norms: "And especially in Latin culture, family time is really important, and also families can be really sexist. Like, my father . . . what he says, goes. My family is very, very strict and very family oriented, so that's why I couldn't come to the retreat last weekend. That's why I'm not allowed to do a lot of things after a certain hour, because my family wants me home."

Indeed, when YP and SRU boys talked about the moments when parental opposition posed an obstacle to student organizing, they talked specifically about girl activists and their parents, rather than about their own experiences. SRU activist Jacob spoke of his frustration with parental power, and indeed adult power, in gendered terms. He explained, "I think a lot of times nowadays you have parents who are really, like, who really annoy me. It's like, 'let your daughter grow up!' But I don't know; it's just possible that's my personal bias against parents, and teachers, and all sorts of people like that."

While SRU activist Suzanne advocated a nonconfrontational strategy to navigate parental control: "Hold it in. Negotiate. Keep calm," SRU activist Jacob's advice was markedly different:

> Never negotiate with your parents at all. I don't think kids should ever negotiate with their parents. I think that is going to actually result in one of the worst relationships ever. . . . If your parents are being ridiculous you shouldn't have to jump through hoops to have

to deal with them. You should try to educate them. I mean, this is a problem with a lot of kids' parents. They don't like SRU, and I just tell those kids, "Don't negotiate with your parents." It doesn't work for every individual, but ... the individual needs to choose and know what the boundaries are.

Here, Jacob expressed a highly individualistic kind of agency, one very different from that of the SRU and YP girls in this study. In some ways, this individualistic agency, pronounced by white, middle-class boys like Jacob, even differed from the agency expressed by YP boys, who did not as explicitly talk about themselves, or their fellow activists, as abstract individuals simply making choices suspended from their familial contexts. For YP organizers, there was a clearer understanding that their activism, although geared toward empowering youth, was one piece of a larger social justice vision for their families and wider communities. In comparison, SRU activists did not necessarily conceptualize youth power as integral to advancing social justice for their families or their entire community in Portland—members of which were overwhelmingly white and middle class. Because of this, it was easier for SRU boys in particular to view their activism in terms of individual autonomy and individual rights. Jacob's vision of individualistic agency resonates with a larger Western liberal individualist discourse that renders specifically male (Acker 1990) and Euro-white experiences as bodiless, abstract, and "universal." This meant that SRU boys tended to view not only their own, but also girls,' activism as a reflection of their individual choices rather than of larger gendered forces. At its core, SRU boys' individualism was also an assertion of autonomy, a masculine construct and central feature of masculine identity. Because parental opposition was perceived as much more manageable and less absolute for SRU boys like Jacob, there was less of a disjuncture in their activist lives between their political consciousness and public participation in social movements.

Because white, middle-class SRU girls did not have access to adult allies who could facilitate their role in community social movement activities, their struggles with their parents became more visible to SRU boys than did YP girls' familial struggles in YP politics. Instead of recognizing girls' struggles with parents as a reflection of their gendered positions in

family life, some SRU boys like Stephen viewed these struggles as indica-
tors of girls' weaker commitment to political action:

> I don't know if they [parents] have whole power over you. This
> might sound sad, but your parents will learn that, especially if it's
> important to you, you're going to do it. And if they have enough
> authority over you, they can tell you not to do that and you don't do
> it. Then it obviously isn't that important to you, 'cause you don't
> have the guts to say, "Whatever, I'm going to do it anyway because
> it's that important."

In Stephen's view, real, committed, and authentic political activity is
defined according to masculine values of confrontational and uncompro-
mising action. As Angela McRobbie and Jenny Garber (1975) argue, it
is precisely this kind of masculine, public, confrontational, and more
"spectacular" activity that has come to define youth subcultures in media
and researcher accounts, effectively rendering girls' participation in
subcultures invisible. For the SRU girls in this study, openly defying
parents in this confrontational way was too risky; thus, they preferred to lie
or withhold information rather than cause family disharmony and risk
punishment. For these girls, lying and withholding information became
a kind of family care work that they performed. However, their strategies
to maintain familial harmony went unrecognized by boys, and even by
girls themselves, as family care work. Because girls tended to perceive their
own negotiations with parental power as struggles rather than as care
work, they could not turn their positions of family caretaking into positions of political power—as many adult women activists have done with
motherhood.[7]

The reasons for parental worry over, or opposition to, student activism
stem from specific intersections of race, ethnicity, class, and gender.
Student strategies to negotiate this worry and opposition are also structured along these same intersecting dimensions. However, there is also a
clear gendered pattern in student conceptions of parental power across
racial, ethnic, and class groups. As evidenced in these accounts, parental
worry, opposition, and control were central themes in narratives from
Shandra, Zoe, Suzanne, Myra, Sara, Kristin, and Pilar about difficulties in
their organizing work. The tension between maintaining familial harmony

and engaging in public activism was much more pronounced in girls' lives in both sites.

In Portland, SRU boys' relative familial independence allowed them the mobility to forge fledgling alliances with adult radical activist groups in their communities. These boys enjoyed even more spatial and civic mobility than did YP boys, who still had to contend with parental worry over their physical safety in navigating Oakland city spaces on a daily basis. SRU boys were more able than SRU girls to attend adult activists' meetings and actions, many of which took place at night. Meanwhile, SRU girls rarely attended these meetings and relied on updates and reports from boys in weekly SRU meetings. Often, these girls did not even know the exact names of these adult organizations, nor what their acronyms stood for. This differential access to adult allies in the community (access shaped by girls' and boys' different relationships to parental worry and constraint) became a powerful source of gendered conflict between boy and girl activists in SRU. This conflict erupted after the mainstream media captured the confrontation between SRU students and the police during "the incident on the bridge."

The "Incident on the Bridge" Revisited: The Retreat of SRU Girls from Community Activism

As described in the last chapter, the turn of adult support for SRU activism—spurred by negative media coverage of antiwar direct action in general and the incident on the bridge in particular—produced a gendered crisis within SRU itself. At the pivotal meeting when SRU students engaged in intense debate over whether or not to keep antiwar activism and proeducation activism separate, it became clear that boys and girls held different stakes in the struggle. For girls who were facing the loss of support from their parents and teachers, radical antiwar activism put organizing efforts to promote funding for education at risk. More concerned about the withdrawal of this support, SRU girls argued that SRU should separate its antiwar and proeducation activism. At the meeting, Amanda suggested formally severing SRU from antiwar direct action. She proposed the creation of two student activist groups: one officially called SRU that advocated for school funding, and a direct action version of the group, sans the SRU title, which would enable SRU youth to take direct action in street protests without incurring adult backlash against SRU. Troy and other SRU boys with stronger ties to older activists vehemently disagreed with this proposal. Not coincidentally, girls' and boys' proposed organizational strategies mirrored their own personal strategies to navigate parental power. Girls proposed complex organizational permutations designed to both facilitate their activism in the public sphere and maintain harmonious relationships to important adults in their lives. Boys counterproposed a defiant and straightforward organizational structure, one consistent with their political ideologies and less responsive to shifts in adult support.

Feeling alienated and angry, Alana and Amanda called the boys "elitist," because they perceived the boys to be abandoning the many high school students who would like to participate in SRU, but who have few or no connections to adult radical organizations and who could not afford the luxury of alienating supportive parents and teachers. These SRU girls never once mentioned gender, sexism, or male domination in their charges against boys during this meeting. As Verta Taylor (1999) and Elaine Brown (1992) have demonstrated, gender has the power to shape the trajectory of movement groups, even if these groups do not explicitly wrestle with the language of gender. In this instance, the girls' language of "elitism" veiled underlying gender tensions that threatened to dismantle the group.

In later interviews, girls explicitly discussed the male dominance in SRU. As Alana bitterly declared after the split: "SRU was started by white, middle-class boys and now it's led by white, middle-class boys." The contingent of girls who left SRU still had activist clubs at their schools and opted to withdraw from larger community politics to focus their energies on school-based activism. While important, this school-based activism took place in after-school meetings and on school grounds, away from the vibrant political life of the Portland streets and adult activist networks that helped to shape collective and public dissent against the war. A few girls without opportunities for activism at their schools either left SRU and largely dropped out of political life, or stayed in the male-dominated SRU and battled for space in the best way they could. The gendered split in SRU sparked by the incident on the bridge revealed to SRU girls the disparity between boys' and girls' mobility, familial autonomy, and their potential to participate on equal footing in adult-dominated community politics.

Adult Allies in YP: Mediating Parental Opposition, Interrupting Sexism

In the preceding section, I have demonstrated how gendered differences in experiences, perceptions, and negotiations of parental constraint can exacerbate patterns of male domination within youth social movement organizations and can result in girls' relative political invisibility both within the youth movement organization and to outsiders. However, the presence of adult movement allies within these organizations can interrupt these patterns of sexism and can mollify the gendered effects of parental constraint. The strong relationship between adult allies and youth organizers in YP challenged me to rethink the relationship between youth empowerment and youth autonomy that I had taken for granted in SRU. More importantly, I increasingly became aware that these strong intergenerational relationships within YP facilitated girls' sustained movement participation and muted the gender divides that eventually destabilized SRU and led to the withdrawal of SRU girls from community activism.

In YP, adult allies buffered the impact of parental worry on girls by serving as a crucial interface to concerned YP parents, which helped to facilitate both girls' and boys' attendance to YP events. In many cases, YP adult allies kept in direct contact with worried parents, negotiating with them over students' involvement in organizing activities. Adult allies would often provide YP teens with the necessary transportation to coalition meetings, retreats, and rallies, which eased parental concern over their children's whereabouts.

YP adult allies went even further to interrupt sexist patterns of domination within the organization to encourage girls' involvement and leadership once they attended YP activities. Although male domination was an issue in YP just as it was in SRU—in the sense that boys talked over girls, and girls were often reluctant to speak and allowed boys to take over—young adult mentors were vigilant about interrupting these patterns and drawing students' awareness to the ways in which sexism and heterosexism played out in their practices and compromised their social justice goals.

At one YP student organizer retreat, young adult mentors broke up YP students into gender caucuses. This kind of open discussion about sexism in youth movements was largely absent in SRU meetings. YP adult ally

Estella, in a ritual dating back thousands of years among indigenous peoples across the Americas, lit copal and blessed each girl with the smoke. Then, she and twenty-five-year-old Yesenia led the girls in a brainstorming discussion on femininity, masculinity, heterosexism, and sexism. What is a woman? How is one expected to behave? What happens when women step out of our expected roles? What are our expectations for our male allies? Girls came up with a list of expectations and requests that they were to present to their male allies: understand that women deal with internalized sexism; be conscious of this and try to make a space for us to participate; take responsibility for unlearning sexism—it is not women's job to teach men about sexism; be conscious of the organizing work women do; and allow a space where women can be more at the forefront of organizing.

After three hours of intense discussion, YP adult allies gathered the two groups together and shared with each other what they brainstormed. In the company of male YP organizers, some YP girls began to contradict their own ideas when they agreed with the objections of some male student organizers that some of the girls' expectations would result in reverse sexism in YP. Yesenia and Estella broke in for a moment and called girls' attention to the ways in which they themselves were now undoing the expectations they had created in the previous brainstorming session. They asked the girls to think about why they were contradicting their own list of expectations and what this might have to do with internalized sexism. After an impassioned group debate about whether or not there is such a thing as reverse sexism, students discussed their expectations of each other as allies in multiracial struggles. Despite the earlier debate on reverse sexism, the gender caucus heightened boys' awareness of sexist practices in their group. After the group finished dinner, boys took it upon themselves to wash dishes and clean up the kitchen.

YP adult allies and YP student organizers themselves continued to interrupt sexist practices in the group throughout YP meetings, programs, and events. At one subsequent event, sixteen-year-old Alisha, an African American girl, tried to get the attention of a roomful of students by standing up on a table and shouting, "Okay, y'all, we're gonna start the workshop, so listen up!" When sixteen-year-old James, a biracial black/Latino YP organizer, noticed that most students were not responding to Alisha's request, he jumped up on the table next to Alisha and shouted, "Listen up, y'all! Alisha is going to lead this workshop!" Immediately, the roomful of students became quiet so that they could listen to what James had to say. He continued, "See? That's an example of sexism right there. How come you listen to me, but you won't give that same respect to Alisha?" With everyone's attention, Alisha began leading her workshop on the history of alliances between racial justice movements.

Conclusion

Teenagers' conceptions of parental power, and their strategies to negotiate with their parents over the limits of their activism, affect their participation in community social movements. Inasmuch as political activism in one's community necessitates a requisite mobility to network with other activists and attend meetings, protests, and rallies, the themes of gender, parental power, and mobility must become central to considerations of how teenagers become community activists. There is also a relationship between gender inequality within youth movements and girls' relational care work or boys' relative autonomy within families, as gendered negotiations of parental power can precipitate and exacerbate gendered movement divisions.

In using SRU's direct action as one example, I do not wish here to privilege boys' direct action as "real" political action, because the school-based activism around educational funding that some SRU girls ultimately chose was also legitimate political action. It is important to recognize, however, that although these two arenas are both significant sites of political action, they are not necessarily equivalent in their potential to bring youth into the larger fold of community politics. Because of their greater mobility and familial autonomy relative to girls, SRU boys were able to form fledgling alliances with adult social justice groups and to access larger social movement networks. This access enabled boys to attend coalition meetings, acquire new organizing skills, form relationships with adult social justice groups, learn about new developments in local city politics, and eventually speak to adult publics as community organizers—even if this access also exposed boys to these groups' periodic ageist betrayals. It is not the confrontational dimension of their activism that gave boys an edge in their sociopolitical development. Rather, it is the public nature of this political arena, and boys' sustained engagement with a larger civic network, that rendered their activism qualitatively different from girls' activism at their individual schools. As Michelle Fine (1991) has argued, schools are not always genuine public spheres. Often, they are institutions disconnected from community social movements. SRU girls without activist clubs at their schools found themselves without any opportunities to engage in collective action at all once they left their youth activist network. Girls' struggles with parental power can contribute to their relative social invisibility as agents of political change, both within their peer networks and to a broader adult network of community activists. As such, they face added barriers to countering the citizenship-in-the-making model and turning it into meaningful and recognized public, political power.

While the issue of parental opposition was paramount to particular YP girls, YP girls' struggles with their parents did not produce the same gendered organizational divisions within YP that surfaced within SRU. Both girls and boys in YP were buffered by young adult organizers, who were able to mollify parents' many concerns over their children's community activism. This meant that despite the centrality of parental worry and opposition in YP girl activists' narratives, YP girls' actual participation in social movement activities was much more consistent than white, middle-class girls' participation in Portland community politics. Absent any stable allies who were informed by feminist consciousness and were committed to developing leadership and organizing skills among both girls and boys in Portland, the potential of SRU girls to become powerful speakers and organizers was hampered. The feminist interventions of YP adult allies in this study suggest that the presence of adult mentors in youth movements is especially important for girls' political development.

However, these feminist interventions are beneficial to girls only if they simultaneously work to interrupt adultist practices and ageism as well. While YP adult allies were committed to interrupting sexist practices, they also conceptualized ageism as a legitimate social oppression on par with racism and sexism and were committed to mentoring youth in ways that did not replicate adultist patterns of interaction between adults and adolescents. This provides us with an opportunity to consider how the intersecting forces of adult power and sexism work to coproduce girls' political subordination within social movements and within society more broadly. In this sense, it is important to recognize the key role that youth peer culture plays in facilitating girls' involvement in adult-dominated community politics, even as male domination in these same peer networks can hinder girls' involvement. Politicized youth peer cultures such as SRU and YP represent an unusual opportunity for girls to express their anger and political outrage. As Lyn Mikel Brown persuasively argues, there is a link between anger, self-respect, and social change in girls' and women's lives: "Without anger there is no impetus to act against any injustice. . . . If we take away girls' anger, then, we take away the foundation for women's political resistance" (1998, 13). Given the social pressures on girls to disconnect from their anger during adolescence, we must recognize the key role that politicized youth cultures play in counteracting these pressures by bringing girls' voices into the public sphere and providing a platform for their political anger. However, without adult allies to help mediate their relationships to parental power and without an explicit antisexist consciousness that guides the internal dynamics of youth organizing, girls' attempt to sustain this public and political link to their outrage becomes a private struggle.

The gendered consequences of young people's navigation of parental power hold the potential to reverberate beyond adolescence. As in the case of SRU, girls' negotiation of parental power, without the counterweight of feminist interventions, influences several dimensions of girls' political participation: it can result in their absences from key organizing meetings and public demonstrations, which in turn compromises their visibility to outsiders as political actors and prevents them from gaining the organizing skills required to become leaders within their activist networks. Girls' negotiation of parental constraint also works to channel their political participation from higher-risk politics, such as protesting war, to what might be perceived as "softer issue" politics, such as rallying for school funding. Might these gendered patterns influence the direction and scope of adult activism? Do girls' experiences during adolescence influence the issues that women take on as adults and the ways in which they approach their political participation around these issues? Do boys' greater independence and mobility during adolescence ultimately provide them with the social capital necessary to develop into movement leaders as adults?

In the end, both YP girls and boys were able to sustain their community activism over the span of their high school years, sharpening their skills as Oakland community organizers and taking with them their activist experiences and knowledge into young adulthood. Although SRU girls began the political project of transforming citizenship-in-the-making into actualized youth political power, they were unable to sustain this work within their larger community over the course of their high school careers. During the brilliant and short-lived historical moment when their brand of high school student activism burst out of the Portland schools and into the streets—becoming noticed, celebrated, then finally criticized by segments of the local community—SRU girls never really had the opportunity to develop the skills that would establish them as leading organizers.

After the exodus of most girls from the SRU network, SRU boys still continued to meet and organize. Recognizing that they had become mostly reactive, they organized what they considered to be proactive school and community events: alternative and politicized school proms, community youth art exhibits, community gardens. However, by the autumn of the following year, SRU had all but lost its vibrance, its drive, and, importantly, much of its membership. The network that SRU activist Megan once described as "the only high school student–run activist group in the whole city . . . a place you can come and be heard" had now become a shadow of its former self. SRU's high-visibility, quick-change, direct action politics faded into the expanse of summer 2004, when SRU seniors had graduated, the war in Iraq raged on despite massive antiwar mobilizations around the world, and the citywide school crisis had been temporarily solved. The historical moment had come to an end, and SRU was no longer that place that Portland youth, not even the boys, could "come and be heard."

Conclusion

In the two years I spent with YP and SRU activists, I witnessed their challenges, successes, and defeats. Anchored in larger historical and contemporary movements, YP organizers in Oakland fundamentally changed their school landscapes: at some schools they successfully instituted youth centers that provided a proyouth, empowering respite from their defeating experiences of schooling. They created student committees to meet with their school administrators over curriculum design and organized multiracial unity days that emphasized racial alliances: radically altering their schools' depoliticized and divided multicultural celebrations of diversity. They protested the California High School Exit Exam and were instrumental in winning a two-year delay in the institution of the test. They protested the war in Iraq, leading massive student walkouts.

In Portland, SRU activists mobilized teens from across the city to lobby adult voters around tax increases for schooling. They created new student unions and new activist clubs in their schools and captured local media attention by orchestrating citywide student sit-ins and walkouts. They threaded the concerns of public school students into the antiwar protests and rallies that shook the city. They marched down to the mayor's office and demanded that she come down to talk to them about why the city was unable to fully fund their public schools. They took the lead in organizing a community-wide free school to fill the educational gap that would be left by early school closures.

Clearly, these accomplishments reflect teens' efforts toward rejecting the model of citizenship-in-the-making, which posits that only as adults will young people ever engage in critical thought, turn critical thought into political action, and dare to change the structures and processes that impact their everyday lives. Their efforts show that adolescents are quite capable of naming social injustices, envisioning the changes that need to be made, and strategizing toward turning those visions into concrete realities.

Processes of Disruption: Youth Resistance and Youth Agency

The creation of underground newspapers, student unions, and campaigns to institute ethnic studies into their classrooms stand as evidence of adolescents' capacities to subvert the many prescriptions for their political passivity, even if these efforts take place at individual schools and ultimately do not come to fruition. As youth movements expand outward from schools into cities, young people access more organizing skills, political action frames, and alternative political educations that subvert their prescribed passivity as youth. Through these connections to larger social activist networks, students transform themselves from passive and disempowered youth into capable organizers and educators. These practices enable adolescents to become political actors, teachers, and organizers long before the state, schools, mainstream media, and even families recognize them as legitimate and capable participants in social decision making.

Racial and class systems of power play key roles in determining the structure of youth political resistance, specifically in relation to the young adult mentors who facilitate their political development. White, middle-class youth in Portland and low-income youth of color in Oakland have structured their movements very differently in relation to these mentors—a reflection of the ways in which youth movement organizations are shaped within larger systems of inequality. In Oakland, for example, students' social locations as racially subordinated, impoverished youth required the strategic integration of adult allies for specific purposes. Adult allies in YP served as links to social services and as adult faces for a particularly devalued student population in ways that relatively privileged white, middle-class students did not require as they became activists. In contrast, SRU activists, to subvert adult power in the making of their movement, formed a youth-only structure and cultivated youth autonomy in ways that impoverished youth in Oakland could not. These different structures of youth movement vis-à-vis adult society, structures that have in part been determined by students' locations in other systems of privilege and power, shaped the ways in which white, middle-class radical youth and low-income youth of color politicized and subverted adult power in their understandings of age inequality.

As teen activists wrestle with ageism and the model of citizenship-in-the-making, they also develop strategies to confront the adult gaze that delegitimizes them as serious and valuable political participants. While both middle-class, white students and impoverished students of color wrestle with this gaze, the strategies they develop to successfully get their wins on campus and in their larger communities are also differentiated by racial and class politics. YP students employed academic achievement as a political strategy in gaining legitimacy in the eyes of school administrators. This strategy helped particularly devalued students of color disrupt the efforts of adult authorities to simply write them off as delinquent failures (a process of youth subordination that represents a particular intersection of racial, class, and ageist oppression). Meanwhile, SRU activists unconsciously drew upon their cultural capital and white privilege, both of which helped them to negotiate directly with school administrators, unmediated by other adults. This white and class privilege meant that middle-class, white student organizers did not need to politicize or employ academic achievement as a means toward challenging their subordinated status as adolescents, and they had more flexibility in demanding autonomous spaces on their school grounds than did low-income youth of color.

Outside the school, the intersection of whiteness and class privilege in SRU activists' lives meant that white, middle-class students sometimes saw their youth status as a distinct advantage in direct action politics, rather than as a hindrance. YP youth of color, in contrast, did not hold this same "youth-as-superhero" conception of themselves, because they did not enjoy the protection of being under eighteen vis-à-vis the state penal system. For them, the adult gaze was not infused with a vision of youth innocence. SRU youth, perceiving themselves as secret superheroes, found limited success with their efforts to play upon specific themes pervasive in the Portland adult gaze: whitened images of childhood innocence and

adults' underlying fears of youth takeover. And the politics of youth invisibility (as a particular intersection of white, middle-class "innocent" youth
who are largely invisible to the public as social actors) and hypervisibility
(an intersection of racist, classist, and ageist imagery) determine different
orientations to mainstream media and different youth resistances to the
adult gaze.

Processes of Youth Subordination: The Social Construction
of Citizens-in-the-Making

Whether or not young people's efforts result in clear political victories, they
unequivocally show that there is nothing inevitable about young people's
political silence, nonparticipation, and exclusion from community decision making. Teenagers' political silence and inaction is neither an outcome of teenage brain function, nor is it hardwired into youth physiology.
It is not a matter of developmental delay and a lack of social maturity, as
compared to the idealized adult political subject. Clearly, some teens are
politically active and thus demonstrate that young people's alienation from
politics does not have to be the status quo. This begs the question: if young
people's political alienation is not a result of their cognitive deficiencies or
developmental inabilities but is instead a socially constructed process,
then what is it, exactly, that produces their alienation from politics?

First, we must recognize how difficult it is to judge how widespread
youth political alienation really is. Alongside Robert Putnam's (2008) opti-
mistic news that a more civically engaged generation of youth is emerging
in the United States, leagues of other scholars are signaling a worldwide
crisis of youth political disengagement. These scholars document a disturbing lack of political knowledge and a growing political apathy among
youth worldwide (Delli Carpini 2000; Henn et al. 2002; Williamson 2002;
Youniss et al. 2002; Thomson et al. 2004). Although these scholars dis-
agree as to what the source of youth disengagement might be (is it a reflection of young people's increasing irresponsibility, selfishness, and
individualism, or are governments to blame for failing to foster young
people's active participation?), they agree that increasing levels of youth
distrust of government is an alarming indicator of youth political alienation. As Jessica Taft and Hava Gordon (2009) point out, however, youth

distrust of government is not necessarily a good measure of youth political alienation. The struggles of YP and SRU activist youth show that young people can be intensely critical and distrustful of their governments and institutional politics, and yet still devote an impressive portion of their teenage years to political activism and engagement. Indeed, when we shift our focus away from how youth feel about and participate in institutional politics to how youth engage in social movements and more dissident forms of youth activism, we find that many youth worldwide are, and would definitely consider themselves to be, politically active.[1] As Marc Flacks (2007) suggests, scholars should be more attentive to the diverse ways in which youth themselves conceptualize "politics," "political identity," and "political engagement" to avoid making sweeping generalizations about a whole youth generation's approach to politics.

Second, when considering levels of youth political alienation, we must not only conceptualize youth as a generational group. Especially in the case of teenagers, youth must also be understood as an age group. Although age and generation are interrelated concepts, they are not the same. By rethinking youth in terms of age and not just generation, we can move beyond analyzing generational differences in political participation and can begin to analyze the role that age inequality might play in facilitating youth political disengagement.

While recognizing that politics means more than just "government" and can be stretched to include social movement activism and that some youth are political participants and even leaders in social justice struggles around the globe, we cannot ignore the many obstacles that youth encounter as they try to mobilize their peers into powerful social justice campaigns. These obstacles provide essential clues to scholars trying to figure out why so many youth are not politically active. In documenting the struggles of YP and SRU activists, I have provided an overview of the many converging processes by which youth are actually diverted from political action and are constructed as citizens-in-the-making. The roadblocks youth movements encounter represent more than just the standard difficulties that adult organizers also face, nor are they simply reflections of young people's poor tactical choices as organizers. Although most scholars of youth political socialization and civic engagement neglect to examine how ageism impacts youth political development, I argue that it plays a major role in constructing youth political alienation. The roadblocks that youth activists encounter signify the specific prescriptions for young people's political silence and passivity; they are part and parcel of the forces that establish age as an axis of inequality. When young people claim political power before they reach adulthood, they confront these road-blocks, violate these prescriptions, and make visible the forces that construct youth political alienation.

So what are these forces? In large part, they are historically and geographically specific. At the turn of the millennium, we see that large-scale historical processes have worked to alienate young people from political power. Social divestment, violence, neighborhood resegregation, school defunding, war, the militarization of schooling, the ascendancy of neoliberal values, and the privatization of public goods all play a role in estranging young people from claiming political power.

Although much is made of youth apathy in popular discourses that blame youth for social problems (Males 1996), apathy and hopelessness are two different processes of social construction—produced along lines of racial and class privilege and oppression—that also work to estrange youth from political power. Clearly, the problems of white, middle-class apathy and the internalized hopelessness and cynicism of working-class and poor people of color are not unique to the youth of these populations. However, in many ways apathy and hopelessness are compounded by adolescents' subordinated status as citizens-in-the-making. Youth of both groups are conditioned to understand themselves as passive social actors who do not participate in political processes, social decision making, or larger political projects before adulthood. Youth in both Portland and Oakland, like adolescents everywhere in modern postindustrial societies, are constructed as passive objects to be seen and not heard and to express agency only in terms of consumption. Thus, adolescents are socialized to see themselves as unable to make change until they become adult citizens, if ever. As youth organizers in Oakland and Portland have pointed out, apathy and hopelessness have made youth organizing particularly difficult. Both movements have aimed to undo these effects among their peers in the course of building student movements.

While neoliberalism, social divestment, school defunding, war, and consumerism have all been powerful in constructing adolescents as beings estranged from political agency, there are specific historical and social processes that affect some youth more than others. In the context of deindustrialized urban Oakland, violence has become paramount in shaping the conditions for adolescent subordination. Importantly, young people's responses and adaptations to violence have also come under the microscope of outside commentators who have further demonized youth in particularly racialized ways. Thus, youth of color must contend with labels like "menaces" and "superpredators" in the construction of their adolescence-as-subordination status, while middle-class, white youth do not. Undoing these distorted stereotypes of gang activity and violence, as part of YP workshops such as The Cycle of Violence, becomes an important mechanism in transforming youth of color from objectified, social problems into engaged political organizers.

The forces that construct youth as citizens-in-the-making are also institutional. Rather than encouraging youth to engage in civil society as active problem solvers, the battles of high school movements to organize on school grounds reveal the ways in which students are actually diverted from political engagement by adult society. SRU activist Sunnie's struggle to establish a GSA at her school, YP students' struggles to institute ethnic studies into their curriculums, and students' attempts to bring antiwar organizing into full view on campuses met with various levels of resistance from teachers and administrators, who often urged students not to stir political controversy and to keep politics out of their schooling. The distanced and hierarchical relationship between the school administration and the students plays a part in sustaining youth subordination, ultimately reminding students that agreements depend on the good will of specific administrators who are capable of betraying students anytime, without reprisal. The power struggles between parents, teachers, and school administrators over proper expressions of student activism reveal the ways in which young people are constructed as voiceless citizens-in-the-making, while it is the adults (especially teacher allies) who are ultimately held responsible for their activism. This makes teacher support of student movements very tricky, because teachers themselves must answer to a higher adult authority. Thus, the power structure of the school limits the extent to which teacher allies can facilitate the transformation of students into engaged citizen activists, even if they support students' autonomy and development as politicized people. This provides one window into the adult politics that work to steer adolescents away from larger social movement activism.

It is not only the relationships between students, teachers, and school administrators that work to produce student political powerlessness on school grounds. It is also the gap between schools and larger community movements that can distance students from the power that local movements hold. Although a few of the schools in this study already had seemingly politicized spaces, such as Gay/Straight Alliances, environmental clubs, and even ACLU or Amnesty International clubs, these spaces were often disconnected from local community movements and from adult organizers. Student organizers featured in this study identified these clubs as ill-equipped to galvanize students into local movements against war or educational justice issues. As Penelope Eckert (1989) has noted, schools turn adolescents "inward" in the process of preparing them to take their places in the capitalist social order. Thus, school rivalries and school spirit are examples of the ways in which students are encouraged to identify with their own school rather than with other schools and nonschool entities. Schooling can disrupt geographical continuity and thus, in many ways, can disconnect students from their larger communities (Eckert 1989; Fine 1991). Although seemingly progressive, school clubs such as GSAs, school newspapers, and environmental clubs often take on the role of producing adolescents as citizens-in-the-making in their own ways, running youth through the motions of civic engagement while severing them from the political content of this engagement. This is most clearly exemplified in the structure of student government, a hierarchical governing structure designed to run students through the motions of electoral politics. Student government holds presidential campaigns and plans dances and school activities and, in this sense, trains youth for future adult citizenship and civic participation. However, the fact that student government is unable to empower students to participate in more fundamental school decision-making processes, such as curriculum design, school budget issues, hirings, and so on, speaks to its structure as an agent of adolescent subordination, one that produces citizens-in-training but not actual political participants with real institutional power.

While I note the sanitizing effect on extracurricular activities in middle-class schools, impoverished schools such as Kendall and Patterson High in East Oakland suffer from a lack of extracurricular opportunities in general. Potential teacher sponsors of student clubs are already stretched thin, and ethnic-specific clubs like the Black Student Union or the Raza club often don't even exist. Without an advisor to agree to sponsor a club, students find that there are simply too few school activities through which they can find an entrance into political activism. Thus, school impoverishment compounds the processes of political alienation, as it stifles the creation of a potential student activist infrastructure on school grounds. In an era when schools are facing landmark budget cuts and schooling is increasingly geared toward standardized testing, potential activist infrastructures such as extracurricular clubs rank low on the list of funding priorities.

Importantly, adolescents are also constructed as subordinated beings without political agency outside of their schools, in their larger communities. Youth who cannot find opportunities to become politically active in their schools do not simply walk out into their communities and join already-existing adult social justice groups. Public civic spaces that are usually reserved for adult participation can be difficult territory for students to break into. Many young people in this study had tried to join already established adult groups. However, adolescents routinely face disregard, patronization, and marginalization by adults in their communities as they try to join their organizations. That many high school students form youth movements rather than participate in already-existing social justice groups reflects the extent to which social movements are profoundly age segregated and adult dominated, as social movement politics (like electoral politics) are naturalized as adult, rather than adolescent, territory.

As youth movements pick up steam, they run into the roadblocks presented by distorted mainstream media coverage. Of course, media distortion poses a roadblock for many social movements. But with its particular adultist overtones, it plays a specific and important role in constructing the image of youth as citizens-in-the-making instead of as full-fledged community organizers, delegitimizing youth critique and dissent. It could be argued that mainstream media rarely portrays any political dissent as legitimate, whether it be adult or youth dissent. But in the case of SRU, the mainstream media delegitimized youth political action through specific adultist imagery that erased young people's political outrage altogether, instead focusing on infantilized images of youth as "happy" or "sad." Once youth activists' antiwar outrage could not be denied, mainstream media portrayed their outrage as pathological and corrupted, a result of the bad influences of older "violent anarchists" rather than generated by youth themselves. In the case of YP, mainstream media was perceived to be such a significant roadblock for low-income youth of color that they wasted little time trying to strategize around this adult gaze. In many instances, they worked to keep mainstream media completely out of their politics.

Finally, the family is another important institution that can work to construct youth as citizens-in-the-making and can play a role in delaying children's political subjectivity. Although parents can be key supporters of children's political and ideological development, and although youth activists in this study routinely named their parents as major influences on their political development, some youth also perceived their parents to be roadblocks to their actual civic participation. To become vocal and publicly visible organizers, teen activists first have to contend with parental opposition, worry, and control. For some teens, the impact of parental consideration is minimal. For others, worried, controlling, or oppositional parents mean the difference between being a person who holds certain ideals about the world (i.e., a citizen-in-the-making with a politicized consciousness), and being an organizer who is able to enact political subjectivity in the public sphere. As the struggles of SRU and YP girls suggest, this difference is profoundly a gendered one. This difference also reflects the crucial distinction between two dimensions of political subjectivity: political *consciousness* and political *engagement*. If we notice only the ways in which parents' facilitate children's political ideologies but neglect to notice their attempts to regulate students' actual political engagement (and the complicated ways in which youth negotiate these attempts), we miss the more complex role that families play in both facilitating and hindering youth political engagement.

Many historical forces and institutional processes converge to distance young people from political power and political action. But as the term "social construction" has always promised: what is socially constructed can, theoretically, be deconstructed. If young people's exclusion from political decision making is not a biological or developmental inevitability but is instead the result of human action, we can envision a different kind of youth: where young people, though still young, are also active participants in community, national, and global political processes. As the struggles of youth activists featured in this book show, young people themselves, through politicized peer cultures, actively wrestle with their status as citizens-in-the-making and disrupt the processes that create their political alienation.

From Citizenship-in-the-Making to Youth Political Power: Peer Culture and Adult Allies

The centrality of peer culture in young people's efforts to disrupt the model of citizenship-in-the-making runs counter to structures of schooling and other political socialization theories that propose a kind of top-down, adult-youth interaction as the key in training youth to become "good citizens." Often, the assumption is that adults need to do this *for* youth. As SRU and YP struggles show, there are many ways in which adult society actually consciously and unconsciously blocks young people's efforts to claim political power, because this precocity runs counter to adultist conceptions of when, where, and under what conditions people should responsibly engage in politics. As we see in the case of both YP and SRU, peer culture plays a crucial role in facilitating youth political engagement in ways that adults cannot do for youth. This calls our attention to the positive role that peer networks play in undermining youth subordination and political powerlessness. This dominant image of youth as dangerous or endangered—what Donna Gaines (1991) has termed "two sides of a social problem"—requires that adults step in to right young people's wrongs and to protect them from the inevitable damage they will do to each other. As young people's movements demonstrate, youth cultivate politicized peer networks to undo the damage wrought by adultist practices and structures of power. These practices and structures not only devalue youth, they also serve to ensure that young people, as citizens-in-the-making but not as valued political participants in their own right, are left with few social or political resources with which to counter their devaluation. Young people's social movements are one path toward developing adolescent political agency, made possible only through politicized peer cultures.

However, as evidenced in the rise and fall of SRU, youth peer cultures can only go so far in shaking up the model of citizenship-in-the-making and ushering in a new, sustainable model for youth political power. Although class and race privilege made it possible for SRU to construct a youth-only movement—and they were intensely proud of building their movement without sustained adult help—SRU student activists felt *compelled* to structure their movement this way, given the near absence of adult allies in Portland's antiauthoritarian movement scene who recognized age inequality to be a real axis of social power. In the end, they could not trust adult allies in community movements to not betray them, belittle them, misrepresent them, or take over their movement. Their choice for a youth-only network was empowering for them on the surface, but it concealed a host of overlapping problems underneath. Because they were youth-only, they threw themselves at the mercy of mainstream media (and the adult gaze that it represents) to broadcast their message: a tactic that ultimately rendered their collective identity as both proeducation and antiwar untenable. Because they would eventually age out of the organization, they could not adequately set long-term goals and sustain long-term social justice campaigns, and instead limited their political engagement to short-term direct actions. Because they intuitively sensed that their organization had a limited lifespan, they cut short important debates and disagreements, focusing on action rather than divisive talk, which allowed group tensions to fester. All of these factors contributed to the fall of SRU. For some SRU youth, especially the girls, this meant that their larger project of resisting, disrupting, and subverting the model of citizenship-in-the-making was left unfinished.

YP survived because it integrated young adult allies into its activist network. This is not to say that youth movements succeed only because of adult participation, but they cannot sustain their organizing work without it. Adults provide organizing tools, political action frameworks, material resources, and alternative political educations to youth as they form their social justice movements. They interface with school administrators, parents, social service agencies, and a host of other powerful adults—brokering resources and mollifying ageism on a variety fronts. In sum, these adult connections allow youth to advance their political power. At times, adults provide feminist interventions into the processes of youth organizing to disrupt tendencies toward male domination, and they help undo internalized oppressions like ageism and racism among youth organizers. They also provide a clear vision for social justice by teaching youth about their social movement legacies.

All of the roles that adult allies play *within* youth movements are tied to the overlapping historical threads and institutions that shape young people's subordination and powerlessness. Adults' role as bridges to past movement legacies would be less necessary if schools included these histories in their curriculums. Their role as connections to needed social services would be irrelevant if all youth had access to health care and real economic and human security. Their negotiations with school administrations would not be needed if administrations were truly held accountable to student visions and needs.

The interactions between YP youth and their adult allies is particularly instructive in providing an alternative model to adult power and youth subordination, where youth autonomy can coexist with adult mentorship and further the goals of youth movements. YP youth organizing has been able to achieve this balance because both adolescents and adult allies in YP have openly recognized, criticized, and politicized age inequality. Most importantly, they have made commitments to disrupt this inequality. What if all adults and youth made this commitment, in a variety of contexts, beyond youth movements? What would families look like? What would schools look like? What would mainstream media look like? Undoubtedly, these institutions would be unrecognizable. Like social movements, these institutions would be enriched by young people's voices, imaginations, leadership, and active participation in ways we could not even begin to imagine.

The story of youth movements is much more than just the story of youth political power. It is ultimately the story of how all of us—teachers, students, activists, parents, allies, policy makers and media makers—facilitate or disrupt youth political powerlessness. It is about our role in helping youth in their struggles to transform from citizens-in-the-making into political powerhouses, valuing them for the strengths they possess and the social justice visions they provide, and not just for the adults they'll become.

APPENDIX: ENTERING THE WORLDS OF YOUTH ACTIVISM

STUDENTS RISE UP IN PORTLAND

I first came across Students Rise Up on a rainy October day in 2002, at one of the first of many peace rallies before the start of the war in Iraq the following March. Gathered with hundreds of people in Pioneer Courthouse Square in the center of Downtown Portland, SRU teens huddled under a huge banner that read, "Students Rise Up." I approached one of them, Curt, a tall guy with long hair. I explained to him that I studied sociology and wanted to learn more about youth and social movements. He smiled and invited me to an SRU meeting before I even asked to attend. At that time, SRU meetings were open to the public and took place in an anarchist café on the east side of town. Curt emphasized to me that rather than sitting in the circle of SRU students during the meetings, I should sit outside and just observe. I took his cue, not quite familiar yet with the dynamics of the group.

For two weeks I returned, and sat at the outer edges of the SRU circle. I pulled Curt aside and said, "Do you think I should just introduce myself to the group now?" He responded with a vehement, "No, just sit and observe—I'll tell them who you are." The third week I took my usual place on the outside of the circle but was feeling increasingly uncomfortable with the group not yet knowing who I was. It was clear that for whatever reason, Curt had not yet told them why I was observing meetings. Students were beginning to stare at me and whisper to each other. I decided right then and there to forego Curt's advice to just sit on the margins and decided to introduce myself at the end of the meeting, as awkward as it would be. It was a moment when I realized that my initial entrée tactic had gone very, very wrong and that Curt was probably not the most effective person to have facilitated my entrée into the group.

As I waited for a good moment to introduce myself, Travis, a teen in a hat and a jean jacket studded with spikes, walked up to me during the meeting. He had been eyeing me throughout the meeting, and I was both relieved and alarmed that he was approaching me. At least this would give me a chance to explain why I was sitting there. He sat down next to me and whispered, "Excuse me, why are you here?" I told him what I was studying and about my interest in SRU. He responded sternly, "Well, a better way to do that is to just introduce yourself to us. 'Cause, see, we thought you were a cop." There it was. I was grateful to him for his honesty, but the charge stung.

Right after the meeting I got up and introduced myself to them and openly apologized for making anyone uncomfortable. Joni, a vocal girl organizer, invited me to sit in on the next meeting and let me know that I could put myself on their next agenda. Even though the gaffe felt somewhat repaired by the time I left the café, a few youth were still looking at me like I was pure evil. That night I scribbled in my notes, "This has to be the worst entrée ever in the history of participant-observer entrées." The worst impression I could have made on these activists is that I was a cop. To me, this charge was particularly hard-hitting because I had spent the last two years active in the Portland Police Accountability Campaign.[1] And yet I had managed to do it. I decided to start all over again, this time without a sponsor. I came back to the meeting the following week and put myself on the agenda. I then explained to the group why I was interested in youth activism, what I taught, what I studied, and why I felt it was important to learn more about youth movements. I asked them if they would allow me to sit in on their meetings. I told them that I would gladly leave the room while they talked about it, or would come back to a subsequent meeting. They had an open discussion in front of me about having a researcher join them in their meetings. After reiterating their policy to each other and to newcomers that they were not to discuss plans for direct actions at the weekly SRU meetings, they agreed to let me sit in and observe.

Later on I found out from several SRU students that Curt was just trying to protect the group, because several progressive teachers had already tried to take over SRU meetings at the café and run them as if the students were in their classrooms. There was also growing suspicion that their group could be infiltrated by police, intensified by rumors that the café was bugged by the FBI. An action SRU had planned just a few weeks before had been foiled by the police, who showed up before the kids did, ready and waiting for them. Nobody knew who leaked the information, but some suspected it was a local news reporter who found out about their planned and unpermitted action. Finally, the media coverage that they so welcomed just a few weeks earlier had done a story on the group that they viewed as distorting of their efforts, tactics, and politics. It was their first experience with distorted media coverage. In this climate, new adult observers were particularly suspect. My appearance was the last straw that crystallized for them, and later for me, the ways in which adult power (whether well intentioned or not) can threaten youth movements. Over time I grew accustomed to their lingering suspicion that I might be an infiltrator, although I never became comfortable with it. Once the initial sting faded, I was able to consider my discomfort to be a measure of their autonomy.

Although the group grew to trust me over the next year, the suspicion that I was a police infiltrator never quite dissipated. The founders of SRU: Bart, Vlad, Paul, and Theo were polite to me but cool, and rarely acknowledged my presence at public protests. I attended meetings, rallies, and SRU demonstrations. However I was never invited to join their affinity groups, nor was I invited to be on their electronic listserv (which they used to discuss issues between meetings). I also knew not to ask to be on this listserv, as much as it would have been a great site in itself for research. When students felt there was something in particular from the listserv that they wanted me to see (authors sometimes specified on the listserv that a certain rant or letter could and should be distributed to the public), they would print out a copy and bring it to me. In this way, students maintained the perimeters of their space and a measure of control over their privacy, both of which were crucial to the development of their collective movement and political selves.

YOUTH POWER IN OAKLAND

My entrée into YP was much smoother than it was with SRU. A major reason for this comparative ease was that an adult helped to facilitate my entry into the group. At first this made me very uncomfortable, because an adult was the gatekeeper, allowing me entrance into this youth movement. The experience of entrée into YP was so different from SRU, I wondered if maybe this was not really a youth movement after all. Was it just a youth movement in name only? YP, unlike SRU, integrated young adults into its structure. The presence of these adult allies also facilitated my entrée into YP, making my presence less freakish because I was not the only adult hanging out with youth activists.

The adult gatekeepers, as well as the student organizers, wanted to make sure that I was not some researcher who would "put them under the microscope." The YP adults and youth were conscious of the role that outside observers, educators, policy makers, and "experts" have played in the larger project of demonizing youth of color. As a sociologist, I represented these outsiders who carry the power to label these youth and reinforce white supremacist notions that make youth of color hypervisible in public debates over welfare, crime, poverty, and even terrorism. They wanted to make sure to integrate me into certain YP activities to keep me from taking this distanced and objective scientific status. Of course, this was agreeable to me as well, as I did not want to be an opportunist and unreciprocal researcher. I wanted not only the finished product but also my active presence as an ethnographer to be as helpful as possible to the group.

While we all agreed that this less objective approach would be the best research strategy, this raised another problem: I was an outsider to their communities. The fact that I would be conducting ethnographic research over several intensive visits but that I didn't live day in and day out in Oakland was problematic.[2] For these youth, adults drift in and out of their lives. In the context of Oakland's racially segregated and impoverished urban communities, teachers and principals don't stick around for too long and family members die early, are incarcerated, or migrate elsewhere in search of work. Adults are always leaving youth. I would be no exception. The fact that I would be bonding with these youth, sometimes integrated into their activities as a participant observer, became the flip side to the problem of being a distanced observer. Any bonding with them would make my departure that much more problematic, contributing to a larger pattern of adult abandonment and compounding young people's sense of hopelessness and low self-worth.

The final concern with my presence as an ethnographer in YP was that I am a white person. The movement openly acknowledged that YP existed to foster multiracial leadership among youth of color. As Estella, a YP adult ally, put it, "We are unapologetic about that. We are not here to build bridges between students of color and white students," much to the chagrin of some local school administrators who wanted YP to play this role in schools with sizeable white student populations. The fact that I am a white person (compounded by the fact that I come from a middle-class background and did not live in Oakland) limited my ability to serve as a mentor to students. YP adult allies are people of color, most of whom are from Oakland themselves and have experienced teenage activism as youth of color. Estella and others advised me to openly acknowledge my whiteness whenever possible when working with the youth. I took their advice and discussed my whiteness, Jewishness, and white privilege openly during discussions and workshops when I was asked or expected to participate.

DATA COLLECTION

To explore the processes of adolescent subordination and agency, I used a combination of participant observation and in-depth interviewing methods. Such a combination of qualitative work is especially important in studying human agency, as Catherine Hakim writes: "If one is looking at the way people respond to . . . external social realities at the micro-level, accommodating themselves to the inevitable, redefining the situation until it is acceptable or comfortable, kicking against constraints, fighting to break out of them, or even to change them, then qualitative research is necessary" (1987, 28). Irena Guidikova and Lasse Siurala note that qualitative research is particularly important for studying youth resistance, because "broad, quantitative questionnaire-based surveys of young people indicate recurrently their conventional aspirations—a desire for social inclusion and modest, mainstream roles and responsibilities. In contrast, more qualitative, ethnographic studies of young people suggest patterns of resistance, even if it is conceded that these may rest largely at the level of 'ritual'" (2001, 14–15). Adolescent agency and resistance, especially in overt political and social movement forms, have been particularly ignored themes in social science research. Therefore, I employed qualitative methods to reach these larger issues of resistance and agency.

PARTICIPANT OBSERVATION: STUDENTS RISE UP

In SRU, my role was mostly observer and sometimes observer-as-participant. Immediately after each participant-observation experience with SRU, I made a habit of going to the same café to write out my field notes before going home. I did this to avoid delay in recording observations and thus to avoid the decay of memory. Because SRU was a youth-only movement, there was really no clear space to participate as an adult ally. I attended weekly meetings, which lasted close to two hours. Each meeting started with introductions, and so I would introduce myself in the same ways each time: as a researcher, educator, and someone who was interested in understanding young people's social movement activism. In keeping with my commitment to contribute to the student activists in the process of the research itself (and not just in an abstract way with the finished product), I offered to serve as a volunteer in any way that would help the youth. Often, my position as an adult and my access to a university proved to be useful to SRU students, who were in need of a copy machine for their flyers or a PA system for their events. My volunteer position with SRU was mostly relegated to doing functional things for SRU activists such as making copies of flyers for events and rallies, and even posting them around town. These solo activities were ways that I could help the students without taking over more important organizing work, as some adults had tried to do (parents and teachers and even other social justice activists), or without making them feel unsafe in case I was a cop.

I researched SRU as cuts to public education threatened to close Portland schools a month early in 2003. SRU organized a community meeting to discuss with concerned parents, teachers, activists, and other students the idea of a liberation school that could continue to educate students even if the schools had to close. The community meeting room, on the campus of a local college, was packed with hundreds of community members—myself among them. Students broke us up into planning groups, one of which was a discussion group with people (both youth and adults) who would be willing to teach free liberation school classes during the furlough period. I volunteered to teach those classes I knew I could teach: Women's Studies, Globalization Studies, and Social Movements. After the meeting, some SRU activists asked more about the resources I had on globalization, and some of the girls were interested in women's and gender studies. From there I began loaning out my books to SRU activists. I did not end up formally teaching any of these subjects to SRU and other Portland area students (because the funding crisis was, in the short term, solved, and liberation schools went by the wayside), and I was wary of taking on any role, even if educational, that would assert authoritative power. They never asked me to give a workshop, and—because they were already allowing me into their youth-only group and making themselves vulnerable to possible adult power/infiltration— they were cautious about giving me any authority, even in the guise of mentorship or education. However, my loaning of books and material resources (such as copying fliers) helped to build trust among the students and give some concrete assistance to the group.

I also attended their rallies and protests. SRU demonstrations around proeducation issues were much more amenable to adult observation and even, at times, participation. I learned to keep my distance from SRU activists during antiwar demonstrations, as those were the times when suspicion of police infiltration was the most heightened and when students took the most risks to take direct action. At some of these demonstrations SRU boys, in particular, who had stronger ties to young adult radicals than did SRU girls, would break off into affinity groups that included both young adults and teens. My suspected status as a cop was particularly dangerous in these moments of street protests. There was a moment, however, when SRU activists faced off with police during the "incident on the bridge," when my participation in an antiwar protest helped to dispel suspicion among SRU that I was an infiltrator. I happened to be in the crowd at the bottom of the bridge with other friends, protesting the war on that day as well. The crowd received word that activists on the bridge were trying to shut down the flow of traffic and were being confronted on the bridge by several police dressed in riot gear.[3] Our whole crowd immediately moved up the bridge to assist the activists who were facing off with police and to take the bridge and shut it down. As I was running up the bridge, SRU students were running back down, having been pepper-sprayed in the face by police. Meeting them halfway, I pulled a few aside and helped them to flush out their eyes with water that I was carrying. That incident, students later told me in individual interviews, was pivotal in changing SRU's perception of me as an undercover cop, because I was on the bridge. However, it did not dispel suspicion among all the organizers.

As discussed in chapter 5, SRU students organized a school-funding rally at the State Capitol in early 2003. There, students played guitar, recited poetry, and made speeches about the importance of education. I was one of just a few adults, mostly teachers and parents, who stood at the margins of the rally. We clapped and whistled in support of students but did not make our own speeches. An hour into the rally, an SRU activist got on the bullhorn and announced that we'd be moving the rally into the Capitol building, so that legislators would be sure to hear us. At first I stood with the other adults, at the edges of the circle of high school students who were now forming a circle inside the stately Capitol and joining hands, shouting, "What do we want? An education! When do we want it? Now!" and singing, "I want to be an educated proletarian!" Whereas outside on the Capitol steps the mood was more peaceful and somber, the move into the Capitol building signaled a transgression, a student invasion, a takeover. Soon, Travis, who had confronted me before at one of those early SRU meetings, approached me again. He gave me a look that said, "Okay, this is your chance. If you're not a cop then come join us" and waved me forward to join the circle of students. It was something of a test, because the students were getting brave and rambunctious, singing louder and louder as security guards were moving closer. The situation was getting tense. I went ahead and joined the circle of kids, skipping with them, singing, and shouting, knowing that if anyone would get arrested, it could be me because I was the adult and might be held liable for the group. There were moments like these when my presence as a researcher in SRU was put to the test and I was asked to demonstrate my allegiance to the group.

PARTICIPANT OBSERVATION: YOUTH POWER

My position in Youth Power oscillated much more between observer and observer-as-participant than it had in SRU. Because there was more room for adult allies, and YP's conception of youth was more flexible than in SRU, I was able to occupy specific roles that were assigned to me. Although I was more of an outsider to YP than to SRU (in the sense that I was an outsider for many more overlapping reasons: I am a white person from a middle-class background; I am not from, nor did I live in, Oakland; and I was a researcher), the participant-observation data from this experience was richer than it was from SRU, because I had many more opportunities to get closer to the students.

I was alternately brought on as a YP intern, a YP tutor, a YP volunteer, as well as a YP adult chaperone, the sound of which initially made me cringe. My shift from participant observation in SRU to participant observation in YP was a jarring one. After meeting activists in SRU, I grew to measure youth empowerment and political leverage in terms of the extent to which adolescents could attain separation and autonomy from adults. My experience with SRU had trained me, as an adult ethnographer, to behave in a very distanced, nonimposing way. Any attempt to participate more overtly in youth activities and discussions would have been an exercise in ageism, an imposition of my adult privilege and control. My active voice and presence would have constituted a violation of an important source of empowerment for these young people, one that only the achievement of youth autonomy can generate.

In contrast, as an ethnographer in YP, I was invited to volunteer in the organization in specific capacities that at first seemed to me to reassert adult power. Over time, however, I began to understand that some of these roles existed in name only and were often more for the benefit of parents, school administrators, and other adults than for the students themselves.

As a YP intern, volunteer, and researcher, I often took on the role of note-taker during YP meetings, workshops, and summer programs. YP adult allies in particular wanted a record of how workshops went, what was discussed, and how students were developing as organizers. With their consent, I gave YP copies of the notes and kept copies for myself, changing the actual names in my own notes to pseudonyms. In addition, I wrote a separate set of my own field notes immediately after my day-long activities with YP. I usually did this on the BART or bus, traveling back to my brother's house in Vallejo or my sister's apartment in San Francisco. Taking immediate field notes was not always possible during my visits when I spent full and nearly sleepless weekends with YP organizers at organizing retreats. In those instances, I waited until I had departed from the group to take my own field notes.

In addition to taking notes, I also volunteered to do more functional work for the group such as cooking and cleaning during YP strategizing retreats. This meant that sometimes I had to break away from particularly rich YP discussions about taking corporate funding, violence, internalized racism, and family histories to prepare breakfasts, lunches, and dinners for about thirty student organizers and five YP adult allies. During the summer-long YP programs for incoming high school freshmen, when YP teenage organizers conducted daily organizing workshops and their own version of ethnic studies, I was in charge of getting food donations from local businesses. Many students at Patterson High, where I was doing most of my interning during the summers, often showed up to YP workshops hungry. At first, I spent mornings alone roaming around Oakland on foot or by bus trying to solicit local grocery stores, bakeries, pizzerias, and donut shops for free food. This experience gave me an unexpected opportunity to hear how local business owners perceived Patterson youth. In one instance, I was asking for a food donation from a prickly grocery store manager about forty blocks away from Patterson High. He stared at me and said, "What, you think I'm going to just give you money?" I tried to explain more about YP and the purpose of the summer program and students' needs. He then shook his head and said, "I remember when Patterson High was a good place to go to school. Now, more kids are dropping out than they are graduating. The neighborhoods are so dangerous." He pulled out twenty dollars from his wallet and said, "I'll give you this on the condition that you tell those kids that I care about them and that this business cares about them. 'Cause they just don't seem to be hearing that."

After a while, YP student organizers Salvador and Alisha began to join me on my quest for food donations. They tried to go themselves but were told by several area businesses that they had to have an adult with them to receive any donations. In these moments, I became the legitimizing face of YP youth to other adults. We would meet in the mornings before the YP summer program began at noon. We walked and took the bus and solicited fast-food restaurant after fast-food restaurant. We celebrated our victories when we got a Pizza Hut to donate a pizza, and we cursed Quiznos for rudely turning us down. We talked about ageism, music, white privilege and racial oppression, Oakland, Portland, Wal-Mart, welfare, the police, and the president. These excursions gave me a more informal opportunity to talk at length with Salvador and Alisha as they showed me around East Oakland.

As an adult "chaperone," I accompanied YP student mentors and new freshmen mentees on day trips to places like Angel Island, where YP student organizers taught new students about the history of Asian immigrant internment in the Bay Area, and to Sacramento, where students converged from all over California to disrupt the state school board meetings and to call for a delay in the California High School Exit Exam. This title of chaperone was mostly for the benefit of parents and other non-YP adults we would encounter, but did not carry much weight within the group. During one retreat, late at night, six YP student organizers wanted to take a night hike outside of the retreat center where we were staying. Part of the agreement made to parents of YP students, and also to the hostel staff, was that the youth would be supervised by an adult at all times. Therefore, I agreed to take them on a night hike. One YP student organizer, James, joked, "Okay, Hava, you lead us. You're the adult, right? So you're the leader!" The students laughed and the joke underscored the gap between my public (i.e., for the benefit of other adults) role as an adult leader and chaperone and the actual practices within YP that consciously subverted adult authority and emphasized student leadership.

Finally, there were moments when I was specifically asked by YP students or adult allies to participate in YP discussion groups instead of taking notes. These were moments when students in the group discussed painful and personal issues that were part of multiracial consciousness raising and bonding. In these moments I was expected to do the same.

These moments when I was expected to participate were designed, by YP organizers, to interrupt power dynamics between researcher/researched and adult/youth and forced me to be vulnerable to the group as they were vulnerable with me. One moment in particular occurred during my first YP weekend strategizing retreat, when we left Oakland to go to the woods and spend the weekend strategizing on present and long-term education campaigns. The activity, called "life maps," was designed to build solidarity among YP student organizers who were usually divided by schools, turf, and racial/ethnic tensions. This required all of us, adult and youth alike, to draw, in large pictures, where our ancestors came from, what brought them to the United States, and how we ended up where we are. The rule was that we could not draw words, only pictures. One by one, we had to get up in front of the group and explain our life maps to each other. We started in order, from oldest to youngest, which meant that I went first. I explained my family's migration from Eastern Europe, the Holocaust, and the grief my mother's parents carried with them to New York, having left their families behind in Poland. I explained that shortly thereafter, their families were murdered by Nazis. I had never presented my family history in front of anyone before and I was surprised at how emotional I had become as I stood in front of the group. I also had to acknowledge my father's role as a World War II veteran, and the GI bill that enabled him to go to college. The GI bill propelled him (like so many other Jewish veterans) into middle-class status and into "whiteness."[4]

My life map as a white and middle-class person was strikingly different from the other YP life maps. Students talked about dangerous border crossings from Mexico, slave ships from Africa, dehumanizing immigration experiences from Vietnam. They talked about extreme poverty, homelessness, and encounters with violent white supremacy. These moments were difficult and humbling for me, as they highlighted my outsider status and made me examine my own white and class privilege and, to a lesser extent, my Jewish identity, in ways I had not been prepared for. However, these instances when I became vulnerable to the youth also helped to build trust and rapport. As Danny Jorgensen writes, "The participant observer's biography may be used to overcome social distance. . . . It represents a gift, a confidence, a sign of respect and trust for the person to whom you reveal yourself" (1989, 77). I was grateful to YP organizers for designing these moments.

IN-DEPTH INTERVIEWS

I supplemented participant-observation data with forty formal, semistructured, in-depth interviews with both SRU and YP organizers. In-depth interviews allowed me to deepen inquiry into themes emerging in the participant-observation research. Each interview lasted anywhere from forty-five minutes to three hours, and most were audio-taped. I also conducted several other informal interviews during my participant-observation experiences in SRU and YP, question-and-answer sessions that approximated free-flowing conversations rather than structured interviews. These were not audiotaped, but I did record, to the best of my ability, the flow of these conversations in my field notes.

I conducted twenty formal interviews with core SRU student organizers. These took place at locations convenient to the youth: cafés, outside in parks, pizza parlors. I waited until I gained some trust with the group before asking for interviews. To my surprise, SRU students were much friendlier and more willing to talk with me in individual interviews than they were in a group setting. Looking back, their keeping me at arm's length in meetings was important to forming their youth-only collective identity and was important in solidifying their anticop and radical activist stance (in which I was perceived as threatening). Of course, keeping me at arm's length was also important in protecting the group from adult interference and takeover.

SRU students' focus on planning actions, direct action, and on doing activism in an almost completely physical sense sometimes meant that they (usually SRU boys) abhorred long drawn-out debates over group conflicts, values, and strategies. To some organizers, this signaled infighting, wasting time, the breakdown of the group, and the rise of a political ineffectiveness that threatened to deflate students' newfound confidence in their own political power. Therefore, many debates among the organizers during meetings were usually cut short and left unresolved. As a result, their interviews with me became a chance for them to vent or continue some of these debates, and many students thanked me for listening and allowing them to vent. This was particularly true in the case of SRU girls, a contingent of which split off from SRU during my research with the group. This was also true for some SRU boys who were struggling with the direction (or rather the lack thereof) of SRU after the antiwar and proeducation rallies died down.

I conducted twenty formal in-depth interviews with YP organizers. Six of these were with YP young adult allies, one was with a YP intern who was twenty (somewhere between high school student and adult ally), and thirteen interviews were with core YP high school student organizers. The YP intern and two adult allies were former teenage activists in YP, while all but one of the other YP adult allies I interviewed were teenage activists in other organizations or movements. I met students and adult allies where it was most convenient for them: most often in a quiet room with the door closed at the YP central office space in downtown Oakland. Sometimes I met them at cafés along bus lines or at their workplaces when they had a lunch break or got off of work. Without the YP central office, however, finding a safe and comfortable meeting place for a private interview would have been a challenge, as youth of color in Oakland don't have access to many such spaces, and I was without a car or a space of my own.

Although my participant observation in YP was much richer and more intense than in SRU, I found it more difficult to get YP students to sit down with me for interviews. Once they did, I found that some YP students were guarded or terse during interviews in ways they weren't in other interactions with me. Much of this problem was a time issue: YP students' time was carefully and rigidly structured, much more so than the students in SRU, who seemed to have more free time, although they too were quite overwhelmed with the time it took to organize a student movement. Many of them kept appointment books to effectively balance all their schoolwork, music lessons, sports activities, and political work and penciled me in for an interview. In contrast, YP students' calendars, for the most part, were not filled with sports activities or music lessons. Because school achievement was a major strategy to gain legitimacy in the eyes of school administrators, YP students' time, when not taken with organizing meetings or working their jobs (one student worked three days a week at a flea market, another worked at a pawn shop), was devoted to homework and studying. Therefore, getting students to make enough time for me to sit for an interview proved to be more challenging and took a few tries.

The difficulty with interviewing YP students went further than just a time issue. While some YP students were comfortable with being interviewed and spoke easily, a few were more reserved and uncomfortable during interviews, more so than they were in other interactions with me. Salvador was one striking example. Over the course of the YP summer program at Patterson, Salvador and I had a chance to spend a lot of time together. Our attempts to get food donations with Alisha gave us all a chance to talk and get to know one another. Salvador smiled easily and joked often, and even invited Alisha and me to his house to cook us "real Mexican food," as he loved to cook. However, when we sat down for an interview, Salvador became quiet and serious, and his conversation became uncharacteristically terse. As much as I tried to emphasize to all my interviewees that this would be more like a semistructured conversation rather than a rigid interview, the interview process ushered in a formality that changed our interaction. There was something in his tone and body language that seemed almost practiced or familiar, as if he had been interviewed by adults several times before.

Earlier, Salvador had shared with me some of his negative experiences with social workers in Oakland, as he and his brother had been through a few foster homes before being reunited with his birth parents just a year earlier. Despite my best attempt to interact with YP youth as an adult ally, visitor, volunteer, and intern, the formal interviewing process might have felt to students like other clinical interchanges they have had with social workers or other adults (those who hold significant power over students), adults whom students did not necessarily view as allies. This discomfort with the formal interview process that I noticed among a few YP youth was not as apparent among middle-class, white youth in Portland, who did not have ongoing interaction with state social workers or were enmeshed in state programs in the same ways that some low-income youth of color in Oakland were. This issue might have overlapped with YP organizers' critique of researchers and social scientists: outsiders who have a track record of misreading and distorting youth of color and their everyday worlds. My more formal taking of their words in interviews might have heightened my status as a white person/outsider/researcher and therefore heightened their suspicion of me.

Finally, as I learned throughout my research in YP, the process of becoming a vocal youth organizer meant finding new confidence in one's abilities to speak face-to-face with adults in power, such as teachers, principals, and even other adult social justice activists. Periodically I would hear students express frustration that they couldn't speak the language that adults speak. Because of their relatively impoverished education compared to middle-class students in Portland, YP students didn't carry the kind of cultural capital that allowed them to speak as equals to powerful adults. SRU youth expressed much more confidence in their abilities to talk with and to adult power, in ways unmediated by other adults, than did YP youth. I believe this issue played out in formal interviews with some YP youth who appeared to be more uncomfortable speaking to me in the more formal setting of a taped interview.

In the end, to different degrees, these youth activists and their adult allies let me into their lives, gave of their words, and shared with me the successes and defeats of their activist journeys. I hope this book has done justice to their stories, and that their stories can serve as both guideposts and warnings to other youth activists (and their adult allies, wherever they may be), who struggle to claim political power from where they stand, challenging the model of citizenship-in-the-making and changing our world for the better.

NOTES

INTRODUCTION

1. See Ariès (1962), Holt (1975), James and Prout (1990), Jenks (1996), and Platt (1977).

2. See Gaines (1991), Lesko (1996), and Males (1996, 1999) for critiques of this dominance in social research and theorizing. Lesko (2001) delineates four "confident characterizations" of teens that operate in popular and scholarly discussions on youth: (1) adolescents "come of age" into adulthood, (2) adolescents are controlled by raging hormones, (3) adolescents are peer-oriented, and (4) adolescence is signified by age. She argues that these confident characterizations help to maintain the dominance of essentialism in discussions on adolescence.

3. For examples of core works in New Childhood Studies, see Adler and Adler (1998), Corsaro (1997), James and others (1998), Lesko (2001), and Qvortrup (1994).

4. Some, such as Clarke and others (1975), suggest that the resistance expressed by some youth subcultures is not fully political because these youth express and resist in a realm of leisure, using the cultural means of style (e.g., music, fashion) made available through the consumer market. These authors argue, however, that subcultural resistance has political *potential*. In contrast, Nehring (1993) offers that to recognize the political elements in youthful cultural resistance, we must expand our definitions of what is political. According to Nehring, it is precisely because young people are so structurally disempowered that they can resist only through cultural means.

5. See Eckert (1989) and Bettie (2003) for excellent examinations of how school cliques are shaped by social inequalities.

6. This multiracial feminist tradition is represented by scholars such as Baca Zinn and Thornton Dill (1996), Collins (1999), Mohanty (1991), hooks (1989), Glenn (1986), and Spelman (1988), among many others.

CHAPTER 1   THE DEVELOPMENT OF URBAN TEENAGE
ACTIVISM: OPPORTUNITIES AND CHALLENGES
AT THE TURN OF THE MILLENNIUM

1. MEChA is the Chicano student organization, Movimiento Estudiantil Chicano de Aztlan.

2. Although nationally hip-hop has become a commodified popular music genre mostly stripped of its overt political messages, it survives in localized forms as overtly political, less commodified, and more tied to community organizing. Oakland and the Bay Area more generally is a stronghold for this type of local hip-hop activism.

3. For an extensive examination of antiyouth and racist discourse, see Males (1999). Examples include articles such as "Wild in the Streets" (Kantrowitz 1993) and "Taming Teenage Wolf Packs" (Gergen 1996), and criminologists such as James Alan Fox, James Q. Wilson, and John Dilulio. Males notes that although these leading criminologists use the term "youth violence," they almost exclusively focus on urban black and Latino youth. Males argues that these new "age theories" of crime, delinquency, and pathology "are caging Blacks and Latinos even more efficiently that the old 'race theories' did" (1999, 37).

4. Dead Prez has been particularly critical of youth subordination, public schooling, and imperialism and has become an important source of consciousness raising among many youth both in Oakland and Portland. In SRU, I encountered several individual students who were fans of Dead Prez. Many SRU students noted how much Dead Prez had awoken them to social injustices. However, unlike in Oakland, I have never witnessed Portland SRU activists actually use Dead Prez as a tool for educating and organizing other youth.

5. George H. W. Bush nicknamed Portland "Little Beirut" after encountering direct action protests during a presidential visit in the early 1990s. The name has stuck and has been reclaimed by Portland leftists, who have even started a progressive newspaper called *Little Beirut*.

6. This equation between anarchism and youth is reflected, for example, in the mainstream media coverage of the WTO protests in Seattle. However, anarchism is not *exclusively* a youth movement, as it has a rich history that predates Marxist communism. It has also been at the center of movements in Latin America as well as in contemporary earth and animal liberation movements.

7. For an excellent examination of how the mechanisms of policing and social control have shifted in response to the decentralized networks of dissent represented by the Seattle WTO anticorporate protests, see Fernandez (2008).

8. "Security culture" refers to practices that direct action groups adopt to keep police infiltrators from destroying movements. Adopting a security culture means assuming that your group is under police surveillance and taking precautions to safeguard discussions through the mail, Internet, telephone, or face-to-face meetings.

9. Goode and Maskovsky recognize that although wealth inequality and a promarket ideology are not necessarily new developments in the United States, "It is their emergence in the current moment, their level of coordination and mutual reinforcement, that represents a situation of historical significance" (2001, 8).

10. For an excellent examination of the politics of welfare reform, see Mink (1999).

11. Fraser and Gordon argue that the evisceration of public goods and social services undermine possibilities for social citizenship, because social citizenship entails not only individual rights but also participation in public life with "an entitlement to social provision" (1998, 113). Thus, social citizenship entails a right to a decent standard of living and the right to access pubic services and institutions. Fraser and Gordon note that the use of public parks, public schools and public health services, for example, all constitute the practice of social citizenship. When these institutions and services are eviscerated and curtailed, so is the very essence of citizenship.

12. Channel One is a twelve-minute video news program broadcasted throughout public classrooms across the United States. It consists of two minutes of advertising. For more discussion on Channel One as it relates to the privatization and the corporatization of schooling, see De Vaney (1994).

13. Saltman (2003) describes the militarization of public schooling as the proliferation of JROTC programs on campuses, the Troops to Teachers programs that places retired soldiers in public schools, the trend of military generals being hired as school superintendents, and the army's vast online education program. He also points to new educational emphases on discipline and standardized testing as manifestations of militarization.

14. Angela Davis (1998) describes the term "prison industrial complex" as the "corporatization of punishment," referring to the profit-generating capacity of prisons. Davis cites private prison companies, prison construction bonds as profitable investments, and the use of prison labor as cheap labor for companies such as Victoria's Secret, IBM, Motorola, Microsoft, and Boeing as elements of the prison industrial complex.

15. See Henwood's (1997) study of poverty rates by race and gender in the United States. Henwood finds that while incomes for rich households have skyrocketed in recent years, this has not been the case for middle-class and poor households.

16. BART is the Bay Area Rapid Transit, the train system that connects various sections of the Bay Area; Muni is the light-rail system in San Francisco.

17. Kozol calls this racial segregation a "dual society," which has intensified since the Reagan era especially in regard to segregated public schooling. He argues that as a result of Reagan-era economic restructuring, "social policy has been turned back almost one hundred years" (1991, 4).

18. Kornbluh argues that there exists an artificial distinction between "civil rights" and "economic rights" movements in many historical works that document

movements of the 1960s. She advocates for a broader understanding of the civil rights movement, one that includes movements for "economic redistribution and macroeconomic planning," such as the welfare rights movement (2003, 199). This broader conceptualization of the civil rights movement helps us to understand more recent backlash in California as not only racist but also fundamentally opposed to the civil rights' antipoverty demands for economic redistribution. For more on backlash against civil rights and antipoverty politics, see M. Davis (1986).

19. For an analysis of the generational race divide in the United States, see Chideya (1999) and Males (1999).

20. Leistyna (2003) argues that the No Child Left Behind Act represents a trend toward educational standardization and knowledge conformity that especially alienates and devalues poor and racially subordinated youth.

21. The California High School Exit Exam has been instituted in recent years as a statewide graduation requirement. By 2003, one hundred thousand teens had failed the exit exam at least twice (see Moore and Hayasaki 2003). The institution of the exit exam has become a focus of youth protests across the state of California, as it holds all students to the same standards despite vast inequalities in school resources, especially for youth of color in impoverished school systems. Student and adult activists argue that the exit exam is a punitive measure and constitutes one more barrier to the education of students of color and one more assault on poor communities of color. Because of these protests, low-income students and communities of color successfully secured a temporary, two-year delay in the exit exam from the California Board of Education in 2003.

22. The term "violent superpredators" was coined by John Dilulio, who in 2001 became the director of the new White House Office of Faith-Based and Community Initiatives under the Bush administration. He, along with his fellow authors, wrote, "America is now home to thickening ranks of juvenile 'superpredators'— radically impulsive, brutally remorseless youngsters, including ever more pre-teenage boys, who murder, assault, rape, rob, burglarize, deal deadly drugs, join gun-toting gangs and create serious communal disorders" (Bennett et al. 1996).

23. For a critique of this oft-repeated characterization of youth, see Males (1996, 1999).

24. Food Not Bombs is a worldwide anticorporate and antiauthoritarian grassroots movement that views healthy food as a human right. In cities around the world, Food Not Bombs chapters regularly distribute free, vegetarian food to hungry and homeless people, as well as to activists at a variety of protests and rallies.

25. For further examination of cynicism and apathy as social constructions and neoliberal accomplishments, see Eliasoph (1998), Putnam (2001), Boggs (2000), and Bauman (1999).

26. For examples of these scholarly discussions, see Youniss and others (1999), Delli Carpini (2000), Siurala (2002), Metz and others (2003), and Putnam (2008).

CHAPTER 2   READING, WRITING, AND RADICALISM: THE POLITICS
OF YOUTH ACTIVISM ON SCHOOL GROUNDS

1. The Oregon Citizens Alliance is a conservative Christian activist organization that has organized against gay rights since the late 1980s.

2. Vinson and Ross call the intensification of standardized testing schemes after 9–11 reflective of "a singular, idealized view of schooling" that "works to enforce, control, and discipline both cultural knowledge and behavior" (2003, 242). The authors argue that standardized testing reflects a politics of education driven by elites, a politics that defines and produces "official" knowledge and "proper" school behavior.

3. Influential progressive educational philosophers include Francis Parker, G. Stanley Hall, and John Dewey. For reviews of their philosophies in shaping education in the United States, see Brantlinger (2003) and Aronowitz and Giroux (1994).

4. See Bowles and Gintis (1976), Bourdieu (1977), Willis (1977), and MacLeod (1995).

5. I do not want to underestimate the importance of ACLU clubs, GSA clubs, environmental clubs, and service learning opportunities. While not necessarily overtly political or closely aligned with social movements in students' own communities, these club infrastructures are nevertheless important. However, activist students' critiques of these structures highlight the extent to which these infrastructures are severed from local or even national social movements, and thus how they often fail to foster political power among students.

6. Both Eckert (1989) and Bettie (2003) argue that structures like student government, in which the "jocks" (Eckert) or the "preps" (Bettie) participate, resonate with the dominant middle-class culture and middle-class students who are the least alienated by schooling. Eckert and Bettie note that through student government, the jocks and preps learn the tools of the management class through "managing" other students at school.

7. In his study of high school community service programs and students' sense of civic obligation, Riedel (2002) notes that public schools often conscientiously avoid political controversy when teaching civics.

8. This YP critique is much in-line with Bourdieu's notion of symbolic violence. In schools, symbolic violence works through the imposition of a dominant cultural ideology and ultimately preserves unequal power relations. See Bourdieu and Passeron (1990).

9. See Aronowitz and Giroux (1994) for an analysis of neoliberal school reforms under the Reagan and Bush administrations.

10. See Chideya (1999) and Miron (1999) for a further critique of multicultural curricula and cultural diversity policies that aim to "celebrate diversity" and difference under the banner of cultural harmony. Miron argues that this approach to multicultural ethnic studies bypasses political struggle, denies cultural conflict, and forecloses opportunities for students to form politicized collective identities as a result of this education.

11. Spirit Week is an annual week-long series of events designed to galvanize school spirit among students.

12. Zines have become particularly popular among girl youth subcultures like Riot Grrrl, who use zine making as a mode of resisting gender subordination (see Schilt 2003).

13. Eckert asserts that there is a "progressive adoption of adult prerogatives with each grade in secondary school" (1989, 109). James and others similarly note that school curricula are age graded: "Children enter the world of the school and they progress with their same-age peers through a fixed series of educational stages linked to an established, spatial hierarchy of classes. Each of these carries differing obligations and duties in relation to levels of educational attainment, the demonstration of social skills and adoption of responsibilities. It is an age-set charter laid out through curriculum design" (1998, 72).

14. These politics of student/adult alliances on campus are consistent with Bowles and Gintis's analysis of schooling as social reproduction. They argue that "the relationships of authority and control between administrators and teachers, teachers and students, students and students, and students and their work replicate the division of labor which dominates the workplace" (1976, 12).

15. For an examination of how political apathy is actively constructed through everyday cultural practices, see Eliasoph (1998).

16. The prohibition of political talk in schools is exacerbated by the growing emphasis on education as measured by standardized testing, which focuses on standardized, quantitative models of learning rather than seminar/discussion formats for education.

CHAPTER 3   ALLIES WITHIN AND WITHOUT: NAVIGATING THE TERRAIN OF ADULT-DOMINATED COMMUNITY POLITICS

1. SRU students, through constructing an autonomous youth-led space, subverted adult power by controlling the entry of adults into their space. They achieved, in Wolfe's terms, the spatial "privacy" that is usually reserved for adults. In this sense, their access to spatial privacy was an important source of their political empowerment.

2. The extent to which youth connections to adult allies are gendered will be discussed further in chapter 6.

3. The late rapper/poet Tupac Shakur, who stands as a contemporary hero and martyr for many black and Latino youth, was named by his mother (a prominent Black Panther) after Tupac Amaru—an Inca warrior who led a rebellion against Spanish occupation and conquest. YP adult allies used students' connection to Tupac Shakur as a bridge to discuss the warrior and the legacy of anticolonial revolution that bears his name.

4. These truncated discussions in SRU were not unlike those taking place within the radical women's movement in the early 1980s, in which participants

debated the issue of racial and class diversity (or lack thereof) within the movement (see Whittier 1995).

5. These discussions, in many ways, were much like those documented by Epstein (1991) in her analysis of the struggles within the nonviolent direct action movement.

CHAPTER 4   TOWARD YOUTH POLITICAL POWER IN OAKLAND: THE ADULT GAZE, ACADEMIC ACHIEVEMENT, AND THE STRUGGLE FOR POLITICAL LEGITIMACY

1. Martínez, an icon of YP, writes, "The commonalities begin with history, which reveals that again and again peoples of color have had one experience in common: European colonization and/or neo-colonialism with its accompanying exploitation. . . . People of color were victimized by colonialism not only externally but also through internalized racism—"the colonized mentality" (1998, 7).

2. As McAdam (1982) observes, when individuals are isolated, they tend to explain the conditions of their existence in terms of individual flaws rather than as functions of structural conditions. When youth of color are able to come together and mobilize mass movements, they begin to see their existence, as youth of color, in structural ways.

3. For an in-depth look at how public schools push out low-income adolescents, see Fine (1991).

4. Carter (2005) argues that underlying the academic disengagement of many low-income black and Latino youth is their strong critique of how schools function according to an arbitrary and unfair hierarchy of cultural meanings, which work to perpetuate social inequalities.

5. However, Carter (2005) warns that students' academic disengagement should not necessarily be read as delinquency and acquiescence to oppression and powerlessness. Rather, it should be recognized as students' criticism of the cultural hierarchies legitimized by schools and as student efforts to create racial-ethnic cultures that give each other comfort, distinction, and the ability to negotiate the systemic and cultural inequalities that they experience in their schools.

6. SRU activists were incredibly busy: their activism competed with music lessons, sports, and other extracurricular commitments and therefore became an especially salient measure of political commitment. Unlike YP organizers, almost all SRU activists possessed day planners and constantly referenced them. See Lareau (2003) for an analysis of why middle-class children's lives are more hectic and more rigidly structured than working-class and poor children's lives.

7. Although these politics of surveillance intensified for low-income students of color at the turn of the millennium, they are consistent with class-based schooling mechanisms that have long served to reproduce class inequalities. Bowles

and Gintis (1976), for example, argue that in working-class neighborhoods, schools are more hierarchical and focused on behavioral control, while schools in middle-class suburbs encourage greater student participation and less direct supervision.

8. Bourdieu's (1977) concept of cultural capital is central to schooling and social reproduction theory. Cultural capital is the broad set of tools and skills that are passed on to upper-class children from upper-class families. Because schools represent class interests and embody the language and values of the dominant culture, upper-class students are rewarded by schools while working-class cultural capital is devalued by schools. See also Berstein (1977), who applies Bourdieu's theory of cultural capital specifically to linguistic structures in schooling.

9. In Alana's particular case, it is important to note that she ended up denouncing SRU and eventually severed her ties to its brand of radical antiwar youth activism. This might have augmented her legitimacy vis-à-vis her teachers and school administration, and saved her from having to hide her SRU identity from her teachers, as Shae did. Girls' split from SRU will be explained further in chapter 6.

CHAPTER 5   TOWARD YOUTH POLITICAL POWER IN PORTLAND: THE ADULT GAZE, MAINSTREAM MEDIA, AND THE PROBLEMS OF SOCIAL VISIBILITY

1. The gendered differences between boys' and girls' relationships to their parents will be discussed further in the next chapter.

2. See Giroux (2003a) for an analysis of how low-income, urban, black, and Latino youth are increasingly subject to constant systems of policing in several spheres of their lives, including the streets, schools, and malls. In 2004, Oakland's *Bay City News* reported on a particularly disturbing instance of police harassment of area high school students. Three students alleged that, while on their lunch break from school, two officers searched the students, exposed their genitals, used racial slurs, and threatened to hit the teens if they did not stop asking the officers why they were being searched. Many YP students had experienced first-hand, or had heard about similar instances of, police harassment happening in their communities.

3. For an explanation of youth as "superpredators" and an argument for why young, urban, poor youth of color signify a coming crime wave that must be stopped, see *Body Count* (Bennett et al. 1996). For a rebuttal to the arguments in *Body Count*, see Males (1999).

4. Many school administrations, parents, media, and other students questioned the appropriateness of the multischool citywide walkout, which protested school budget cuts. Critics questioned whether walking out of school (and thus allegedly draining more money from schools) was the best way to demonstrate how much students wanted to save their schools. The SRU citywide sleep-in was an answer to these criticisms.

5. This depiction of "happy" or "sad" children in mainstream media coverage aligns with the image of youth as innocent victims in the victimizer/victim dichotomy of youth in public discourse (see Gaines 1991).

6. Local news coverage tended to depoliticize the meanings behind the antiwar protests on the day of bombing and focused instead on the spectacular imagery of "violent" protesters. This media portrayal of dissent resonates with what Fernandez (2008) terms the "violent anarchist frame," a social control tactic that frames dissent as a threat to public security, creating a chilling effect on protest movements and their links to local communities.

CHAPTER 6   GENDERING POLITICAL POWER: GENDER POLITICS IN YOUTH ACTIVIST NETWORKS

1. For notable studies on how systems of gender affect women's activism and resistance, see Abrahams (1996), Brown and Ferguson (1995), Naples (1998), Robnett (1997), Ruddick (1989), and Whittier (1995).

2. See Habermas (1989). Although new information technologies allow youth to access virtual publics in cyberspace like never before, electronic communication cannot completely substitute for face-to-face movement participation (see Bandy and Smith 2005).

3. For analyses of how and why young people are often barred from public space, see M. Davis (1991), Lucas (1998), Sibley (1995), and Valentine (1996).

4. However, in some cases adult women activists must contend with opposition from their spouses and, like teenage girls, also have to navigate family barriers to civic mobility. This is documented in studies on women's organizing in immigrant communities in the United States, and in women's labor organizing in maquiladora and export processing zones. See Louie (2001) for an example of these issues in women's organizing.

5. For an examination of gendered parenting patterns, see Fiese and Skillman (2000), Orenstein (1994), Taylor and others (1995), and Weitzman and others (1985).

6. However, some SRU girls, especially those who were still freshmen or sophomores, discussed their curfews as obstacles to participating in evening and night activist meetings and events.

7. For an analysis of women's political resistance and specifically the ways in which women's antimilitarist movements take politicized symbols of traditional femininity and motherhood into the public sphere, see Ruddick (1989).

CONCLUSION

1. For a fascinating look at teenage girls' activism in global justice movements throughout the Americas, see the work of Jessica K. Taft. Taft also calls attention to the role that nation plays in cultivating youth political engagement and disengagement. For example, she notes that leftist political parties throughout

Latin America include "youth wings" designed by and for politically active youth in their teens and twenties. This may signal to us that levels of youth political alienation also depend on national context (see Gordon and Taft 2008), and the deeper political alienation of youth in the United States may very well be a feature of North American political life.

APPENDIX: ENTERING THE WORLDS OF YOUTH ACTIVISM

1. I joined the now-defunct Portland Police Accountability Campaign, which had been working to establish an independent citizen review board of police abuses in Portland.

2. Between March of 2003 and June of 2004, I made five visits to Oakland to conduct research with YP. Two of these visits lasted a few months; one of these visits lasted only a week. The other two visits took place over a few weeks. Each visit was intensive, however, and allowed me an opportunity to conduct ethnographic research during periods when YP students met every day during summer-long YP programs or even spent whole weekends together during YP strategizing retreats. However, I missed their more regular weekly meetings during the course of the school year.

3. As in San Francisco, the goal of the antiwar protest in Portland on the day President Bush announced the war in Iraq (what activists call "the Day of Bombing" or "Day X") was to shut the city down. Flyers posted to telephone poles all over the city in the days preceding the war read, "When the bombs drop, Portland stops!" The goal was to impede traffic and business as usual, making the cost of waging war in Iraq too high in terms of national security and economic viability in cities at home. This follows the same direct action antiwar tactics used during the Vietnam-era protests.

4. For an historical overview of how Jews became racialized as white, see Brodkin Sacks (1994).

REFERENCES

Abrahams, Naomi. 1996. "Negotiating Power, Identity, Family, and Community: Women's Community Participation." *Gender & Society* 10 (6): 768–796.

Acker, Joan. 1990. "Hierarchies, Jobs, Bodies: A Theory of Gendered Organizations." *Gender & Society.* 4 (2): 139–158.

Adler, Patricia, and Peter Adler. 1998. *Peer Power.* New Brunswick, NJ: Rutgers University Press.

Anderson, Lenore, Daniel Macallair, and Celina Ramirez. 2005. *California Youth Authority Warehouses: Failing Kids, Families, and Public Safety.* Issue Briefing. Oakland, CA: Books Not Bars.

Ariès, Philippe. 1962. *Centuries of Childhood.* London: Cape.

Aronowitz, Stanley, and Henry A. Giroux. 1986. *Education under Siege: The Conservative, Liberal, and Radical Debate over Schooling.* London: Routledge.

Baca Zinn, Maxine, and Bonnie Thorton Dill. 1996. "Theorizing Difference from Multiracial Feminism." *Feminist Studies* 22:321–333.

Bandy, Joe, and Jackie Smith. 2005. "Factors Affecting Conflict and Cooperation in Transnational Movement Networks." In *Coalitions across Borders: Transnational Protest and the Neoliberal Order*, ed. Joe Bandy and Jackie Smith, 231–252. New York: Rowman and Littlefield.

Bauman, Zygmunt. 1999. *In Search of Politics.* Stanford, CA: Stanford University Press.

Bay City News. 2004. "Oakland Students Allege Abuse at the Hands of Police." February 26.

Beckerman, Gal. 2003. "Edging Away from Anarchy: Inside the Indymedia Collective, Passion versus Pragmatism" *Columbia Journalism Review* 42 (3): 27–30.

Bennett, William, John Dilulio, and John Walters. 1996. *Body Count: Moral Poverty and How to Win America's War against Crime and Drugs.* New York: Simon and Schuster.

Bernstein, Basil. 1977. "Social Class, Language, and Socialization." In *Power and Ideology in Education*, ed. Jerome Karabel and A. H. Halsey, 473–486. New York: Oxford University Press.

Best, Amy L. 2006a. *Fast Cars, Cool Rides: The Accelerating World of Youth and Their Cars.* New York: New York University Press.

———. 2006b. "Freedom, Constraint, and Family Responsibility: Teens and Parents Collaboratively Negotiate around the Car, Class, Gender, and Culture." *Journal of Family Issues* 27 (1): 55–84.

———. 2007. Introduction to *Representing Youth: Methodological Issues in Critical Youth Studies*, ed. Amy L. Best, 1–38. New York: New York University Press.

Bettie, Julie. 2003. *Women without Class: Girls, Race, and Identity*. Berkeley: University of California Press.

Bloom, Marissa, and Marianne Cariaso. 2004. "A Voice to Be Heard: Diverse Bay Area Youth Building Community through Arts Activism." Presentation, annual meeting of the American Sociological Association, San Francisco, CA, August 14.

Boggs, Carl. 2000. *The End of Politics: Corporate Power and the Decline of the Public Sphere*. New York: Guilford.

Bourdieu, Pierre. 1977. "Cultural Reproduction and Social Reproduction." In *Power and Ideology in Education*, ed. Jerome Karabel and A. H. Halsey, 487–510. New York: Oxford University Press.

———. 1998. "The Essence of Neoliberalism." *Le Monde Diplomatique*. December.

———. 1999. *Acts of Resistance: Against the Tyranny of the Market*. New York: New York Press.

Bourdieu, Pierre, and Jean-Claude Passeron. 1990. *Reproduction in Education, Society and Culture*. 2nd ed. Newbury Park, CA: Sage.

Bowles, Samuel, and Herbert Gintis. 1976. *Schooling in Capitalist America*. New York: Basic Books.

Brantlinger, Ellen. 2003. *Dividing Classes: How the Middle Class Negotiates and Rationalizes School Advantage*. New York: RoutledgeFalmer.

Brodkin Sacks, Karen. 1994. "How Did Jews Become White Folks?" In *Race*, ed. Steven Gregory and Roger Sanjek, 78–102. New Brunswick, NJ: Rutgers University Press.

Brown, Elaine. 1992. *A Taste of Power: A Black Woman's Story*. New York: Pantheon.

Brown, Enora. 2003. "Freedom for Some, Discipline for 'Others.'" In *Education as Enforcement*, ed. Kenneth Saltman and David Gabbard, 127–152. New York: RoutledgeFalmer.

Brown, Lyn Mikel. 1998. *Raising Their Voices: The Politics of Girls' Anger*. Cambridge, MA: Harvard University Press.

Brown, Phil, and Faith Ferguson. 1995. "'Making a Big Stink': Women's Work, Women's Relationships, and Toxic Waste Activism." *Gender & Society* 9:145–172.

Bucholtz, Mary. 2002. "Youth and Cultural Practice." *Annual Review of Anthropology* 31:525–552.

Cahill, Spencer. 1990. "Childhood and Public Life: Reaffirming Biographical Divisions." *Social Problems* 37:390–402.

California Institute for Federal Policy Research. 2002. "New Poverty Numbers Released by Census Bureau." *California Capitol Hill Bulletin* 9 (September 26): 4–5.

Carter, Prudence. 2005. *Keepin' It Real: School Success beyond Black and White*. Cambridge: Oxford University Press.

CCSRE (Center for Comparative Studies in Race and Ethnicity). 2002. "Race and Poverty Rates in California: Census 2000 Profiles." *CCSRE Race and Ethnicity in California: Demographics Report Series* 12 (November): 1–20.

Chideya, Farai. 1999. *The Color of Our Future: Race for the 21st Century*. New York: Morrow.

Clarke, John, Stuart Hall, Tony Jefferson, and Brian Roberts. 1975. "Subcultures, Cultures and Class: A Theoretical Overview." In *Resistance through Rituals: Youth Subcultures in Postwar Britain*, ed. Stuart Hall and Tony Jefferson, 9–74. London: Hutchinson.

Clay, Andreana. 2006. " 'All I Need Is One Mic': Mobilizing Youth for Social Change in the Post–Civil Rights Era." *Social Justice* 33 (2): 105–121.

Cohen, Jean, and Andrew Arato. 1992. *Civil Society and Political Theory*. Cambridge, MA: MIT Press.

Collins, Patricia Hill. 1999. *Black Feminist Thought: Knowledge, Consciousness, and the Politics of Empowerment*. 2nd ed. London: HarperCollins.

Corsaro, William. 1997. *The Sociology of Childhood*. Thousand Oaks, CA: Pine Forge.

Cullinan, Cris. 1999. "Vision, Privilege, and the Problem of Tolerance." *Electronic Magazine of Multicultural Education* 1 (September). www.eastern.edu/publications/emme/1999spring/cullinan.html (accessed March 13, 2008).

Davis, Angela. 1998. "Masked Racism: Reflections on the Prison Industrial Complex." *Colorlines*. Fall.

Davis, Mike. 1986. *Prisoners of the American Dream*. New York: Verso.

———. 1991. *City of Quartz*. New York: Verso.

Dawson, Michael. 1999. "Globalization, the Racial Divide, and a New Citizenship." In *Race, Identity, and Citizenship: A Reader*, ed. Rodolfo D. Torres, Louis F. Miron, and Jonathan Xavier Inda, 373–386. Oxford: Blackwell.

Delli Carpini, Michael. 2000. "Gen.com: Youth, Civic Engagement, and the New Information Environment." *Political Communication* 17:341–349.

Delpit, Lisa. 1995. *Other People's Children: Cultural Conflict in the Classroom*. New York: New Press.

De Vaney, Ann, ed. 1994. *Watching Channel One: The Convergence of Students, Technology, and Private Business*. Albany: State University of New York Press.

Eckert, Penelope. 1989. *Jocks and Burnouts: Social Categories and Identity in the High School*. New York: Teacher's College Press.

Education State Rankings. 2004. *Pre K-12 Education in the 50 United States*. Lawrence, KS: Morgan Quitno.

Ehlers, Scott, Vincent Schiraldi, and Eric Lotke. 2004. *Racial Divide: An Examination of the Impact of California's Three Strikes Law on African Americans and Latinos*. Washington, DC: Justice Policy Institute.

Eisenstadt, Shmuel Noah. 1978. *Revolution and the Transformation of Societies*. New York: Free Press.

Eliasoph, Nina. 1998. *Avoiding Politics: How Americans Produce Apathy in Everyday Life*. Cambridge: Cambridge University Press.

Epstein, Barbara. 1991. *Political Protest and Cultural Revolution: Nonviolent Direct Action in the 1970s and 1980s*. Berkeley: University of California Press.

Erikson, Erik H. 1968. *Identity: Youth and Crisis*. New York: Norton.

Evans, Sara, and Harry C. Boyte. 1986. *Free Spaces: The Sources of Democratic Change in America*. New York: Harper and Row.

Farson, Richard. 1974. *Birthrights*. New York: Macmillan.

Ferguson, Ann Arnett. 2001. *Bad Boys: Public Schools in the Making of Black Masculinity*. Ann Arbor: University of Michigan Press.

Fernandez, Luis. 2008. *Policing Dissent: Social Control and the Anti-Globalization Movement*. New Brunswick, NJ: Rutgers University Press.

Ferreira, Jason M. 2004. "Medicine of Memory: Third World Radicalism in San Francisco and the Politics of Multiracial Unity." Presentation, annual meeting of the American Sociological Association, San Francisco, CA, August 14.

Feuer, Lewis Samuel. 1969. *The Conflict of Generations*. New York: Basic Books.

Fiese, Barbara H., and Gemma Skillman. 2000. "Gender Differences in Family Stories: Moderating Influence of Parent Gender Role and Child Gender." *Sex Roles* 43 (September): 267–283.

Fine, Michelle. 1991. *Framing Dropouts: Notes on the Politics of an Urban Public High School*. Albany: State University of New York Press.

Flacks, Marc. 2007. "Label Jars Not People": How (Not) to Study Youth Civic Engagement." In *Representing Youth: Methodological Issues in Critical Youth Studies*, ed. Amy L. Best, 60–83. New York: New York University Press.

Flacks, Richard. 1971. *Youth and Social Change*. Chicago: Rand McNally.

Fordham, Signithia. 1996. *Blacked Out: Dilemmas of Race, Identity, and Success at Capital High*. Chicago: University of Chicago Press.

Fordham, Signithia, and John Ogbu. 1986. "Black Students' School Success: Coping with the 'Burden of "Acting White." ' " *Urban Review* 18 (3): 176–206.

Forman, Murray. 2002. *The "Hood" Comes First: Race, Place, and Space in Rap and Hip-Hop*. Middletown, CT: Wesleyan University Press.

Forman, Tyrone A. 2004. "Color-Blind Racism and Racial Indifference: The Role of Racial Apathy in Facilitating Enduring Inequalities." In *The Changing Terrain of Race and Ethnicity*, ed. Maria Krysan and Amanda E. Lewis, 43–66. New York: Russell Sage Foundation.

Fraser, Nancy, and Linda Gordon. 1998. "Contract versus Charity: Why Is There No Social Citizenship in the United States?" In *The Citizenship Debates*, ed. Gershon Shafir, 113–130. Minneapolis: University of Minnesota Press.

Gaines, Donna. 1991. *Teenage Wasteland: Suburbia's Dead End Kids*. New York: Harper Perennial.

Gamson, Josh. 1989. "Silence, Death, and the Invisible Enemy: AIDS Activism and Social Movement 'Newness.'" *Social Problems* 36 (4): 351–367.

Garrison, Ednie. 2000. "U.S. Feminism-Grrrl Style! Youth (Sub)Cultures and the Technologics of the Third Wave." *Feminist Studies* 26:141–171.

George, Susan. 1999. "A Short History of Neoliberalism." Presentation, Conference on Economic Sovereignty in a Globalising World, Bangkok, Thailand, March 24.

Gergen, David. 1996. "Taming Teenage Wolf Packs." *U.S. News & World Report*, March 25.

Giroux, Henry. 1996. *Fugitive Cultures: Race, Violence, and Youth*. New York: Routledge.

———. 2003a. *The Abandoned Generation: Democracy beyond the Culture of Fear*. New York: Macmillan.

———. 2003b. *Public Spaces, Private Lives: Democracy beyond 9–11*. Oxford: Rowman and Littlefield.

Glenn, Evelyn Nakano. 1986. *Issei, Nisei, War Bride: Three Generations of Japanese American Women in Domestic Service*. Philadelphia: Temple University Press.

Goode, Judith, and Jeff Maskovsky. 2001. Introduction to *The New Poverty Studies: The Ethnography of Power, Politics, and Impoverished People in the United States*, ed. Judith Goode and Jeff Maskovsky, 1–36. New York: New York University Press.

Gordon, Hava R. 2007. "Allies Within and Without: How Adolescent Activists Conceptualize Ageism and Navigate Adult Power in Youth Social Movements." *Journal of Contemporary Ethnography* 36 (6): 631–668.

———. 2008. "Gendered Paths to Teenage Political Participation: Parental Power, Civic Mobility, and Youth Activism." *Gender & Society* 22 (1): 31–55.

Guidikova, Irena, and Lasse Siurala. 2001. "A Weird, Wired, Winsome Generation: Across Contemporary Discourses on Subculture and Citizenship." Introduction to *Transitions of Youth Citizenship in Europe: Culture, Subculture, and Identity*, ed. Andy Furlong and Irena Guidikova, 5–16. Strasbourg, France: Council of Europe Publishing.

Habermas, Jürgen. 1989. *The Structural Transformation of the Public Sphere: An Inquiry into a Category of Bourgeois Society*. Cambridge, MA: MIT Press.

Hakim, Catherine. 1987. *Research Design: Strategies and Choices in the Design of Social Research*. Boston: Allen and Unwin.

Hall, Stuart, and Tony Jefferson, eds. 1975. *Resistance through Rituals: Youth Subcultures in Postwar Britain*. London: Hutchinson.

Harris, Cheryl I. 1995. "Whiteness as Property." In *Critical Race Theory: The Key Writings That Formed the Movement*, ed. Kimberle Crenshaw, Neil Gotanda, Gary Peller, and Kendall Thomas, 276–291. New York: New Press.

Hayasaki, Erika. 2003. "Districts Taking On Recruiters." *Los Angeles Times*. February 13.

Hebdige, Dick. 1979. *Subculture: The Meaning of Style*. London: Methuen.

Henn, Matt, Mark Weinstein, and Dominic Wring. 2002. "A Generation Apart? Youth and Political Participation in Britain." *British Journal of Politics and International Relations* 4 (2): 167–192.

Henwood, Doug. 1997. "Trash-o-Nomics." In *White Trash: Race and Class in America*, ed. Matt Wray and Annalee Newitz, 177–192. New York: Routledge.

Hill, Shirley A., and Joey Sprague. 1999. "Parenting in Black and White Families: The Interaction of Gender with Race and Class." *Gender & Society* 13 (4): 480–502.

Holt, John. 1975. *Escape From Childhood*. New York: Ballantine Books.

Hondagneu-Sotelo, Pierrette. 1994. *Gendered Transitions: Mexican Experiences of Immigration*. Berkeley: University of California Press.

Hooks, Bell. 1989. *Talking Back: Thinking Feminist, Thinking Black*. Boston: South End.

———. 1994. *Teaching to Transgress: Education as the Practice of Freedom*. New York: Routledge.

James, Allison. 1998. "From the Child's Point of View: Issues in the Social Construction of Childhood." In *Biosocial Perspectives on Children*, ed. Catherine Panter-Brick, 45–65. Cambridge: Cambridge University Press.

James, Allison, Chris Jenks, and Alan Prout. 1998. *Theorizing Childhood*. New York: Teacher's College Press.

James, Allison, and Alan Prout, eds. 1990. *Constructing and Reconstructing Childhood*. New York: Falmer.

Jenks, Chris. 1996. "The Postmodern Child." In *Children in Families: Research and Policy*, ed. Julia Brannen and Margaret O'Brien, 13–25. London: Falmer.

Jorgensen, Danny. 1989. *Participant Observation: A Methodology for Human Studies*. Newbury Park, CA: Sage.

Kantrowitz, Barbara. 1993. "Wild in the Streets: Murder and Mayhem, Guns and Gangs; A Teenage Generation Grows Up Dangerous and Scared." *Newsweek*, August 2.

Kaplan, Elaine Bell. 1997. *Not Our Kind of Girl: Unraveling the Myths of Black Teenage Motherhood*. Berkeley: University of California Press.

Katz, Alex. 2004. "1 Year Later, Is Takeover Working?" *Oakland Tribune*. June 2.

Kearney, Mary Celeste. 1998. "'Don't Need You': Rethinking Identity Politics and Separatism from a Grrrl Perspective." In *Youth Culture: Identity in a Postmodern World*, ed. Jonathan Epstein, 148–188. Malden, MA: Blackwell.

Keniston, Kenneth. 1968. *Young Radicals*. New York: Harcourt, Brace and World.

———. 1971. *Youth and Dissent*. New York: Harcourt Brace Jovanovich.

Kornbluh, Felicia. 2003. "Black Buying Power: Welfare Rights, Consumerism, and Northern Protest." In *Freedom North: Black Freedom Struggles Outside the South, 1940–1980*, ed. Jeanne Theoharis and Komozi Woodard, 199–222. New York: Macmillan.

Kozol, Jonathan. 1991. *Savage Inequalities: Children in America's Schools*. New York: Harper Perennial.

Kurz, Demie. 2002. "Caring for Teenage Children." *Journal of Family Issues* 23 (6): 748–767.

Labaree, David. 1997. "Public Goods, Private Goods: The American Struggle over Educational Goals." *American Educational Research Journal* 34 (1): 39–81.

Lareau, Annette. 2002. "Invisible Inequality: Social Class and Child Rearing in Black Families and White Families." *American Sociological Review* 67 (October): 747–776.

———. 2003. *Unequal Childhoods: Class, Race, and Family Life*. Berkeley: University of California Press.

Leistyna, Pepi. 2003. "Facing Oppression: Youth Voices from the Front" In *Education as Enforcement*, ed. Kenneth Saltman and David Gabbard, 101–125. New York: RoutledgeFalmer.

Lesko, Nancy. 1996. "Denaturalizing Adolescence." *Youth and Society* 28:139–162.

———. 2001. *Act Your Age! A Cultural Construction of Adolescence*. New York: RoutledgeFalmer.

Lipset, Seymour Martin, and Philip G. Altbach, eds. 1969. *Students in Revolt*. Boston: Houghton Mifflin.

Lorber, Judith. 1991. *The Social Construction of Gender*. Newbury Park, CA: Sage.

Lorde, Audre. 1984. "Age, Race, Class, and Sex: Women Redefining Difference." In *Sister Outsider: Essays and Speeches*, 114–123. Freedom, CA: Crossing.

Louie, Miriam Ching Yoon. 2001. *Sweatshop Warriors: Immigrant Women Workers Take on the Global Factory*. Cambridge, MA: South End.

Lucas, Tim. 1998. "Youth Gangs and Moral Panics in Santa Cruz, California." In *Cool Places: Geographies of Youth Cultures*, ed. Tracey Skelton and Gill Valentine, 146–161. London: Routledge.

MacLeod, Jay. 1995. *Ain't No Makin' It: Aspirations and Attainment in a Low Income Neighborhood*. Boulder, CO: Westview.

Males, Mike. 1996. *Scapegoat Generation: America's War on Adolescents*. Monroe, ME: Common Courage.

———. 1999. *Framing Youth: Ten Myths about the Next Generation*. Monroe, ME: Common Courage Press.

Males, Mike, and Dan Macallair. 2000. *The Color of Justice: An Analysis of Juvenile Adult Court Transfers in California*. Washington, DC: Justice Policy Institute.

Martínez, Elizabeth (Betita). 1998. *De Colores Means All of Us: Latina Views for a Multi-Colored Century*. Cambridge, MA: South End.

———. 2000. "Where Was the Color in Seattle? Looking for Reasons Why the Great Battle Was So White." *Monthly Review*. July–August.

Massey, Douglas S., and Nancy A. Denton. 1993. *American Apartheid: Segregation and the Making of the Underclass*. Cambridge, MA: Harvard University Press.

McAdam, Doug. 1982. *Political Process and the Development of Black Insurgency, 1930–1970*. Chicago: University of Chicago Press.

McRobbie, Angela, and Jenny Garber. 1975. "Girls and Subcultures: An Exploration." In *Resistance through Rituals: Youth Subcultures in Postwar Britain*, ed. Stuart Hall and Tony Jefferson, 209–222. London: Hutchinson.

Melucci, Alberto. 1989. *Nomads of the Present: Social Movements and Individual Needs in Contemporary Society*. Philadelphia: Temple University Press.

Metz, Edward, Jeffrey McLellan, and James Youniss. 2003. "Types of Voluntary Service and Adolescents' Civic Development." *Journal of Adolescent Research* 18 (2): 188–203.

Mink, Gwendolyn, ed. 1999. *Whose Welfare?* Ithaca, NY: Cornell University Press.

Miron, Louis F. 1999. "Postmodernism and the Politics of Racialized Identities." In *Race, Identity, and Citizenship: A Reader*, ed. Rodolfo D. Torres, Louis F. Miron, and Jonathan Xavier Inda, 79–100. Oxford: Blackwell.

Mohanty, Chandra. 1991. "Under Western Eyes: Feminist Scholarship and Colonial Discourses." In *Third World Women and the Politics of Feminism*, ed. Chandra Mohanty, Ann Russo, and Lourdes Torres, 51–80. Bloomington: Indiana University Press.

Molnar, Alex. 1996. *Giving Kids the Business*. Boulder, CO: Westview.

Moore, Solomon, and Erika Hayasaki. 2003. "L.A. School Board Votes to Oppose State Exit Exam." *Los Angeles Times*. April 9.

Muñoz, Carlos, Jr. 1989. *Youth, Identity, Power: The Chicano Movement*. New York: Verso.

Naples, Nancy. 1998. *Community Activism and Feminist Politics: Organizing across Race, Class, and Gender*. New York: Routledge.

Neal, Mark Anthony. 1999. *What the Music Said: Black Popular Music and Black Public Culture*. New York: Routledge.

Nehring, Neil. 1993. *Flowers in the Dustbin: Culture, Anarchy, and Postwar England*. Ann Arbor: University of Michigan Press.

Ogbu, John. 1991. "Immigrant and Involuntary Minorities in Comparative Perspective." In *Minority Status and Schooling: A Comparative Study of Immigrant and Involuntary Minorities*, ed. Margaret Gibson and John Ogbu, 3–33. New York: Garland.

Omi, Michael, and Howard Winant. 1986. *Racial Formation in the United States: From the 1960s to the 1980s*. New York: Routledge.

Ong, Aihwa. 1999. "Cultural Citizenship as Subject Making: Immigrants Negotiate Racial and Cultural Boundaries in the United States." In *Race, Identity, and Citizenship: A Reader*, ed. Rodolfo D. Torres, Louis F. Miron, and Jonathan Xavier Inda, 262–294. Oxford: Blackwell.

Orenstein, Peggy. 1994. *Schoolgirls: Young Women, Self-Esteem and the Confidence Gap*. New York: Anchor/Doubleday.

Osler, Audrey, and Hugh Starkey. 2003. "Learning for Cosmopolitan Citizenship: Theoretical Debates and Young People's Experiences." Educational Review 55 (3): 243–254.

Parker, Robert. 1994. *Flesh Peddlers and Warm Bodies: The Temporary Help Industry and Its Workers*. New Brunswick, NJ: Rutgers University Press.

Platt, Anthony. 1977. *The Child Savers: The Invention of Delinquency*. Chicago: University of Chicago Press.

Putnam, Robert. 2001. *Bowling Alone: The Collapse and Revival of American Community*. New York: Touchstone Books.

———. 2008. "The Rebirth of American Civic Life." *Boston Globe*. March 2.

Qvortrup, Jens. 1994. "Childhood Matters: An Introduction." In *Childhood Matters: Social Theory, Practice, and Politics*, ed. Jens Qvortrup, Marjatta Bardy, Giovanni Sgritta, and Helmut Wintersberger, 1–23. Aldershot, VT: Avebury.

Riedel, Eric. 2002. "The Impact of High School Community Service Programs on Students' Feelings of Civic Obligation." *American Politics Research* 30 (September): 499–527.

Roberts, Dorothy. 1997. *Killing the Black Body: Race, Reproduction, and the Meaning of Liberty*. New York: Vintage Books.

Robinson, Catherine. 2000. "Creating Space, Creating Self: Street-Frequenting Youth in the City and Suburbs." *Journal of Youth Studies* 3 (4): 429–443.

Robnett, Belinda. 1997. *How Long, How Long? African-American Women in the Struggle for Civil Rights*. New York: Oxford University Press.

Ruddick, Sara. 1989. *Maternal Thinking: Toward a Politics of Peace*. Boston: Beacon.

Saltman, Kenneth. 2000. *Collateral Damage: Corporatizing Public Schools; A Threat to Democracy*. Boulder, CO: Rowman and Littlefield.

———. 2003. Introduction to *Education as Enforcement*, ed. Kenneth Saltman and David Gabbard, 1–24. New York: RoutledgeFalmer.

Saltman, Kenneth, and David Gabbard, eds. 2003. *Education as Enforcement*. New York: RoutledgeFalmer.

Saltman, Kenneth, and Robin Truth Goodman. 2003. "Rivers of Fire: BPAmoco's iMPACT on Education." In *Education as Enforcement*, ed. Kenneth Saltman and David Gabbard, 37–60. New York: RoutledgeFalmer.

Schilt, Kristen. 2003. " 'I'll Resist with Every Inch and Every Breath': Girls and Zine Making as a Form of Resistance." *Youth and Society* 35 (September): 71–97.

Sibley, David. 1995. *Geographies of Exclusion: Society and Difference in the West.* New York: Routledge.

Sigel, Roberta, and Marilyn Hoskin. 1981. *The Political Involvement of Adolescents.* New Brunswick, NJ: Rutgers University Press.

Siurala, Lasse. 2002. *Can Youth Make a Difference? Youth Policy Facing Diversity and Change.* Strasbourg, France: Council of Europe.

Sleeter, Christine. 1999. Foreword to *Subtractive Schooling: U.S.-Mexican Youth and the Politics of Caring*, by Angela Valenzuela. Albany: State University of New York Press.

Smith, Noel, Ruth Lister, Sue Middleton, Lynne Cox. 2005. "Young People as Real Citizens: Towards an Inclusionary Understanding of Citizenship." *Journal of Youth Studies* 8 (4): 425–443.

Spelman, Elizabeth. 1988. *Inessential Woman: Problems of Exclusion in Feminist Thought.* Boston: Beacon.

Starr, Amory. 2000. *Naming the Enemy: Anti-Corporate Movements Confront Globalization.* New York: Zed Books.

Taft, Jessica, and Hava Gordon. 2009. "Youth Civic Engagement and Constrained Democracy." Forthcoming presentation, annual meeting of the American Sociological Association, San Francisco, CA, August 10, 2009.

Taylor, Jill McLean, Carol Gilligan, and Amy M. Sullivan. 1995. *Between Voice and Silence: Women and Girls, Race and Relationship.* Cambridge: Harvard University Press.

Taylor, Verta. 1999. "Gender and Social Movements: Gender Processes in Women's Self-Help Movements." *Gender & Society* 13 (1): 8–33.

Thomson, Rachel, Janet Holland, Sheena McGrellis, Robert Bell, Sheila Henderson, and Sue Sharpe. 2004. "Inventing Adulthoods: A Biographical Approach to Understanding Youth Citizenship." *Sociological Review* 52 (2): 218–239.

Thorne, Barrie. 1993. *Gender Play: Girls and Boys in School.* New Brunswick, NJ: Rutgers University Press.

Touraine, Alain. 1985. "An Introduction to the Study of Social Movements." *Social Research* 52 (4): 749–787.

Valentine, Gill. 1996. "Children Should Be Seen and Not Heard: The Production and Transgression of Adults' Public Space." *Urban Geography* 17 (March): 205–220.

Valenzuela, Angela. 1999. *Subtractive Schooling: U.S.-Mexican Youth and the Politics of Caring.* Albany: State University of New York Press.

Vinson, Kevin D., and E. Wayne Ross. 2003. "Controlling Images: The Power of High Stakes Testing." In *Education as Enforcement*, ed. Kenneth Saltman and David Gabbard, 236–253. New York: RoutledgeFalmer.

Ward, Janie. 2000. *The Skin We're In: Teaching Our Children to Be Emotionally Strong, Socially Smart, Spiritually Connected.* New York: Free Press.

Watts, Roderick J., and Omar Guessous. 2006. "Sociopolitical Development: The Missing Link in Research and Policy on Adolescents." In *Beyond Resistance! Youth*

Activism and Community Change, ed. Shawn Ginwright, Pedro Noguera, and Julio Cammarota, 59–80. New York: Routledge.

Weitzman, Nancy, Beverly Birns, and Ronald Friend. 1985. "Traditional and Non-traditional Mothers' Communication with Their Daughters and Sons." *Child Development* 56:894–896.

Whittier, Nancy E. 1995. *Feminist Generations: The Persistence of the Radical Women's Movement*. Philadelphia: Temple University Press.

Williamson, Howard. 2002. *Supporting Young People in Europe: Principles, Policy and Practice*. Strasbourg, France: Council of Europe.

Willis, Paul. 1977. *Learning to Labour: How Working Class Kids Get Working Class Jobs*. New York: Columbia University Press.

Wolfe, Maxine. 1978. "Childhood and Privacy." In *Children and the Environment*, 175–222. New York: Plenum.

Youniss, James, Susan Bales, Marcelo Diversi, Verona Christmas-Best, Milbrey McLaughlin, and Rainer Silbereisen. 2002. "Youth Civic Engagement in the Twenty-First Century." *Journal of Research on Adolescence* 12 (1): 121–148.

Youniss, James, Jeffrey McLellan, Yang Su, and Miranda Yates. 1999. "The Role of Community Service in Identity Development: Normative, Unconventional, and Deviant Orientations." *Journal of Adolescent Research* 14 (2): 248–261.

Zavella, Patricia. 2001. "The Tables Are Turned: Immigration, Poverty, and Social Conflict California Communities." In *The New Poverty Studies: The Ethnography of Power, Politics, and Impoverished People in the United States*, ed. Judith Goode and Jeff Maskovsky, 103–134. New York: New York University Press.

INDEX

dropping out of, 142; early closure of, 199, 217; health and, 48; hierarchy of classes in, 230n13; immigrant students and, 77; isolation from larger community of, 69, 89, 94, 97, 99, 196, 206; lack of political framework in, 23, 74; liberation, 34, 217; maintenance of unequal relationships in, 76–77; middle-class liberal, 26; obedience in, 66; overcrowding of, 153; politicized spaces within, 82, 83, 96; politics and, 61–62, 64, 68–69, 74, 75–76; power dynamics in, 96; role of in youths' lives, 45; sit-ins at, 32, 150, 185; sleep-ins at, 118, 149, 161, 162, 163, 232n4; student government in, 72–73, 90, 94, 206, 229n6; violence in, 3–4, 9, 41–42, 46, 48, 98, 113–114, 153; walkouts of, 21, 150, 161, 163, 165–166, 167–168, 232n4; war and, 41; youth organizing in, 11, 60–65, 81, 92–93, 95, 97, 135–136, 139

schools, impoverished, 16, 37, 45, 53–54, 65, 113–114, 142–143; bathroom campaigns in, 81, 144; ethnic studies at, 77–78; high administrator turnover at, 85–87; lack of school clubs at, 65, 95, 207; lack of services at, 48, 106; media and, 144; militarism in, 20, 34–35, 58, 137–138, 187, 227n13; police in, 158; portable classrooms in, 143; prisonlike appearance of, 34–35; racial tensions at, 79; security guards in, 148; student government at, 73; teacher support for youth activism at, 93; youth centers and, 85–87; youth political alienation and, 207; YP and, 70, 219

school spirit, 72, 79, 206, 230n11
security culture in radical social movements, 30
security guards, 34–35, 148
senior high school students, status of, 88
September 11th attacks, 39, 41, 55; on Pentagon, 38–39; on World Trade Center, 38–39
service programs, 55
sexism, 3, 5; adult allies and, 193–195, 196; adult power and, 196–197; lack of curricular attention to, 74; models of youth and, 9; reverse, 194; safety and, 64; in SRU, 189–191, 193–194; youth subordination and, 14–15; in YP, 193–195. See also gender
Shakur, Tupac, 12, 230n3
Siurala, Lasse, 216
slave rebellions, 112
Sleeter, Christine, 76
Smith, Noel, 9
SNCC (Student Nonviolent Coordinating Committee), 34

social constructionism, 5–6, 7, 10, 14, 19–20, 208–209
social divestment, 36, 58, 106, 204
social inequalities, schooling and, 66
social movement activism, 1, 12, 19, 72, 98, 203
social movement groups, 4, 19, 26, 68, 99–100, 120
social movement histories: adult allies and, 111–115, 130, 211; lack of in curricula, 78, 112–113; of Oakland, 21–22, 32, 112; of Portland, 32; SRU and, 122–123, 123–124, 131; youth empowerment and, 113, 125; YP and, 111–112, 130
social reproduction theories, 66
social services, youth access to, 106–107, 130
social workers, 223
spaces: adult allies in youth-led, 116; adult domination of public, 11, 99; gendered access to, 177–178; necessity of for youth organizing, 91; privacy and, 230n1; race and access to, 116–117; turf warfare and, 45–46; youth access to, 21, 26, 100–101, 116–117, 207; youth occupation of adult, 165, 166–167; youth-run vs. adult-run, 86. See also mobility
Spirit Week, 79, 230n11
sports participation, 12, 33
SRU (Students Rise Up), 1–2, 12, 15, 19, 213–215; academic achievement and, 136, 145–146, 150–151; adult allies' absence from, 102, 115–118, 123, 126, 128, 130–131, 183, 196; adult gaze and, 162, 174, 210; adultism and, 120; adult power and, 125; adults and, 101–102; advantage of youth legal status in, 156–157, 159–160; ageism and, 121, 125, 130; alternative schools and, 26–27; anarchist movement and, 32; antiwar organizing of, 64–65, 92, 147, 167–170, 217; consumerism and, 50; counterdemonstrations to, 64; crisis within, 169–170, 176, 191–192; critique of ineffective movements by, 124; definition of youth in, 127, 130; direct action and, 115, 140, 158, 169, 195, 221–222; discontinuity in, 127; end of, 198; founders of, 101–102, 146, 214; gendered navigation of parental worry in, 183–184, 189–190, 192, 197, 233n6; gender issues in, 146–147, 156–157, 169–170, 176–178; girls' departure from, 191–192, 198; goals of, 56, 58, 121–122, 199; GSAs and, 67; health care and, 38; imperialism and, 39; "incident on the bridge" and, 167–168, 176, 191–192,

ABOUT THE AUTHOR

HAVA RACHEL GORDON is an assistant professor of sociology at the University of Denver. She has published articles on youth activists in the *Journal of Contemporary Ethnography* and *Gender & Society*. Her research and teaching interests include the intersections of age, race, class, and gender inequalities; youth cultures; social movements; globalization; and schooling. She is currently working on her next project, an ethnographic study of community struggles over urban school reform.